AMERICA ENCOUNTERS INDIA

GARY R. HESS is Associate Professor of History at Bowling Green State University. He is the editor of *America and Russia: From Cold War Confrontation to Coexistence,* and the author of *Sam Higginbottom of Allahabad: Pioneer of Point Four to India* and of articles in the *Journal of American History, Pacific Historical Review,* and *Agricultural History.*

AMERICA ENCOUNTERS INDIA, 1941–1947

Gary R. Hess

THE JOHNS HOPKINS PRESS
Baltimore and London

The passages from Winston S. Churchill, *The Hinge of Fate,* are reprinted by permission of Houghton Mifflin Company and Cassell & Company Ltd. The passages from V. P. Menon, *The Transfer of Power in India,* are reprinted by permission of Princeton University Press and Orient Longmans Private Ltd. The passage from Robert Sherwood, *Roosevelt and Hopkins,* is reprinted by permission of Harper & Row, the original publishers. One passage is reprinted from *Nehru: The First Sixty Years,* edited by Dorothy Norman, copyright © 1965 by Indira Nehru Gandhi, by permission of The John Day Company, Inc., publisher.

Copyright © 1971 by The Johns Hopkins Press
All rights reserved
Manufactured in the United States of America

The Johns Hopkins Press, Baltimore, Maryland 21218
The Johns Hopkins Press Ltd., London

Library of Congress Catalog Card Number 72-163196
ISBN 0-8018-1258-5

To Rose

Contents

Preface

THE DEVELOPMENT OF RELATIONS between the United States and India has attracted increasing interest among scholars of both countries in recent years. While doing research on my dissertation in India seven years ago, I became one of those fascinated by Indo-American relations. In 1965 I began research on the American response to the Indian nationalist movement, focusing on the popular and official attitudes toward Indian political developments from 1941 to 1947. World War II brought the two countries into a much closer relationship and forced from the administration of Franklin D. Roosevelt a response to the demands of the Indian National Congress.

The topic of Indo-American relations attracted me for another reason. In defining its policy toward Indian nationalism, the United States was forced to choose between supporting a prized ally and aiding a nationalist movement which was demanding independence from that ally. This dilemma has frequently confronted the United States in the period since World War II, but India posed the problem initially, and so it provides a case study on which the historical record is nearly complete.

Several individuals and agencies have been of assistance in this study. I am indebted to the staffs of the Library of Congress, New York Public Library, Yale University Library, University of Michigan Library, Toledo Public Library, Carnegie Library of Pittsburgh, Houghton Library of Harvard University, and Alderman Library of the University of Virginia.

Several officers and staff members in the Department of State rendered considerable assistance, including Edwin S. Costrell, chief of the Historical Studies Division; Arthur G. Kogan, special assistant to the director, Historical Office; Wilmer P. Sparrow, supervisor, Reference Services, Records Services Division; and Marvin Kranz, formerly of the Historical Office staff. At the National Archives, Milton O. Gustafson and Mrs. Patricia Dowling, of the Legislative, Judicial, Fiscal Records Division, were very helpful, as were Elizabeth B. Drewry, Edgar B. Nixon, and William Stewart of the Franklin D. Roosevelt Library.

A research grant from the National Foundation on the Arts and Humanities enabled me to devote the summer of 1967 to research in Washington, Hyde Park, and elsewhere.

Bowling Green State University supported my efforts in various ways. The Faculty Leaves and Research Committee financed a reduction in my teaching load and made funds available for the purchase of materials and student assistance. Professor Stuart Givens, former chairman of the History Department, arranged teaching schedules that left much time for research and writing. Miss L. Emily Grimm, formerly the university's Research Resources Librarian, aided in locating and securing materials from other libraries.

To Mrs. Pamala German and Mrs. Phyllis Wulff, who typed the original and revised manuscripts respectively, I am deeply indebted for their highly efficient work. William Dillon and Lou Berry assisted in some of the early research, and Patricia Bogni and Julia Cardone have helped in proofreading.

My colleague Professor William Rock offered much valuable advice. Finally, I acknowledge Professor Edward Younger, of the University of Virginia, who directed my attention to Indo-American relations as a field of research and encouraged the completion of this study.

A Note on Sources

IN THE INTEREST of keeping footnotes within reasonable limits and of providing a comprehensive biblographic essay, I have followed several guidelines. First, the notes are largely restricted to references to documents and contemporary newspapers, periodicals, and books. I have endeavored to discuss secondary sources, on which I have also relied, in the Bibliographic Essay. Of course, some secondary works must be cited in the notes, but, insofar as it was possible, the above delineation was utilized.

Second, in citing State Department documents, I have included the decimal file designation of the unpublished documents and references to the department's *Foreign Relations of the United States* series for the published documents. The first reference to a volume in that series includes the title of the volume and the year of publication by the Government Printing Office. Subsequent references to a given volume include the shortened title *FRUS*, the year of the documents, and the volume number.

Finally, I have endeavored to eliminate the cumbersome language commonly used in referring to State Department documents. Correspondence between American diplomatic missions and the State Department has been reduced to "to" or "from" the mission. Thus "Telegram, Consul at Bombay (Donovan) to Secretary of State, October 21, 1942, becomes "Telegram from Bombay, October 21, 1942." Similarly, citations of memoranda within the State Department do not include the full titles of the author and recipient. The names of the officers are cited, but their positions are included only if they are not evident in the text. Thus the prolix "Assistant Secretary of State (Berle) to Under Secretary of State (Welles)" becomes "Berle to Welles."

I

Pearl Harbor and the Transformation of U.S. Relations with India

THE JAPANESE ATTACK ON PEARL HARBOR thrust upon the United States a formidable military challenge as well as many diplomatic questions and far-reaching responsibilities. Among the more important problems accompanying world leadership was formulating a response to nationalism in Asia and Africa. During and after World War II, nationalism frequently presented a dilemma to the American government and public, for in many instances independence movements challenged the empires of nations allied to the United States. In an era of constant menace from unfriendly powers, it has been difficult to interfere in the imperial affairs of valued allies. Nationalism, however, has appealed to American idealism. Never comfortable with its own empire, and proud of its reputation as an enlightened ruler of the Philippines, the United States naturally sympathized with nationalist movements that had often received inspiration from the American example. Moreover, failure to champion nationalism would have risked the loss of confidence among the emerging nations.

That now distant Sunday morning in December of 1941 brought the United States into its initial encounter with this question. India, the heart of the British Empire and the very symbol of the imperial order, was demanding independence from Great Britain, America's most prized ally. The demand came from the Indian National Congress, the principal voice of Indian nationalism. The National Con-

1

gress represented the most advanced and certainly the most widely known nationalist movement of the colonial area. Under the leadership of Mohandas Gandhi it had become the symbol of the nationalist strivings of the Asian peoples.

To nationalists throughout Africa and Asia the American response to the impasse between the British and the National Congress came to be regarded as the critical test of Allied war aims. The Atlantic Charter, issued by President Franklin Roosevelt and British Prime Minister Winston Churchill four months before Pearl Harbor, had seemingly affirmed the self-determination of peoples as one of their goals. Britain's refusal to implement this vaguely phrased pledge in India raised doubts as to whether the United Nations was seeking to preserve or to end imperialism. Indian nationalism challenged America's idealism, political wisdom, and diplomatic skill.

Prior to World War II the public and official interest in India had been nominal and sporadic. Americans knew little of Indian civilization, history, and politics beyond a few distorted generalizations that had been cultivated for a century. Commercial relations and contacts between the two peoples had not been extensive. India had been a field of Christian missionary activity, and American missionaries had assisted in economic, educational, and social advances in India. The small number of Indians who had come to America, however, had experienced discrimination and alienation. The nationalist movement had occasionally attracted the interest of the public and government, but few had ever suggested any American responsibility for India.

To meet the wartime challenge, Americans were thus called upon to develop quickly an understanding of a people and a country that had long been considered Great Britain's problem and had suffered from an unfavorable popular image. Indeed, according to a 1942 poll, 60 per cent of a nationwide sample of Americans could not even locate either India or China on a map.[1]

For nearly one hundred years India had been a popular subject in American books, magazines, and films. Prior to the Mutiny of 1857, India had been viewed as a distant land of mystery, but the uprising

[1] The following description of the development of Indo-American relations through 1940 is based on the secondary sources discussed in the section of the Bibliography on this chapter.

and the development of American interest in Asia produced an increased awareness of India as reflected in the publication of many books and articles during the last decades of the nineteenth century. Nearly all of the early books were travelers' accounts, most of which were written by missionaries and casual visitors whose descriptions represented American middle-class values. They emphasized the features of Indian culture which offered the greatest contrast with the West, a pattern which generally continued until after World War II.

Popular magazines of the late nineteenth century carried many features on India. Short stories, serialized novels, and poems centered on the maharajas, fakirs, and the exalted Englishmen. Informative accounts were somewhat more realistic but still drew attention to the unusual. From these sources Indians were seen as inscrutable fakirs, wealthy princes, or downtrodden untouchables. India was the land of bizarre religious customs, stringent caste taboos, and the sacred cow. The popular writings of Rudyard Kipling reinforced many of these biases. This literary tradition culminated in the publication of Katherine Mayo's *Mother India* in 1927. A best seller for two years, Mayo's criticism of Indian civilization influenced American attitudes toward India for at least a generation.

Motion pictures added to these distorted views. Beginning with *Hindoo Fakir* in 1902, some thirty-five important movies with Indian themes, locales, and characters were produced before World War II. The most popular theme was the suppression of rebellious mountain tribesmen by the British army. Mysterious religious cults were also emphasized; these cults usually were not clearly identified with any known religious faith, but they sometimes bore a vague resemblance to Buddhism. Motion pictures glorified Britain's accomplishments in India and ignored Indian nationalism, even as late as the 1930s. The Indian people emerged as one of several stock characters: the rebellious primitive tribesmen; the good raja loyal to the British; the evil raja plotting with tribesmen against the British; the Bengali soldiers loyal to the British. These themes and characterizations resulted, in part, from Hollywood's reliance on the British India Office for cooperation and, along with Katherine Mayo and British writers, as a source of information. It was not until the release of *The Rains Came* in 1939 that India and its people were seen realistically and favorably.

In that story a benevolent maharaja governed effectively, Indians administered a progressive state, and the heroic role was played by an Indian doctor. The usually dominant English characters remained in the background. Yet, in the same year, the popular movie version of Kipling's *Gunga Din*, with its stock characters and traditional theme, was also released.

Formal education concerning India did nothing to correct these impressions. India received little attention in textbooks used in American public schools, and the limited treatment was usually distorted. Geography texts played on exaggerated dangers from snakes and tigers. History textbooks discussed India primarily in terms of its contact with the West. Alexander the Great, Vasco da Gama, and Robert Clive emerged as the chief characters of Indian history, and the only native Indian who generally received any attention was Buddha. The British conquest was described favorably, and the "Black Hole" incident was related in embellished versions. The British were seen as a civilizing and unifying influence, and nationalism, if mentioned, was viewed as a minor development. Poverty was taken for granted, and its causes were never explored. The sacred cow and caste taboos always warranted space. Hinduism was often ignored, but, when described, it was as a fanatical religion with a multitude of gods. The other religions received no attention, although texts did usually mention the diversity and disunity of India. Even at the higher level of American education, few curriculums included courses in Indian civilization; the most notable work was that in Sanskrit studies at the University of Pennsylvania under the leadership of W. Norman Brown.

Extensive contact between India and the United States might have corrected these impressions, but commercial and diplomatic relations had been restricted. Beginning in 1784, American ships traded in India, and the Jay Treaty gave the United States most-favored-nation status in the East Indian trade. The trade became considerable during the Napoleonic Wars, when Indian trade with Europe was curtailed, but after 1815 Indo-American trade declined. During the late nineteenth century some Americans tried with little success to get a larger share of the Indian market and to promote American investment in industrial development in India. Throughout the period from the Civil War to World War II, Indo-American trade concentrated on jute, jute products, tea, and cotton in exchange for manufactured goods, ice, coal, and oil. World War I temporarily increased the volume of trade, with the United States becoming India's second largest trader, but, despite predictions of continued expansion, the postwar period brought a decline as a result of the efficiency of British firms in regaining lost markets and in the wake of high American tariffs. Over-all, between 1900 and 1940 the United States secured from 2 to 4 per cent of its imports from India and sent from 1 to 2 per cent of its exports there. Proportionately the trade was more important to India, with the United States accounting for 6 per cent of India's imports and taking 10 per cent of its exports. Shortly before World War II, Indian businessmen made an effort to promote the American market. In 1937 a handful of Indian businessmen in New York City organized the Indian Chamber of Commerce, and a year later the Government of India established a trade commission in New York.

The development of trade encouraged the establishment of official representation in India. In 1792 President Washington nominated Benjamin Joy to be consul at Calcutta. Upon his arrival in 1794, East India Company officials said they lacked authority to grant an exequatur acknowledging consular status, but they allowed him to remain as a commercial agent. After Joy's resignation in 1796, William James Miller was appointed and apparently was permitted consular status by the British. After 1801, however, the United States left the Calcutta post vacant until James Higginson was sent in 1843. The position was broadened in 1855 to that of consul general for British India. Earlier, in 1838, a consul was sent to Bombay, which soon was to become the principal center of American trade in India. Again British authorities initially permitted only commercial-agent status, but eventually they acknowledged the representative as consul. A consular agency under the jurisdiction of Calcutta was also established at Madras in 1867. The American representatives were mostly political appointees who had sought European posts and for whom India was a temporary and unwelcome stop. They were concerned mostly with commercial problems, and many of the consuls worked also in business enterprises. Few were interested in the Indian people or culture. Their terms were brief because of health problems, the opening of better positions elsewhere, and modest income. The pay of American representatives was substantially less than that of other foreign representatives, so that Americans usually could not take part in the diplomatic social life.

Missionaries played the predominant role in the development of American ties with India. Beginning with a Congregational mission at Bombay in 1813, the missions grew rapidly, but they never achieved much success in their primary goal of proselytizing. The obstacles to converting were considerable: the inclusiveness of Hinduism, the incompatibility with traditional Indian beliefs of the Christian concept of reward and punishment based on a single lifetime, and the popular identification of Christianity with imperialism. Yet, along with liberal British administrators, English business interests, and Indian reformers, the missionaries contributed to the modernization of India. During the early nineteenth century, when the East India Company government took little interest in education and indigenous education was on the decline, the missions established schools and colleges and introduced Western learning. Later in that century the missions led the way in establishing hospitals and schools of medicine and nursing. Criticism in the Christian press influenced the government to suppress *sati* (the cremation of widows on the funeral pyres of their husbands), *thugi* (murder and robbery by a religious sect), infanticide, and taxation at places of public worship. In the early twentieth century, missionaries pioneered in rural development efforts led by Sam Higginbottom, founder of the Allahabad Agricultural Institute, which became a unique center of practical teaching, extension work, and research.

A few missionaries attempted to bridge the gap between Christianity and Hinduism and to break the identity of missionaries with imperialism. Higginbottom cultivated a friendship with Gandhi, who shared his concern for rural problems. In the 1920s Methodist Bishop Frederick B. Fisher sponsored interreligious meetings and advocated home rule. Through his writings and speeches the evangelist Eli Stanley Jones sought to translate the Christian message into an Indian setting. He also established ashrams and became a close associate of Gandhi. Although strongly opposed to imperialism, Jones avoided open criticism of the British until after 1940. Missionaries were discouraged from championing nationalism because they were obliged to the British for their presence, and after 1925 they were required to take the "missionary pledge" promising no political activity.

The experience of the Indian community in the United States helped reduce the sentiment that America was a land of brotherhood, an image generated by the American democratic experiment and implicit in the teachings of the missionaries. "Hindus," as Indian immigrants were called regardless of religion, had come in small numbers during the nineteenth century, mostly as students and businessmen. After Swami Vivekananda's famous appearance at the Chicago World Conference of Religions in 1893, some swamis supported by the Ramakrishna Mission had also arrived. Between 1898 and 1914 some 6,000 Indian laborers entered the United States, settling in the Pacific Coast states. They were quickly subject to the prevalent antioriental bias, being in fact regarded as the most undesirable of all the oriental immigrants. The "barred zone" of the 1917 immigration law prohibited further labor immigration. In 1923 the U.S. Supreme Court ruled in the appeal of Bhagat Singh Thind that "Hindus" were ineligible for citizenship. Dismissing the Aryan origins of Indian peoples, which would have affirmed the Indians as "white persons" and thus eligible for citizenship, the Court based its decision on the assumption that the American public did not consider "Hindus" as "white persons." A year later the Johnson Immigration Law denied Indians a quota, which was limited to peoples eligible for citizenship. The *Thind* decision led to much criticism of the United States in the nationalist press. In 1926 the central legislature in New Delhi passed the Indian Naturalization Act, which denied Indian citizenship to nationals of any country that denied the same privilege to Indians. Comments made during the legislative debates indicated that this provision was directed at the United States. The barring of Indians and the denial of citizenship left a scar on U.S. relations with India. Beginning in the 1930s a few Indians and a handful of Congressmen began to work for remedial legislation. Yet the "Hindu" suffered from a most unfavorable reputation in America. A 1928 sample of a cross-section of Americans on the degree of intimacy desired with peoples of forty foreign countries placed India at the bottom of the list. Only 13 per cent desired Indians as neighbors, 21

7

per cent wanted them as fellow workers, and 23 per cent favored allowing them citizenship.

Educated Indians also derived an unfavorable view of America
from their press. News about America came mostly from British con-
trolled sources and Indian students and professors in the United
States. Alienated by racial discrimination and the *Thind* decision,
Indian sources frequently emphasized the undesirable elements of
American life, particularly crime, materialism, and intolerance.

Against this background, American interest in Indian nationalism
slowly developed. Beginning early in the twentieth century, Indian
students and professors in America, a few American visitors and missionaries to India, and some liberals in the United States promoted the
nationalist cause. Historically and ideologically Indians were attracted
to America for its revolutionary example and its seeming commitment
to self-determination as reflected in Woodrow Wilson's Fourteen Points
and the generally liberal treatment of the Philippines. Although
Americans had many misconceptions about India, what they knew of
the nationalist struggle appealed to their idealistic instincts.

During the first twenty years of its history the Indian National
Congress pursued moderate policies that did not attract much attention from the outside world. But, beginning with the boycott and
swadeshi campaigns protesting the partition of Bengal in 1905, Indian
nationalism embarked on a revolutionary course that Indian intellectuals in America sought to publicize. Taraknath Das, who came to
America in 1906 to study at the University of Washington, began
publishing *Free Hindustan* in 1908. The result of cooperation with an
Irish-American publisher working for Irish independence, Das's
journal flourished for three years before it was suppressed at the
instigation of the British Embassy.

American attitudes toward nationalism reflected the political division of the country on the question of U.S. imperialism. The foremost
critic of American rule in the Philippines, William Jennings Bryan,
visited India early in 1906. The agitation he witnessed served to reinforce his anti-imperialist position. He criticized British rule on the
grounds that it served only Britain's interests while refusing to
acknowledge the aspirations of the Indians for representative government. But American officials in India revealed little sympathy for the

nationalists. Consular reports defended the British position and maintained that India was not ready for self-government. In January, 1909, President Theodore Roosevelt affirmed unequivocally his belief in the civilizing and stabilizing benefits of British rule.

World War I stimulated renewed nationalist activity in America on revolutionary and constitutional levels. On the West Coast, Har Dayal and Chandra Chakravarty organized the so-called Hindu conspiracy, intending to use the United States as the base for a revolt against the British. Dayal, a native of Delhi, came to the United States in 1911 and taught briefly at Stanford University before being dismissed for overplaying his affiliation with the university. He had been organizing rallies and a Pacific Coast Hindustan Association aimed at preparing the Indian community in America for revolutionary activities in their homeland. In 1913 Dayal began editing the weekly newspaper *Ghadr* (meaning "mutiny" or "revolution") in San Francisco, and his political group became known as the Ghadr party. The revolutionary journal attracted the attention of British authorities, however, and Dayal fled to Germany in 1914. There he secured financial backing for his American operations, which, after the outbreak of the war, were planned by the German Foreign Office. Working through Dayal's political heir, Ram Chandra, schemes to send arms to India met with repeated failures in 1915. Early in 1916 the Germans sent Chakravarty to reorganize the work and carry out an ambitious but ill-conceived revolutionary scheme. In the spring of 1917 the conspirators were arrested for violating American neutrality laws. British agents had collected much of the information that resulted in the indictment of fifty-six Indians, twenty-six Germans, and thirteen Americans. The farcical and tragic trial ended in the conviction of most of the defendants, who included Taraknath Das and several other intellectuals, and in the assassination of Chakravarty by one of the other defendants. The publicity given to the "Hindu conspiracy," which was uncovered on the eve of America's entry into World War I, cast the Indians in the image of enemy agents.

The peaceful, constitutional program advocated by Lala Lajpat Rai offset much of this unfavorable image of Indian nationalism. Born in 1865, Rai had been active in the National Congress before coming to America in 1914. In New York, he founded the India Home Rule

League of America. With the exception of a six-month stay in Japan, Rai spent five years in America, lecturing widely and attracting many to the nationalist position. Among his early supporters was J. T. Sunderland, a Unitarian minister who had visited India in 1895–96 and 1913–14. An outspoken critic of British rule, Sunderland in 1919 wrote *India in Bondage*. A New York publisher, B. W. Huebsch, produced Rai's writings, which included the periodical *Young India* and a book, *England's Debt to India*. The Home Rule League succeeded in winning many American liberals, including Oswald Garrison Villard, George Kirchwey, Norman Thomas, Roger Baldwin, J. G. Phelps Stokes, Robert Morss Lovett, and John Haynes Holmes.

Indian nationalists were encouraged by President Woodrow Wilson's peace program, and particularly by the ideal of self-determination of peoples. Although Wilson primarily intended this concept to be the basis of the settlement in Europe, his pronouncements appealed to nationalists throughout Asia. Many Indians believed that because Britain had accepted Wilson's program in principle, it could not deny India's claim to self-government within the empire. Most nationalists were convinced that the United States would support their position. At its annual meeting at Delhi in December, 1918, the Indian National Congress demanded recognition by the Paris Peace Conference as one of the progressive nations to whom self-determination should be applied and elected representatives to the conference. Madan Mohom Malaviya, president of the Congress, spoke glowingly of Wilson as the architect of a new world order. The Congress delegation was refused recognition at Paris, where India was represented by delegates designated by the Government of India. The nationalists and their sympathizers in America then sought assistance from the U.S. Senate. In August, 1919, Rai and Dudley Field Malone, chairman of the League of Oppressed Peoples and assistant secretary of state briefly in 1913, appeared before the Senate Foreign Relations Committee but failed to secure any support.

In India, however, the portentous events of 1919 overshadowed concern about the peace settlement. The Government of India Act of 1919, which embodied a scheme for the progressive evolution of self-government, was accompanied by the passage of the Rowlatt Acts, which provided for the suspension of civil liberties in cases involving political terrorism. Indian resentment touched off a wave of *hartals* (cessation of all activities for a day) by the National Congress and its followers. These in turn generated riots in the Punjab, which led the British to fear revolution. At Amritsar on April 13, 1919, General R. E. H. Dyer broke up a prohibited meeting by firing into a crowd which numbered from ten to twenty thousand, killing (by official count) 379 and wounding 1,200. Martial law and public humiliations followed in the Punjab. The days of imperial order were numbered. In 1920 Gandhi led the National Congress in a non-cooperation campaign, thus leaving no doubt of the nationalists' strength and determination. The consuls at Bombay, Calcutta, and Madras reported extensively to the State Department on the non-cooperation movement. Becoming less defensive of the British, American officials expressed admiration for Gandhi's goals and determination, although some questioned his methods.

The American public knew comparatively little of the events of 1919, and most information came from British sources. Former civil servants in India wrote extensively in English journals, some of which were also published in America, and individual articles were frequently reprinted in American journals. Sir Valentine Chirol, Sir Andrew Fraser, and Charles Johnston presented the official view of the Government of India Act of 1919. Most of the American press, including *The Nation, The New Republic,* and *Literary Digest,* was also favorably impressed by the reforms. The Amritsar massacre received little attention, and the few editorial comments that did appear followed the Government of India's argument that outsider agitators had been responsible for the rioting that preceded General Dyer's actions. In the Senate, George Norris of Nebraska condemned the policy of repression, but his speech was followed by several defending the British as guardians against chaos.

The non-cooperation movement, however, generally received favorable coverage in American newspapers and magazines. The outbreak of violence in the Chauri Chaura incident of February, 1921, was virtually ignored, but Gandhi's fast to bring his followers back to the non-violent technique attracted much attention. Between 1920 and 1923, many detailed articles and several books on India were published; the nationalist view was perhaps best presented in the articles

11

of Gertrude Emerson, with a British apology argued most persuasively by historian Claude H. Van Tyne in *India in Ferment.*

Nationalist activities continued in America, but they lacked the leadership and direction that Rai had provided. After his release from prison, Taraknath Das, in association with Sailendra Nath Ghose, organized the Friends of Freedom for India, which attracted most of the American supporters of the former Home Rule League. In December, 1921, thirty-eight Americans, including two senators (Norris and David Walsh of Massachusetts) and a few congressmen, sent a Christmas message of sympathy to the Indian National Congress. In the early 1920s two Indian spokesmen for the nationalist cause came to America: Syud Hossain, a Muslim and former subeditor of the *Bombay Chronicle,* spoke and wrote extensively, particularly attempting to refute the political importance of communalism; Haridas T. Muzumdar, a student at Columbia University, founded the Young India Association and wrote a biography of Gandhi. John Haynes Holmes, minister of the Community Church in New York City, emerged as the foremost American apologist for Gandhi. In his sermons and writings, Holmes professed unbounded admiration for Gandhi, describing him as the greatest man alive. In 1925 Holmes journeyed to India where, attired in Western suit and Gandhi cap, he spoke before the annual session of the National Congress.

From Gandhi's arrest in 1922 until the designation of the Simon Commission in 1927, politics faded into the background of Indian life. But, when Britain appointed an all-British commission under Sir John Simon to carry out the review of constitutional progress which had been stipulated in the act of 1919, the indignant National Congress organized a successful boycott of the commission, and it was everywhere greeted with hostile demonstrations. Gandhi returned to active leadership of the Congress, but was forced to accommodate the more extreme elements pushing for an immediate showdown with Britain. In 1928 the Congress declared that *purna swaraj,* complete independence, was its goal. The viceroy, Lord Irwin, persuaded the British government to agree to a declaration that dominion status was the aim of British policy and that a round-table conference should be held to consider the next step. Gandhi, however, insisted that the conference be obliged to prepare a plan for full dominion status which would take effect immediately. The British refused that demand, and in March, 1930, Gandhi launched a civil disobedience movement. In April, Gandhi's one-hundred-sixty-five-mile walk from his Sabarmati ashram to the sea at Dandi, where he illicitly manufactured salt, captured the public mood and touched off a mass uprising. After a year of widespread civil disobedience and ensuing mass arrests, however, a Gandhi-Irwin truce brought an end to the movement in return for the release of political prisoners and representation for the Congress at the second round-table conference in London. The failure of that conference and a corresponding hardening of the British position led Gandhi to initiate a second civil disobedience movement in January, 1932. After the arrest of Gandhi and his followers, another interlude of comparative inactivity ensued.

These developments coincided with increasing contact of Indian nationalists with the United States, but four events between 1927 and 1929 caused some Indian leaders to doubt American appreciation of nationalist feeling. First, Jawaharlal Nehru's experience as the Congress delegate to the Brussels Congress of Oppressed Nationalities awakened him to the political threat of U.S. imperialism. Besides strongly influencing his favorable attitude toward the Soviet Union, the Brussels meeting brought Nehru into contact with Latin American delegates preoccupied with U.S. domination of the Western Hemisphere. After the conference Nehru spoke of the rise of U.S. imperialism, which, he feared, might foreshadow an Anglo-Saxon move to dominate the world. This apprehension had earlier been a recurrent theme in the articles by Taraknath Das in the *Modern Review* of Calcutta and in his 1923 book, *India in World Politics*.

Second, the popularity of *Mother India* underscored the appeal of anti-Indian propaganda in America. Mayo's emphasis on the unfavorable aspects of Indian life produced a wave of resentment against the author and the American public which made *Mother India* a best seller. Gandhi replied to Mayo's work in an article entitled "The Drain Inspector's Report," while Lala Lajpat Rai responded with *Unhappy India*, and another Indian wrote an anti-American diatribe, *Uncle Sham*. Dalip Singh Saund, who had migrated to the United States in 1920 and graduated from the University of California before becoming a farmer in the Imperial Valley, answered Mayo with *My*

13

Mother India. While the Mayo incident brought much misunderstanding and contributed to the American image of a backward India, it appears to have had little influence on American attitudes toward Indian nationalism.

Next, the American attachment to the imperial order seemed to be reinforced by the Pact of Paris outlawing war as an instrument of foreign policy. Partly to counteract Mayo's picture of India, Mrs. Sarojini Naidu, former president of the Indian National Congress, and Charles F. Andrews, the British champion of Indian freedom, came to America in 1929. Their lectures and the publicity given to their visit drew much favorable attention to the nationalist movement. Offsetting that achievement, Mrs. Naidu failed to gain senatorial backing for the National Congress' objections to the antiwar treaty. Republican Senator John J. Blaine of Wisconsin did read the nationalist position into the *Congressional Record.* The National Congress maintained that India had been made a party to the treaty by the British, but that Indians could not be bound by a pledge which restricted their aspirations for freedom. Moreover, when Britain accepted the U.S. offer to sign the treaty, the foreign secretary stipulated that the British would not tolerate any interference under the treaty's provisions within their empire. Blaine's resolution of senatorial refusal to accept the British reservation was not accepted.

Finally, in 1929, Tagore, America's most renowned visitor from India, canceled a lecture tour of the United States because of insulting treatment by an immigration official. Tagore's widely publicized comment that the official reflected a prevalent antioriental bias again brought American prejudice to Indians' attention.

Despite the limitations of American understanding of Indians and their culture, the public did reflect pronationalist sentiment as it witnessed the upheaval of the early 1930's. Gandhi's march to the sea, the first civil disobedience campaign, and Gandhi's arrest in 1930 were all front page news. The picture of the slight holy man dressed in loin cloth defying the British Empire captured the American imagination. His illicit manufacture of salt was frequently compared to the Boston Tea Party. Of the more than twenty books published on India in 1930, William James Durant's *The Case for India* and Gertrude Emerson's *Voiceless India* presented the nationalist viewpoint most persuasively.

Expressions of sympathy for the nationalists came from American liberals. *The Nation* and *The New Republic* consistently defended the policies of the National Congress. After Gandhi's arrest, Blaine introduced a resolution urging that the United States use its good offices to bring about a settlement which would acknowledge the Indian claims. Holmes formulated a petition signed by more than one hundred clergymen calling upon British Prime Minister Ramsay Mac-Donald to reach an accord with Gandhi. Roger Baldwin wrote to Nehru, whom he had met at Brussels in 1927, that American sentiment was on the nationalist side and advised the Congress to stand firm.[2] Muzumdar publicized the identification of the Indian movement with the American independence movement. On January 26, 1931, the first anniversary of the independence day proclaimed by the National Congress, he led a group of Americans and Indians to Independence Hall in Philadelphia, where he read the Indian Declaration of Independence. After agreeing to the pact with Irwin, Gandhi expressed gratitude to Americans and other peoples who had supported the Congress.

Gandhi's participation in the second round-table conference brought India back to the front pages of American newspapers, but much of the coverage focused on the peculiarities of Gandhi's behavior. Aside from the liberal journals that defended the Congress and *The Christian Science Monitor* and *Philadelphia Inquirer*, which expressed the British position, editorial comment from 1930 to 1932 was not extensive.

From 1932 until the outbreak of World War II, Indo-American relations again were distant. In the American press, the Government of India Act of 1935 and the ensuing provincial elections were overshadowed by the domestic questions of the Depression years and the collapse of international order in Europe and East Asia. Americans did become acquainted with Nehru, and thus decreased the usual equating of Gandhi with the nationalist movement. Feature stories on the emerging leader appeared in *Time, Newsweek,* and *The Christian Science Monitor.* Nehru presented the Congress' case in his "Unity of India" published in *Foreign Affairs* in 1938. A few Indians continued

[2] Baldwin to Nehru, February 13, 1931, in Jawaharlal Nehru, *A Bunch of Old Letters Written Mostly to Jawaharlal Nehru and Some Written by Him* (London: Asia Publishing House, 1960), pp. 97–99.

15

their efforts on behalf of the nationalist cause. Muzumdar lectured extensively and wrote a dozen books and pamphlets. Anup Singh, who had received a doctorate in political science from Harvard and then studied international affairs in London and Geneva, became a regular contributor to *Asia* and other journals. The need for coordination of this work led to the founding of the India League of America in 1937. Originally composed only of Indians, the league's first president was N. R. Checker, Muzumdar its first secretary. Also in 1937 the India Welfare League, intended primarily to aid "Hindu" immigrants by securing citizenship privileges, was organized by Mubarak Ali Khan.

Prior to World War II the administration of Franklin Roosevelt had faced a few innocuous problems regarding India. In 1936 Margaret Woodrow Wilson suggested that Roosevelt address a message to India on the centenary of Ramakrishna's birthday.[3] Intrigued with the idea, Roosevelt wrote to Stephen Early:

Take this up with the State Department. Because he was a very great saint this would have a very great effect all through the East.

F.D.R.

P.S. If you do not know about him—go and find out![4]

The State Department, however, noted that this could lead to difficulties with the British and with many Americans who would resent the President celebrating the birthday of a Hindu saint, and the suggestion was dropped.[5] In 1938 Yusuf Meherally, secretary of the Congress Socialist party, visited America and sought to meet Roosevelt or at least a member of his staff. A year later Baburo Patel, president of the Film Journalists' Association of India, was in America seeking a more favorable portrayal of India in American films and also to greet Roosevelt on behalf of the Indian people. Because of the reservations of the British Embassy, neither of these visits materialized.[6]

[3] Margaret Woodrow Wilson to Roosevelt, January 8, 1936, Box O.F. 48-H, India, 1933–39, Roosevelt Papers, Franklin D. Roosevelt Library, Hyde Park, N.Y.

[4] Roosevelt to Early, January 21, 1936, *ibid.*

[5] William Phillips to Early, February 2, 1936, and Early to Margaret Woodrow Wilson, February, 1936, *ibid.*

[6] Chief of Protocol to H. M. McIntyre, *ca.* August, 1938, and Louis Ogull to Roosevelt, August 31, 1939, *ibid.*

16

The beginning of the European War in September, 1939, precipitated a deterioration of British relations with the Indian National Congress. As events in Europe and Asia gradually led the United States toward non-belligerency beside the British, American concern with the Indian problem steadily increased. Since the provincial elections of February, 1937, the Congress and other parties had cooperated with the Indian government in forming responsible provincial ministries. But, when Lord Linlithgow proclaimed India to be at war with Germany, the Congress immediately opposed being led into a war without popular consent. In mid-September the Working Committee of the Congress issued a statement challenging the British to state their war aims. If the war was being fought against aggression and for democracy, the Congress pledged that a free India would fight with other free nations. The other Indian parties supported the war, but the Muslim League added the condition that Britain permit no constitutional changes without its consent. On October 17 the viceroy responded to the Congress that the British aim remained dominion status for India, but that immediate independence was impossible. After the war the Government of India Act of 1935 would be reconsidered in consultation with representatives of the Indian communities. In the meantime a wartime consultative council of representatives of all Indian parties was to be established. Because the viceroy did not meet the demands of the Congress and seemed to be supporting the Muslim League's position, the Congress condemned the October 17 declaration. On November 8 its members resigned from India's provincial governments.

Britain's policy led to renewed hope that outside pressures, particularly from the United States, would force an abandonment of imperialism. Nehru wrote:

We know now, beyond a peradventure, that Britain clings to her imperialism and fights to preserve it, howsoever her statesmen may cover this ancient habit of theirs by soft and pleasing words. What of the British Labour Party now and all those radicals and lovers of freedom in England who talk so eloquently of the brave new world that is coming? What of America, that great land of democracy, to which imperialist England looks for support and sustenance during this war? Does Britain think that the people of the United States will pour their gold and commodities to make the world safe for British imperialism? . . . The aims and objectives of this terrible war are clear at last, at least as far as the present British Cabinet is concerned. Let no man doubt them.[7]

The consulate general at Calcutta reported extensively on these developments. In the State Department the Indian situation was viewed from the standpoint of its effect on the war; in a memorandum of November 14 Wallace Murray of the Division of Near Eastern Affairs summarized the department's position. He concluded that, while the problem caused by disagreement among Britain, the Muslim League, and the National Congress endangered support of the war effort by Muslims of the Middle East, it remained essentially a British-Indian matter.[8]

Events in India were overshadowed by the European war, but they received much attention in the American press. Generally the position of the Indian National Congress was endorsed, not only by the liberal journals, but by such traditionally pro-British newspapers as the *New York Times* and *The Christian Science Monitor*. The conservative *Reader's Digest* carried a favorable portrayal of Nehru written by John and Frances Gunther. The previously noncommittal *Catholic World* presented an article which was critical of British imperialism, and a *Collier's* report entitled "India Won't Wait" reflected so much anti-British sentiment that the issue was banned in India.

In early 1940 the "missionary pledge" first came to public attention in India and the United States when four American missionaries were required to leave India for having endorsed the National Congress' position on the war. The return of J. Holmes Smith, a missionary at Lucknow for nine years, Ralph and Lila Templin of Muttra, and Paul Kenne of Mussoorie led Nehru to write that he could now appreciate the difficulties under which missionaries worked, but he questioned whether Christians should permit themselves any identity with imperialism. In a letter to Smith, Nehru expressed the conviction that

---

[7] Dorothy Norman, ed., *Nehru: The First Sixty Years, Presenting in His Own Words the Development of the Political Thought of Jawaharlal Nehru and the Background against Which It Evolved* . . . , 2 vols. (New York: John Day Co., 1965), 1:662.

[8] Letter from Calcutta, September 15, 1939, 740.0011 E.W./917; letter from Calcutta, October 26, 1939, 845.00/1124; telegram from Calcutta, November 2, 1939, 845.00/1114; memorandum, Near Eastern Affairs (Murray), November 14, 1939, *ibid.*

American knowledge of the Indian situation would strengthen nationalist sympathy in the United States.

Nehru and his ideas did come increasingly to the attention of Americans. Anup Singh wrote a biography which was intended to introduce Nehru to the American public. Nehru's commitment to freedom, democracy, and internationalism was underscored in Singh's sympathetic portrayal. In *The Atlantic Monthly* of April, 1940, Nehru himself presented the National Congress' case in the skillfully developed "India's Demand and England's Answer." Emphasizing the nationalists' willingness to fight fascism, provided India was freed, Nehru accused the British of divide-and-rule tactics and assured Muslims that they would have nothing to fear under a system of provincial autonomy, which should accompany independence. An article in *Pacific Affairs* called attention to Nehru's record in championing nationalism throughout Asia, particularly in China, which he had recently visited. To make certain that the Congress' position had a constant voice in the United States, the India League of America began publishing *India Today*. A three- or four-page monthly, it was edited by Anup Singh. In late 1939, Government of India censorship curtailed the Congress' foreign publication *News from India*, but it reappeared for a brief period in 1940.

American interest in the Congress' position aroused the concern of the Muslim League. In early March, 1940, the chairman of the league's Foreign Committee called upon the United States to intercede with the National Congress on behalf of the Muslims, who he claimed had no common interests with the Hindu majority. The league, however, had no effective spokesmen in the United States, and this resulted in general American ignorance of the Muslim League's policies. In fact, the American press gave little coverage to the league's monumental demand of March 23, 1940, for the creation of Pakistan.[9]

[9] *New York Times*, February 12, March 4, March 25, and July 4, 1940; *India Today*, April, 1940, p. 1; Jawaharlal Nehru, "India's Demand and England's Answer," *The Atlantic Monthly*, April, 1940, pp. 449–55; Anup Singh, *Nehru: The Rising Star of India* (New York: John Day Co., 1939), pp. 3–160; Irving S. Friedman, "Indian Nationalism and the Far East," *Pacific Affairs*, March, 1940, pp. 17–29; Jawaharlal Nehru, *The Unity of India: Collected Writings, 1937–1940* (New York: John Day Co., 1948), pp. 50–52; All-India Congress Committee, Foreign Department, *News from India*, February 1, 1940, p. 1.

The six-month "phony war" in Europe had encouraged leisurely British and Indian approaches to their problem. But, when Germany's blitzkrieg in the spring of 1940 overran the Low Countries and then France, political conditions were altered in both countries. In England the blitzkrieg brought to power the imperialist Winston Churchill, a critic of previous concessions to Indian nationalism. In India the National Congress modified its demands and in July offered full military cooperation in return for a declaration of independence and the establishment of a provisional government. England's "August offer" reiterated the goal of dominion status, but held that minority interests had to be considered and that no fundamental constitutional changes would be possible during the war. While after the war a body representing various political elements would be established to draft a constitution, the only immediate changes would be the expansion of the viceroy's executive council to include representatives of various parties and the initiation of the war advisory council promised the previous October.

Americans followed these events with continued sympathy for the Congress, although the minority issue raised doubts in some journals. The "August offer" was condemned as insufficient by *The New Republic, The Nation,* and *Time.* Editorials in *The Christian Science Monitor, New York Times,* and *Los Angeles Times* showed skepticism and little enthusiasm for the British position. When the National Congress held that the offer failed to meet its demands and authorized Gandhi to launch a civil disobedience campaign, a few newspapers criticized it for taking advantage of Great Britain in its moment of trial. The arrest of Congress leaders in November met with criticism, although most of the comment came from the liberal press and from the American League for India's Freedom, a group led by John Haynes Holmes, Frances Gunther, and J. Holmes Smith. The month he was sent to jail, another article by Nehru was published in an American journal; in "The Parting of the Ways" in *Asia,* Nehru explained the reasons for the rejection of the "August offer."

While the arrests were regretted in the press and by the government, the prevalent attitude remained that India was not of immediate American concern. The *New York Times* deplored the imprisonment of patriots but said that American sympathy could go no further. American Consulate General Thomas Wilson reported extensively from Calcutta, but a bystander approach prevailed in his dispatches.[10]

Yet, as the American commitment to the British war effort unfolded, culminating with the passage of the Lend-Lease Act in March, 1941, more official attention was focused on all of Great Britain's problems. In April, 1941, Wilson reported extensively on the Pakistani demand, which had received little analysis from his predecessor at the time of the Lahore session. The consulate general held that the movement lacked the support of many Muslims, but he predicted that the longer the constitutional issues remained unsolved the stronger the movement would become. Wilson became increasingly critical of British policy, particularly of Secretary of State for India, Leopold S. Amery, who "continues . . . to repeat himself and refuses to take a realistic view of what is taking place."[11]

Nationalist sentiments were expressed in the American press. From jail, Nehru addressed a message to the American people. Published in *India Today* and reprinted in other journals, the message revealed the depth of his frustration and the strengthening of his conviction that the United States had a special obligation to uphold freedom and democracy against fascism and imperialism. *The Nation* carried another story by Nehru, and Anup Singh detailed the careers of Gandhi and Nehru in *Current History*. Nehru's autobiography, *Toward Freedom*, was published by the John Day Company and generally received sympathetic reviews. Another modest nationalist journal, *India and the USA*, was launched in New York by P. G. Krishnayya, a follower of the Congress. Shiva Rao, Indian correspondent for the *Manchester Guardian* and vice president of the National Trade Unions Federation in India, also began writing in America. His article in *Foreign Affairs*

10 *New York Times*, November 10 and 15, 1940; Walter C. Mackett, "Some Aspects of the Development of American Opinion on India, 1918–1947" (Ph.D. diss., University of Southern California, 1957), pp. 276–84; letter from Calcutta, August 10, 1940, 845.00/1189.

11 Letter from Calcutta, May 8, 1941, 845.00/1232; letter from Calcutta, April 5, 1940, 845.00/1174; letter from Calcutta, April 5, 1940, 845.00/1226.

21

held that a settlement was possible only if the British were willing to make concessions.[12]

The British government showed concern over the widespread nationalist propaganda. The chief British spokesman in America, Ambassador Lord Halifax, commanded much respect owing to the general public support of Britain's war effort. He also could claim special competence in Indian affairs, for, known then as Lord Irwin, he had served as viceroy in India from 1926 to 1931. From his dealings with Gandhi in the early 1930s, which had been followed in America, he had gained the reputation of an enlightened viceroy. After serving as foreign secretary from 1938 to 1940, Halifax had been assigned by Churchill to the Washington Embassy in December, 1940. Concerned with sustaining public enthusiasm for his country's war effort, he presented the British view not only in Washington but in speeches throughout the country. At a press conference in March, 1941, Halifax defended Britain's policy in India; in response to a question concerning his country's reluctance to set a date for dominion status, he said:

I happen to be the person who made the original promise about dominion status, and I therefore know something about it. And Mr. Gandhi and others have often said to me "Can you give us a date when dominion status will be effective?" And that, of course, has never been possible and will never be possible.[13]

A few days later Halifax proposed to the State Department the addition to the British Embassy of an Indian with ministerial rank to be designated as agent general for India. The official was to serve as the embassy's advisor on Indian affairs and to assist in resolving non-political problems between the United States and India.

In the State Department the Halifax memorandum, coupled with the tone of reports from Wilson and the nationalist sentiment in America, led to the first serious top-level discussion on India. The diffi-

[12] *India Today*, March, 1941, p. 3; Anup Singh, "Gandhi and Nehru, Saint and Politician," *Current History*, May, 1941, pp. 44–46; Jawaharlal Nehru, "India and the War," *The Nation*, February 1, 1941, pp. 121–24; *India and the USA*, February 26, 1941, pp. 1–2; *ibid.*, March 19, 1941, pp. 1–4; B. Shiva Rao, "Vicious Circle in India," *Foreign Affairs*, July, 1941, pp. 842–51.

[13] *India Today*, April, 1941, p. 2.

culty of following events in India without representation in New Delhi had long been obvious. Accordingly, the United States suggested that it be permitted to send a minister to the Indian capital in return for the agency general in Washington, but this was rejected by Halifax. On May 5 Assistant Secretary of State Adolph A. Berle proposed that the United States urge the British to seek a settlement with India which would acknowledge India as a full and equal partner in the British Commonwealth. Berle urged that approval of the Halifax request be made conditional on the British making such an effort. The Berle memorandum of May 5 stands out as the initial suggestion by a high-ranking official in the State Department that the United States should pressure the British to solve the Indian problem.

In a conversation with Halifax two days later, Secretary of State Cordell Hull presented the substance of the Berle suggestion. Halifax rejected the need for a settlement, claiming that pro-British sentiment was strong in India and that the Indians already enjoyed self-government in the provinces and virtually at the national level, aside from defense, foreign affairs, and finance.

In late May, with the British adamant in refusing to acknowledge the American suggestion, the United States retreated to its initial demand for a minister at New Delhi in return for the agency general. On June 28 the British accepted, but they insisted that the rank of minister not be publicized, for the Government of India was not permitted to receive ministers, and this could cause embarrassment with other countries. After further discussions, the American representative was designated "commissioner" and his rank was kept secret. On July 21, 1941, the exchange was announced, with the British designating as agent general Sir Girja Shankar Bajpai, a member of the viceroy's executive council and a veteran Indian civil servant. Wilson, the career diplomat then serving at Calcutta, was appointed by the United States as commissioner at New Delhi. Wilson had served in China, Australia, Canada, and the consuls at Bombay and Madras before going to Calcutta in June, 1940.

This unique exchange meant that the United States had established direct diplomatic relations with the imperial Government of India, and an Indian under British direction was stationed in Washington. The exchange served the American need for more extensive, reliable, and direct information from India and underscored to Indians, Americans, and the British the official interest in India. From the British viewpoint, Bajpai's presence in Washington gave them an Indian with official status to defend their position; he also symbolized the influence of Indians within the British order in India.

Wilson remained at Calcutta until the formalities of the diplomatic exchange were completed late in 1941. During the summer his reports showed general sympathy for the National Congress. He drew attention to the nationalist habit of exaggerating the American interest in India and the tendency in the nationalist press to seize on all American criticisms of British imperialism as indications of sympathy for their cause. When the Government of India in late July announced the expansion of the viceroy's executive council to include five more Indians, Wilson reminded Washington that this gesture did not end the political deadlock.[14]

In early August, 1941, President Roosevelt and Prime Minister Churchill issued the Atlantic Charter, destined to become the ideological focus of American concern with Indian nationalism. On August 9, 1941, Roosevelt, Churchill, and their political and military advisers met in secrecy at Placentia Bay, Newfoundland. The purposes of the Atlantic Conference were to provide an opportunity for the two leaders to become acquainted and to discuss military strategy. While the participants regarded the cementing of the Anglo-American alliance as their primary accomplishment, the press and peoples throughout the world gave most attention to the Atlantic Charter, a statement of war aims which had been agreed to without much deliberation.

Prior to the Atlantic Conference the British and American governments had hesitated to issue statements of war aims. In his January, 1941, message to Congress, Roosevelt had affirmed dedication to

[14] Secretary of State to British Ambassador, May 28, 1941, *Foreign Relations of the United States, 1941*, vol. 3, *The British Commonwealth, the Near East and Africa* (1959), pp. 170–71; British Ambassador to Under Secretary of State (Welles), June 28, 1941, *ibid.*, pp. 171–72; Welles to British Ambassador, July 2, 1941, *ibid.*, pp. 172–73; British Ambassador to Welles, July 15, 1941, *ibid.*, p. 174; memorandum by Berle, May 5, 1941, *ibid.*, pp. 176–77; memorandum of conversation by Hull, May 7, 1941, *ibid.*, p. 178; report from Calcutta, "India's War Effort," June 20, 1941, 740.0011 E.W. 1939/13463; letter from Bombay, June 10, 1941, 845.00/1244; letter from Calcutta, July 28, 1941, 845.00/1243.

a world order based on the "Four Freedoms." Hull had talked occasionally of the necessity to eliminate trade discrimination. In July, 1941, upon learning of secret treaties between Great Britain and the Soviet Union involving territorial changes in Europe, Roosevelt became concerned about Allied war aims and instructed Sumner Welles to warn Churchill of American disapproval of territorial changes made during the war. A speech by Welles at the Norwegian Legation on July 22 indicated the direction of Roosevelt's thinking; the under secretary of state spoke of arms reduction, equal economic opportunities for all peoples, and a world of independent and secure peoples. The Churchill government had also refused to state war aims, beyond the general support expressed by Foreign Secretary Anthony Eden for the "Four Freedoms."

While the major wartime challenge to the Atlantic Charter came from India, the Indian question was not on the agenda of the conference and apparently did not influence the drafting of war aims. The week before the conference, Welles, who accompanied Roosevelt to Placentia Bay, had been confronted with the Indian question. On August 1, John Gilbert Winant, the American ambassador in London, cabled that only at Roosevelt's suggestion would Churchill reconsider the Indian situation, which the ambassador saw as endangering security in Asia. Four days later, Berle proposed to Welles that the ambassador should be instructed to raise the question with Churchill and Eden. Hull, upon Welles's recommendation, declined to have the United States suggest an Indian policy to the British government. Welles, however, believed that Roosevelt could talk the matter over personally and confidentially, although not officially, with Churchill.[15]

At dinner on August 9, Churchill and Roosevelt discussed the possibility of a joint statement, and the next morning the British submitted a draft declaration of five aims. The third read: "they respect the right of all people to choose the form of government under which

---

[15] William L. Langer and Everett S. Gleason, *The Undeclared War, 1940–1941* (New York: Harper & Bros., 1953), pp. 663–81; Cordell Hull, *Memoirs of Cordell Hull*, 2 vols. (New York: Macmillan, 1948), 2:1482–84; memorandum of trip to meet Churchill, August, 1941, PSF: Atlantic Charter, Roosevelt Papers; telegram from London, August 1, 1941, *FRUS, 1941*, 3:178–79; Berle to Welles, August 5, 1941, *ibid.*, pp. 179–81; Welles to Hull, August 6, 1941, *ibid.*, p. 181.

they will live; they are concerned only to defend the rights of freedom of speech and of thought without which such choosing must be illusory."[16] Roosevelt and Welles regarded the British aims as generally appropriate, but Welles doubted whether Congress and the public would support such a universal pledge to defend human rights, in view of the fact that every Axis country had abrogated them. Accordingly Welles suggested deleting the latter half of the third article. Roosevelt, however, chose to add a new second clause: "and they hope that self-government may be restored to those from whom it has been forcibly removed."[17]

When Churchill and Roosevelt met on the morning of August 11, Roosevelt presented this and two other changes. He readily agreed to Churchill's view that "sovereign rights and" should be added before "self-government" in the Roosevelt revision of Article 3. The discussions on Article 3, and, indeed, those on the entire statement, took little time.[18]

Bearing many idealistic similarities to Wilson's Fourteen Points, the Atlantic Charter pledged: no territorial aggrandizement, no territorial changes without consent of the peoples involved, access by all nations to trade and raw materials, collaboration for economic improvement, security from fear and want, freedom of the seas, abandon-

[16] Memorandum of conversation by Welles, August 10, 1941, *Foreign Relations of the United States, 1941*, vol. 1, *General: The Soviet Union* (1958), pp. 354–55.

[17] Sumner Welles, *Where Are We Heading?* (New York: Harper & Bros., 1946), pp. 7–10.

[18] Memorandum of conversation by Welles, August 11, 1941, *FRUS, 1941*, 1: 356–63. According to Elliott Roosevelt, who accompanied his father to the Atlantic Conference, the president pressed the imperialism question with Churchill. Elliott Roosevelt's reliability has been challenged, however; he wrote *As He Saw It* in 1946 in the belief that the country needed to return to the policies charted by his father during the war. Moreover, his picture of Roosevelt questioning Churchill at the Atlantic Conference is not corroborated in the available documents, nor in Welles's and Churchill's accounts of the conference; Hopkins, who was present at the meeting where the issue was presumably raised, apparently left no record of the confrontation. See Elliott Roosevelt, *As He Saw It* (New York: Duell, Sloan & Pearce, 1946), pp. 35–38; Robert E. Sherwood, *Roosevelt and Hopkins: An Intimate History*, rev. ed. (New York: Grosset & Dunlap, 1950), pp. 353–65; Winston S. Churchill, *The Second World War: The Grand Alliance* (Boston: Houghton Mifflin, 1950), pp. 431–43.

ment of force through a system of general security, and the destruction of Nazi tyranny.

Issued as a press release and not a formally signed document, the eight-point declaration was interpreted as an unequivocal statement of war aims. In the United States the Atlantic Charter was praised for clarifying aims and bringing closer ties with Britain. In general the press focused on the non-aggrandizement, equal access to markets, and disarmament pledges. The reaction to Article 3 was nominal and was regarded as applying to Nazi-occupied areas, an understandable reaction since the war was still limited to Europe. Even the *Far Eastern Survey*, *The New Republic*, *The Nation*, and *The Christian Century* ignored any possible application of the third article to Asia. In a letter to the *London News Chronicle*, the English historian Edward Thompson raised the question of whether Article 3 applied to India with its 5,000 political prisoners, many of whom had been serving the Government of India at the beginning of the war.

Elsewhere the Atlantic Charter was welcomed, with little concern for specific problems. The State Department instructed its embassies and legations to report on press and government reactions. Throughout the Western Hemisphere the Charter was hailed in newspapers and by political leaders. In the Soviet Union, *Pravda* and *Izvestia* praised the anti-Nazi position, while the Chinese Nationalist press and government took heart from the commitment to oppose aggression. The press in the Middle East and those parts of Europe not under Nazi control echoed these sentiments.[19]

Yet, within a week of the Atlantic Conference, the third article was being challenged by events in Burma and Iran. On August 16 the premier of Burma and members of the central legislature asked the British when self-government would be carried into effect in that part

[19] *New York Times*, August 14, 1941; *Commonweal*, August 29, 1941, pp. 435–36; *The Christian Century*, August 27, 1941, pp. 1045–46; *The Nation*, August 23, 1941, pp. 152–53; *Asia*, November, 1941, pp. 526–27; *Far Eastern Survey*, August 25, 1941, p. 181; *The New Republic*, August 25, 1941, pp. 239–40; *Newsweek*, August 25, 1941, pp. 11–14; *U.S. News*, August 22, 1941; *London News Chronicle*, August 20, 1941; Hull to Roosevelt, August 19, 1941, PSF: China, Roosevelt Papers.

For reports on the reaction to the Atlantic Charter from London, Ottawa, Santiago, Panama, Lima, Mexico City, Havana, Quito, Montevideo, Moscow, Chungking, Lisbon, Ankara, Baghdad, see 740.0011 E.W./14019–177.

of the British Empire. The next day Britain and the Soviet Union sent notes to the Iranian government suggesting joint occupation to guard against German fifth-column activities. Ignoring the Iranian government's opposition, British and Soviet forces occupied Iran on August 25. The Iranian minister in Washington appealed to the State Department to uphold the Atlantic Charter against this infringement of Iranian sovereignty. Hull replied that the invasion was justifiable militarily, which was the same position taken by Roosevelt in response to a subsequent appeal by the shah of Iran. While the Iranian controversy was demonstrating the difficulties of moral pledges, the first Indian challenge came from the president of the Hindu Mahasabha, V. D. Sarvarkar, who cabled Roosevelt on August 28 asking whether the United States could, under the Atlantic Charter, guarantee Indian independence within one year.[20]

The association of the Atlantic Charter with India came to general public and official attention on September 9, when Churchill told the House of Commons that Article 3 did not apply to the British Empire. The article had been intended for peoples living under the Nazi yoke; problems of countries under allegiance to the British crown were another matter.

Because the speech contained references to the joint policy, Churchill sent an advance copy to the American Ambassador, who was convinced that the statement would intensify charges of British imperialism and the feeling that the Churchill government was pursuing a "do nothing policy" toward India. Before Churchill spoke to the Commons, Winant attempted to dissuade him from qualifying Article 3, but to no avail, for the prime minister said he could not alter a policy agreed to by the cabinet.

Winant's apprehensions were borne out by India's response. Moderate opinion, represented by individuals and groups normally willing to cooperate with the Government of India and to mediate between the British and the National Congress, was disappointed and critical. The premier of the Punjab, Sir Sikander Hyat Khan, termed the qualification the biggest rebuff India had ever received. On be-

[20] Telegram from Rangoon, August 16, 1941, 740.0011 E.W./14095; Maung Saw to Roosevelt, November 26, 1941, PSF: Burma, Roosevelt Papers; radiogram, V. D. Savarkar to Roosevelt, August 28, 1941, Box O.F. 48-H, India, 1940–41, *ibid.*

half of the Non-Party Leaders' Conference, Sir Tej Bahadur Sapru said the statement raised doubts among all Indians as to Britain's willingness to part with power. On November 18 the Indian Council of State adopted by a ten-to-six vote a resolution that the viceroy convey to the British government the council's deep discontent over the Churchill speech, adding that it would likely prejudice the war effort.[21]

The political situation in India and the British attitude toward the Atlantic Charter were the subjects of most official concern and popular writings in the fall of 1941. American liberal reaction to Churchill's speech reflected disillusionment. Journals that earlier had ignored the implications of Article 3 toward Asian nationalism responded that Churchill had undermined the integrity of the Atlantic Charter. *The New Republic, The Christian Century,* and Richard Walsh in *Asia* criticized the imperial stand. The nationalist line was taken by persuasive writers. In *Harper's,* Anup Singh suggested that a settlement was possible if the British would release political prisoners, enlarge the viceroy's council to include all political groups, and then regard the council as a national government. Krishnalal Shridharani's *My India, My America* was published in the fall of 1941. A popular work, it described Indian culture realistically and presented the Congress' arguments for unity and immediate freedom. Shridharani, who had received a doctorate from Columbia University in 1939, said that the Atlantic Charter offered hope but that further American involvement in India was inevitable.

Continued American sympathy for the nationalist position aroused concern in Britain. British visitors, who included Minister of Information Duff Cooper, were impressed by the effectiveness of nationalist propaganda and suggested countermeasures. T. A. Raman, an Indian journalist and London editor of the United Press of India, toured America and through his speeches and writings became one of the chief spokesmen of the British view. An imposing volume, *India and Democracy,* by Sir George Schuster and Guy Wint, was published in

[21] Telegram from London, November 4, 1941, *FRUS, 1941,* 3:181–83; telegram from New Delhi, November 28, 1941, *ibid.,* pp. 188–89; telegram to New Delhi, November 25, 1941, 740.0011 E.W./15960; *New York Times,* November 19, 1941; *India Today,* September, 1941, pp. 3–4, and December, 1941, p. 4.

America and presented an elaborate defense of British policy. Schuster, a member of Parliament and former civil servant in India, and Wint, who had spent two years doing research on the book, presented India as a land of political and religious disunity. Its problems could be solved only by a gradual program of self-government and close cooperation between the Indians and the British. In the *Pacific Historical Review*, Professor John Christian of the University of Washington offered a similar view of India. In November, Bajpai arrived in New York and in his press conferences affirmed Indian support of the war effort, holding that the National Congress' opposition had been "symbolic," since none of the nationalists desired to interfere with the war effort.[22]

From India, Wilson continued to be critical of the British and of Amery. On October 12, 1941, Gandhi issued his first direct appeal to the United States for assistance against the British. He argued that Americans should think seriously before giving further assistance to Britain without assurances on imperial policy. "She should withdraw any help unless there are guarantees of human liberties. If America is true to her tradition, she should say what Abraham Lincoln would say. America would lose nothing by making stipulations concerning her war help."[23] Gandhi's sentiments were endorsed in *The Christian Century* and *Asia*, and a *New York Times* editorial reflected substantial agreement that America should be committed to freedom in India.[24]

In early November, after reviewing Wilson's reports of political

---

[22] *Asia*, November, 1941, pp. 594–95; *The New Republic*, November 17, 1941, pp. 638–39; *The Christian Century*, December 3, 1941, p. 1492; Anup Singh, "Britain's Last Chance in India," *Harper's Magazine*, September, 1941, pp. 358–65; *Great Britain and the East*, July 13, 1941, p. 71; John L. Christian, "The Other Side of India," *Pacific Historical Review*, December, 1941, pp. 447–60; *Asia and the Americas*, August, 1941, pp. 428–31; *New York Times*, August 2, November 15, and December 3, 1941; Krishnalal Shridharani, *My India, My America* (New York: Duell, Sloan & Pearce, 1941), pp. 349–607; Sir George Schuster and Guy Wint, *India and Democracy* (New York: Macmillan, 1941), pp. ix–xvi, 231–35, 429–44, *et passim*.

[23] *New York Times*, October 13, 1941; letter from Calcutta, August 4, 1941, 845.00/1250.

[24] *The Christian Century*, October 29, 1941, p. 1323; *Asia*, December, 1941, pp. 662–63; *New York Times*, November 24, 1941.

disintegration, Murray again suggested that Winant raise the Indian question in London. While agreeing with Murray that the Atlantic Charter had to be universal, Welles responded that no one in the American government was sufficiently familiar with the Indian situation to suggest a policy to Britain. Welles deferred to the position of Halifax, whom he described as "probably the most liberal Viceroy India has ever had," that immediate political changes would produce chaos. Thus, as he had prior to the Atlantic Conference, Welles again blunted a proposal for more direct American involvement in India. He continued to accept the British imperial view that India was a hopelessly complicated problem. Of the higher-ranking officials who dealt with the Indian question, Welles alone inclined toward the British side. Roosevelt frequently preferred to deal with the State Department through the under secretary, who was a long-time friend, and this, of course, placed Welles in an unusually strong position.[25]

The Atlantic Charter and its application to the British Empire could not be fully ignored. Burmese Prime Minister Maung Saw, who had failed to gain any promises from the British during a visit there, came to the United States and met briefly with Roosevelt on November 15. Under the dyarchy arrangement in Burma, the prime minister lacked diplomatic status and thus the competence to discuss implementation of the Atlantic Charter. Nonetheless, he raised the question at his meeting with Roosevelt, and in a letter to Roosevelt upon his deparure on November 26 he questioned whether the president agreed with the Churchill speech of September 9. In reply, the Roosevelt administration stated that such discussions would be inappropriate.[26]

In those November days of a worsening crisis with Japan, Roosevelt naturally regarded India, Burma, and the Atlantic Charter as secondary problems. But Roosevelt and Hull were unquestionably opposed to imperialism. Since the 1920s, when he had spoken out against American policy in Latin America, Roosevelt had been critical of imperial-

[25] Welles to Hull, November 15, 1941, *FRUS, 1941*, 3:186–87; memorandum Near Eastern Affairs (Murray), November 7, 1941, *ibid.*, pp. 184–86; Welles, *Where Are We Heading?* pp. 324–26.

[26] Maung Saw to Roosevelt, November 26, 1941, and memorandum, Hull to Roosevelt, December 15, 1941, PSF: Burma, Roosevelt Papers.

ism. Within the State Department, Hull's anticolonial inclination was strongly supported by Berle and increasingly so by the officers in the Division of Near Eastern Affairs and at the American missions in India. While Roosevelt avoided any open pronouncements on India, he sympathized with the nationalist position. Shortly after his return from the Atlantic Conference, he received a note from his wife inquiring about his position on India. In response, Roosevelt wrote: "I cannot have probable feelings on India."[27] When Pearl Harbor brought the United States into a world-wide struggle for survival, the president's feelings about India would become more obvious.

[27] Franklin Roosevelt to Eleanor Roosevelt, August 21, 1941, Box O.F. 48-H, India, 1940–41, *ibid.*

II

The Louis Johnson Mission:
An Attempt to Avert
Political Collapse

COINCIDING WITH THE PEARL HARBOR ATTACK, Japanese sea-borne inva-
sions were launched against the Philippines, Malaya, Hong Kong, and
the lesser islands of the Pacific. On December 8 the United States and
Great Britain declared war on Japan but were unable to halt the
Japanese advance. Within three days the American outpost at Guam
had fallen, and on December 23 the Japanese took Wake Island. On
the Russian and African fronts, the Allied position was equally
desperate. In those dark December days the United States mobilized
its resources. The necessity for full cooperation among all non-Axis
nations and the prospect of a continued Japanese advance toward
South Asia brought India to military as well as political significance.

During the first five months of the war, the United States accordingly
assumed a more active role in British-Indian relations. Official interest
increased steadily, culminating in the April, 1942, mission of Louis
Johnson to India. As the President's "personal representative" to
India, Johnson attempted to bring about a settlement during and after
the unsuccessful British mission headed by Sir Stafford Cripps. This
official concern reflected an unparalleled public interest in India. In
1942, American periodicals carried three times as many articles as they
had in any previous year; editorial comment was extensive, and public opinion polls indicated a high degree of awareness of Indian
developments.

Initial concern was expressed briefly during Churchill's visit to America in late December. On December 22 Churchill arrived in Washington to discuss military strategy, the formation of the United Nations, and other matters with Roosevelt. On one occasion during their meetings, Roosevelt raised the India question with the prime minister, who promptly explained the necessity for a continuation of British rule. According to Churchill, "I reacted so strongly and at such length that he never raised it again."[1] A mood of unity with the British prevailed during Churchill's visit and was underscored by his December 26 message before Congress. After briefly visiting Ottawa, Churchill returned to Washington and on New Year's Day, 1942, signed the Declaration of the United Nations, affirming the Atlantic Charter as the statement of Allied war aims. Among the twenty-six signers was Bajpai for the Government of India.

While Roosevelt and Churchill conferred in Washington, the Working Committee of the Indian National Congress was meeting at Bardoli. Nehru, Congress president Maulana Abul Kalam Azad, and other leaders who had been released just before Pearl Harbor, turned their attention to the war, which now threatened India. As the Bardoli session began on December 23, Rangoon was bombed by the Japanese, and on Christmas Day Hong Kong fell. Again rejecting Gandhi's pacifism, the Congress resolution on December 30 reaffirmed its willingness to support the Allied war effort in return for recognition of independence.

The United States thus became more concerned with India's political and military situation. On January 8 the American commissioner at New Delhi was instructed to report extensively on the political situation, particularly the popular strength of Gandhi, the Muslim League, and the Working Committee's position. On January 12 the American and British chiefs of staff agreed that, while only minimum resources necessary for safeguarding Asian interests should be diverted from operations against Germany, Japan should be prevented from conquering Singapore, the East Indies, the Philippines, and Burma. India's potential contribution to this effort, however, required con-

[1] Winston S. Churchill, *The Second World War: The Hinge of Fate* (Boston: Houghton Mifflin, 1950), p. 209.

siderable assistance from the United States, a point which Bajpai had emphasized a month earlier in drawing State Department attention to a Government of India report on India's war effort. In late January, Roosevelt directed that further study be made of the question of military assistance to India.[2]

The fall of Singapore on February 15 and the visit of Chiang Kai-shek to India focused the attention of the press, State Department, and Senate Foreign Relations Committee on India and led to Roosevelt's decision to raise the Indian question again with Churchill. The surrender of the supposedly impregnable naval base at Singapore left the remainder of Malaya, Burma, and India vulnerable to Japanese conquest. In his article "Post-Singapore War in the East," Walter Lippmann argued that a reorientation of British imperial policy was necessary, but he acknowledged that it would be difficult unless the United States assumed responsibility for the war in Asia. The Hearst newspapers, the columnist John Thompson, and editorials in *The Christian Science Monitor* and the *New York Journal and American* echoed the same sentiment.[3]

The visit of Chiang Kai-shek, highly respected in America for his nation's resistance to the Japanese, focused more attention on the Indian situation. The Chinese leader intended primarily to discuss military operations with the Government of India, but he also sought to persuade Nehru and Gandhi to support the war effort. Resenting this seeming interference by a man who was known to favor the National Congress' view, the Churchill government insisted that meetings with the nationalist leaders be arranged through the imperial government. Roosevelt, however, encouraged Chiang's visit; upon receiving word of the fall of Singapore, he cabled Churchill that the

2 Telegram from New Delhi, January 2, 1942, 845.00/1271; memorandum, Near Eastern Affairs (Murray), December 10, 1941, 845.00/1270; telegram from New Delhi, January 8, 1941, 845.00/1271; Berle to Hull, December 12, 1941, 845.00/1263; Berle to Hull, December 20, 1941, *Foreign Relations of the United States, 1942*, vol. 1, *General: The British Commonwealth, the Far East* (1960), pp. 593–95; Berle to Roosevelt, January 29, 1942, *ibid.*, pp. 599–601.

3 *New York Journal and American*, February 13, 1942; *Los Angeles Times*, February 24, 1942; *The Christian Science Monitor*, February 26, 1942; *Los Angeles Examiner*, February 17, 1942; *San Francisco News*, February 26, 1942.

mission would be useful. Despite British reservations, Chiang did meet with Nehru in New Delhi and with Gandhi at Calcutta, and, at the close of his visit on February 24, he publicly expressed hope that the British would give political power to the Indians. Through his ambassador in Washington, T. V. Soong, Chiang informed Roosevelt that he had been shocked by the military and political situation, which he believed could be improved only if the British transferred political responsibility and did "not allow different parties in India to cause confusion."[4]

While Chiang Kai-shek was in India, Berle was again urging that the United States bring pressure to bear on the British. Wilson's reports from New Delhi noted the increasing Indian resentment of the British and the first criticism in the Indian press of seeming American indifference to India. On February 17 Berle, with the support of the Division of Near Eastern Affairs, drafted a memorandum arguing that the fall of Singapore warranted another American approach to the Churchill government on the Indian situation. Berle outlined an involved plan for a settlement which the United States might suggest. Roosevelt, however, was not yet to the point of attempting to define British policy, but he did accept the essence of the Berle memorandum. On February 25 the White House cabled Winant that Ambassador W. Averell Harriman, serving as the president's special representative dealing with matters related to Lend-Lease for the British Empire, should confidentially discuss with Churchill the possibility of a new approach to the Indian problem.[5]

Also on February 25, as Chiang's parting comments were being reported in America and his message was received at the White House, several members of the Senate Foreign Relations Committee expressed exasperation with British policy. At a closed session Senators Tom Connally, Arthur Vandenberg, Theodore Green, Wallace White, and

---

[4] Chinese Minister, via Foreign Affairs, to Roosevelt, February 25, 1942, *FRUS, 1942*, 1:605; Churchill, *Hinge of Fate*, pp. 206–7; Robert E. Sherwood, *Roosevelt and Hopkins: An Intimate History*, rev. ed. (New York: Grosset & Dunlap, 1950), p. 512.

[5] Letter from New Delhi, February 19, 1942, 845.00/1323; Berle to Welles, February 17, 1942, *FRUS, 1942*, 1:602–4; telegram to London, February 25, 1942, *ibid.*, p. 604.

Robert La Follette, Jr., argued that extensive assistance to Britain justified participation in imperial decisions. Furthermore, the Japanese menace to India implied that the United States should exert influence to bring Indian manpower into the conflict.[6]

The sentiments of the senators, Chiang Kai-shek, State Department officials, the White House, and the consensus of the American press ran counter to the attitude of Churchill. In his history of the war, Churchill prefaced his description of the American overtures thus:

Before Pearl Harbor, India had been regarded as a lamentable example of British imperialism, but as an exclusive British responsibility. Now that the Japanese were advancing towards its frontiers the United States Government began to express its view and offer counsel on Indian affairs. In countries where there is only one race, broad and lofty views are taken of the colour question. Similarly, states which have no overseas colonies or possessions are capable of rising to moods of great elevation and detachment about the affairs of those who have.[7]

When Harriman discussed the Indian question with Churchill on February 26, the prime minister retorted that Britain could not risk alienation of the Muslims, who contributed three-fourths of the manpower to the Indian army. Moreover, India had ample manpower ready to fight the Japanese; the real problem was training and equipping an enlarged Indian army.[8]

Churchill's adverse reaction to Roosevelt's gesture failed to lessen American concern with India, and, despite his contention of Indian support for the war, he was being forced by events in Asia and pressures within his government to seek a settlement which would assure full Indian cooperation. During late February and early March, 1942, the United States moved on the Indian question at four levels: continued contact with the British on Indian policy, Roosevelt's suggestion of a specific policy to Churchill, the designation of an American economic and supply mission to India, and the appointment of Louis Johnson as the president's "personal representative" to India.

[6] Assistant Secretary of State (Long) to Welles, February 25, 1942, *FRUS, 1942*, 1: 606–7.

[7] Churchill, *Hinge of Fate*, p. 209.

[8] Telegram from London, February 26, 1942, *FRUS, 1942*, 1:608.

The Japanese advanced steadily in Burma, making an invasion of India and Australia seem imminent. In February, German and Japanese naval assaults destroyed 679,000 tons of Allied shipping. Allied control of the Indian Ocean and Middle East was tenuous. With the military situation worsening, the Churchill government considered making another effort to settle the Indian question. On March 4 Churchill advised Roosevelt that he was contemplating a declaration of postwar dominion status, but reaffirmed that Britain could not abandon its obligations to the Muslims, untouchables, and princes of India. To reinforce this argument, Churchill sent a series of statements made by non-Congress leaders: Jinnah criticizing the Sapru group as a tool of the Congress and holding the British to their pledge of August, 1940; Sir Firoz Khan Noon, a Muslim on the viceroy's executive council, foreseeing disorder if the Congress were given immediate power; and the military adviser to the secretary of state for India warning that any undermining of British authority would unsettle the martial classes in the army. Three days later Churchill sent the comments of the Muslim governor of the Punjab, who said that Indians at this time of crisis wanted the stability of British rule.

With the entry of Japanese troops into Rangoon on March 8, 1942, pressures from within the British government and from the United States and China forced a commitment to attempt a settlement. While Churchill himself did not favor any change in policy, he did get together a committee to plan a special mission to India. The committee was comprised of Sir Stafford Cripps, who was to head the mission, Leopold S. Amery, Clement Attlee, and former Indian officials John Anderson and P. J. Grigg. On March 10 Churchill informed the viceroy of the government's plan with the following explanation: "It would be impossible, owing to the unfortunate rumours and publicity and the general American outlook, to stand on a purely negative attitude, and the Cripps Mission is indispensable to prove our honesty of purpose and to gain time for the necessary consultations."[9]

While these plans were still at the rumor stage, and as the military situation worsened, American newsmen became more critical of

[9] Churchill, *Hinge of Fate*, pp. 214–15; Churchill to Roosevelt, March 4, 1942, *FRUS, 1942*, 1:612.

38

British policy and some called upon Roosevelt to exert his influence. Advocacy of the Congress' demand for immediate independence, with American assurances if necessary, came from Krishnalal Shridharani in *The Nation*, Kumar Goshal in *Amerasia*, editorial comment in *The New Republic*, the column of William Randolph Hearst in his papers, and, of course, in the statements of the India League of America and the American League for India's Freedom. Impatience with the British was expressed in the popular weeklies *Newsweek* and *Time*, but without suggestion of any solutions. A feature article on India in *Time* summarized the British and National Congress' positions, but its tone was derisive of the divergence in British war aims and Indian policy. Editorials in *The Nation* typified another view, one which sympathized with nationalist aspirations but asked Indians to concentrate on the war.[10]

Journalists did not know that on March 10 Roosevelt had suggested a definite Indian policy to Churchill. Attempting to respond to the Churchill argument of Indian diversity and the inability of the National Congress to represent all Indian groups, Roosevelt wrote a lengthy letter which drew parallels between the Indian situation and that of the American colonies immediately after their independence. The Articles of Confederation had been a stop-gap measure by which the nation, through trial and error, discovered the need for a stronger government. Perhaps, the president suggested, India could undergo similar constitutional developments. A temporary dominion government, bringing together different castes, occupations, religions, and representing the British provinces and princely states, could function for a few years or until the end of the war, when it would set up a body to consider the formation of a permanent government. The temporary central government would control certain executive and administrative services such as finance, communication, and transportation. Roosevelt then closed: "For the love of Heaven don't bring me into this, though I do want to be of help. It is, strictly speaking,

[10] *Amerasia*, March, 1942, pp. 36–41; *The New Republic*, March 2, 1942, pp. 290–92; *Time*, March 16, 1942, pp. 26–28; *New York Times*, March 11, 1942; *The Nation*, March 14, 1942, pp. 300–301; *ibid.*, March 28, 1942, pp. 365–67; Walter C. Mackett, "Some Aspects of the Development of American Opinion on India, 1918–1947" (Ph.D. diss., University of Southern California, 1957), pp. 307–8.

none of my business, except insofar as it is a part and parcel of the successful fight that you and I are making."[11]

While a unique departure, Roosevelt's message left much unanswered. Was ultimate responsibility to rest with the temporary central dominion government, or would it remain with the viceroy? Use of the term "dominion" indicated an independent government, but its limited powers foreshadowed the continuation of British authority. Most important, would the interim government control defense? Obviously Roosevelt intended to offer an outline and not a definitive policy. The limitations in his message, however, enabled Amery to claim later that the Cripps plan reflected the essence of the Roosevelt suggestion.[12]

Churchill remained unwilling to accept American assistance. As Robert Sherwood observed in *Roosevelt and Hopkins*:

It is probable that the only part of that cable with which Churchill agreed was Roosevelt's admission that it is "none of my business." Hopkins said a long time later that he did not think that any suggestions from the President to the Prime Minister in the entire war were so wrathfully received as those relating to the solution of the India problem. As one of Churchill's closest and most affectionate associates has said to me, "The President might have known that India was one subject on which Winston would never move a yard." It was indeed one subject on which the normal, broad-minded, good-humored, give-and-take attitude which prevailed between the two statesmen was stopped cold. It may be said that Churchill would have seen the Empire in ruins and himself buried under them before he could concede the right of any American, however great and illustrious a friend, to make any suggestions as to what he should do about India.[13]

In his history of the war, Churchill's disregard for the overture was succinctly stated:

The document is of high interest because it illustrates the difficulties of comparing situations in various centuries and scenes where almost every material

[11] Roosevelt to Churchill, March 10, 1942, *FRUS, 1942*, 1:615–16.

[12] L. S. Amery to Myron Taylor, July 2, 1942, enclosed in memorandum from Taylor to Roosevelt, July 16, 1942, Box O.F. 48-H, India, 1942, Roosevelt Papers, Franklin D. Roosevelt Library, Hyde Park, N.Y.

[13] Sherwood, *Roosevelt and Hopkins*, pp. 511–12.

fact is totally different, and the dangers of trying to apply any superficial resemblances which may be noticed due to the conduct of the war.[14]

At the time of this message to Churchill, Roosevelt was also deciding to send Louis Johnson and an American economic and production mission to India. Initially the State Department planned that Johnson would head the economic mission and replace Wilson as the American commissioner in New Delhi. When the personnel of the mission were formally announced on March 9, however, Johnson was designated as chairman, but no mention was made of his diplomatic function. Sumner Welles, who was acting secretary of state at the time, had resolved that Johnson should not head both the economic mission and the diplomatic post at New Delhi. He reversed the March 9 press release and the expectations of Johnson by appointing former Assistant Secretary of State Henry Grady chairman of the economic mission. Johnson in turn objected to the title "commissioner," observing that in his native South the title connoted an unsuccessful lawyer and was therefore aggravating to the head of a large law firm in West Virginia. On March 24 the State Department announced that Johnson would serve as Roosevelt's "personal representative" to the Government of India.

These two missions publicized America's concern with India militarily and with the forthcoming Cripps mission. In much of the press, the United States was seen as taking a hand in Indian politics. The title "personal representative," while carrying the same ministerial rank as commissioner, indicated a closer personal presidential involvement. Freed from the technical mission, Johnson could act as a political observer and perhaps participant. The degree to which Roosevelt anticipated that Johnson would assume an active role is uncertain. Welles quoted the president as being primarily concerned with having a person with military experience in India. Besides serving as assistant secretary of war from 1937 to 1940, Johnson had been a captain in World War I and an organizer of the American Legion. Welles quoted Roosevelt on the military angle in his message of March 11 informing Wilson of the changes at the New Delhi office. As such, it may have been a convenient rationalization in easing Wilson from

[14] Churchill, *Hinge of Fate*, p. 214.

his post, for Roosevelt had twice within two weeks of the Johnson appointment indicated a personal interest in India which he showed no sign of abandoning. Moreover, Roosevelt knew Johnson to be aggressive and outspoken; as assistant secretary of war he had engaged in an open fight with Secretary Harry Woodring over the question of preparedness. If Roosevelt had intended to withdraw from the Indian problem, he would have sent someone other than Johnson.[15]

The Cripps mission was followed more extensively in the American press than any previous event in Indian history. The selection of Cripps was favorably received in the United States, Britain, and India, for he had long championed nationalist aspirations. A friend of Nehru and sharing with Gandhi a deeply religious approach to life, Cripps understood the legal and psychological complexities of Indian politics. But Cripps encountered an India that had become intensely suspicious of British intent. The Japanese conquest of Southeast Asia, virtually completed with the surrender of Rangoon on March 10, and General Douglas MacArthur's retreat from the Philippines seven days later, failed to alter the mixed reactions to the war. The majority of educated opinion opposed the Japanese, but some elements in the National Congress, led by Subhas Chandra Bose, sought to secure independence through cooperation with the Axis powers. Nehru continued to view the conflict in its Indian and world setting, hoping that India would be freed to fight the Japanese. Gandhi still preached non-violent resistance to the invader, but the Nehru approach continued in ascendancy within the Congress. Jinnah and the Muslim League demanded safeguards for the Muslim minority. Engaged in the ceaseless struggle for survival, the Indian masses were indifferent.

The Cripps mission arrived in New Delhi on March 22, but the plan was not made public until a week later. In the interim Cripps ex-

[15] Transcript of Roosevelt press conference, March 16, 1942, Roosevelt Papers; memorandum of conversation by Berle, February 28, 1942, *FRUS, 1942*, 1:609–10; press release, March 9, 1942, *ibid.*, p. 613; memorandum of conversation by Assistant Secretary of State (Shaw), March 11, 1942, *ibid.*, pp. 616–17; telegram to New Delhi, *ibid.*, pp. 617–18; memorandum of conversation by Welles, April 1, 1942, *ibid.*, p. 618; memorandum, Welles to Near Eastern Affairs, March 12, 1942, 845.24/28; memorandum, Near Eastern Affairs to Welles, March 18, 1942, 123 Johnson, Louis/18; memorandum, Near Eastern Affairs (Murray), February 26, 1942, 845.01/130; Sherwood, *Roosevelt and Hopkins*, pp. 134–36.

plained the plan to the Government of India and held discussions with Indian leaders. The American mission at New Delhi reported on apparent trends, while State Department concern focused on determining the strength of the Muslim League. Memorandums from the department's British Empire Section and the Division of Near Eastern Affairs concluded that the league spoke for most Muslims. While some groups and leaders opposed the league, Jinnah was seen as becoming more tenacious and determined to secure his demands. At the least, some safeguards for the Muslim community were necessary to gain cooperation in the war effort. The Chinese government continued to press Washington on the Indian impasse. In a conference with the American ambassador in Chungking, Chiang Kai-shek reiterated his concern, and Madame Chiang argued that Indians would accept nothing less than immediate political responsibility. The day after Cripps's arrival, Sun Fo, the son of Sun Yat-sen and president of the Legislative Department of the Chinese government, publicly urged Roosevelt and Churchill to announce a "Pacific Charter" pledging the United Nations to the independence of India, Indo-China, Korea, and the Philippines.[16]

The United States learned formally of the Cripps plan on March 28, when Halifax sent an advance copy to Welles asking that it be brought to Roosevelt's attention. In this oblique manner Churchill responded to Roosevelt's March 10 suggestion. The State Department earlier had reason to suspect that the plan would be more acceptable to the Muslim League than to the National Congress; the American officer at New Delhi had reported that, after their conversations with Cripps, Jinnah appeared pleased and Azad downcast. The draft declaration, presented by Cripps at a press conference on March 29, affirmed that the goal of British policy remained the creation of an

---

[16] Telegram from Chungking, March 10, 1942, *FRUS, 1942*, 1:614–15; telegram to Chungking, March 25, 1942, *Foreign Relations of the United States, 1942: China* (1956), p. 730; telegram from Chungking, *ibid.*, pp. 730–31; telegram from London, March 12, 1942, 845.01/126; telegram from Chungking, April 4, 1942, 845.01/150; U.S. Department of State, British Empire Section, Report, "How Strong Is Muslim Hostility to a Self-Governing India?" 745.00/1310; U.S. Department of State, Division of Near Eastern Affairs, Report, "Indian Moslems," March 16, 1942, 845.00/1313.

Indian Union as an independent dominion. At the conclusion of the war, the new constitution would be drafted by an Indian body representing British India and the princely states. Any province could remain outside the proposed union and would retain the right to form its own government. A treaty between the British and the Indian constitution-making body would protect religious and racial minorities. Major changes during the war, however, remained impossible. During the war crisis, control of defense had to remain with the British. It was hoped that all Indian political groups would cooperate in supporting the war effort.[17]

The Cripps offer met with almost unanimously favorable response in America. In general it was hailed as proof of the sincerity of Britain's promises and as an offer of reasonable compromise which the National Congress should accept. *The New Republic*, long a critic of the British in India, argued that the National Congress could not reject a plan which permitted provinces the right of non-accession, for that would be inconsistent with the Congress' avowed belief in democracy. *The Nation*, until recent months a champion of the Congress, described the offer as reasonable and the non-accession principle as a necessary guarantee for minorities. *Time, Newsweek, The Christian Science Monitor*, the *Los Angeles Times, New York Times*, and *New York Herald Tribune* all viewed the plan as an enlightened departure from British policy. Several senators joined in the chorus of approval, seeing the plan as a vindication of Britain's support of the Atlantic Charter. Although Roosevelt was not questioned on the plan at his press conference of March 31, Welles had told the press the day before that the American government hoped it would be a satisfactory solution to the Indian problem. Only *The Christian Century* and Kate Mitchell, in *Amerasia*, interpreted the proposal from the viewpoint of the National Congress, which was that the Cripps offer encouraged the division of India, left real power in the hands of the British, and failed to differ substantially from the offer of August, 1940. The

---

[17] Telegram from New Delhi, March 20, 1942, *FRUS, 1942*, 1:621; Halifax to Welles, March 28, 1942, *ibid.*, pp. 621–22; telegram from New Delhi, March 31, 1942, *ibid.*, pp. 622–23; Welles to Roosevelt, March 30, 1942, PSF: Great Britain, 1941–42, Roosevelt Papers; telegram from New Delhi, March 26, 1942, 845.01/133; telegram from New Delhi, March 28, 1942, 845.01/134.

dominant mood was expressed in a *New York Times* editorial: "But we can see that simple things that make for human brotherhood are good and true in India as in our own country; and we can say to the Indian leaders that if they refuse this gift of freedom for petty, or personal, or spiteful reasons, they will lose the American sympathy and the offer of American comradeship that is now theirs for the asking."[18]

Somewhat contrary to the tone of the press, the findings of the American Institute of Public Opinion indicated that the general public favored immediate dominion status. In a poll taken on March 31, the institute asked two samples if they had heard of the plan to give self-government to India, and, if so, whether dominion status should be granted immediately or after the war. While the term "dominion status" may not have been fully understood, and some may have viewed it as less than full independence, the two samples indicated that a majority of those familiar with the question inclined toward the National Congress' position (see Table I).

Within the State Department, the Cripps offer met with unequivocal praise. A memorandum by Wallace Murray, adviser on political

Table I. Sample of American Opinion, March 31, 1942

Have you heard or read about the plan to give India self-government? If so, should England give India dominion status now or after war?

	Sample A	Sample B
Familiar with plan	78%	70%
Favor dominion status now	41	37
Favor dominion status after war	24	19
Never favor dominion status	2	2
Didn't say when	11	12
Unfamiliar with subject	22	30

Source: Prepared by Mildred Strunk, American Institute of Public Opinion, cited in *American Opinion, 1935–1946,* ed. Hadley Cantril (Princeton: Princeton University Press, 1951), p. 327.

[18] *New York Times,* March 31, 1942; *The Nation,* April 4, 1942, pp. 381–82; *The New Republic,* April, 6, 1942, pp. 443–44; *The Christian Century,* April 8, 1942, pp. 454–55; *Amerasia,* April, 1942, pp. 58–60; *The Christian Science Monitor,* March 31, 1942; *Los Angeles Times,* March 31, 1942; *Business Week,* March 21, 1942, pp. 40–42; transcript of Roosevelt press conference, March 31, 1942, Roosevelt Papers.

relations, to Berle and Welles held that the Congress would probably accept, provided Gandhi did not interfere. Murray was confident the Congress would agree to British control of the army and would not object to the non-accession option, since it first gave the Congress the opportunity to fulfill its claim that Indians, left alone, could draft a constitution which would assure unity.

This buoyancy in the State Department and in the American press contrasted sharply with the response of the National Congress and illustrated the degree to which much of American and Indian nationalist opinion had become estranged. To a people still recovering from the shock of Pearl Harbor, the Indian situation was viewed primarily in terms of its military implications. To most Indian nationalists the assumption of immediate political responsibility remained the priority, despite the trend of the war. American information about India was sparse and unreliable. No American newspaper had an office in India, which meant reliance on British sources. A few special reports from India, the Indian nationalist journals in America, and the handful of Indian writers for American magazines reached a limited audience. Throughout March, 1942, the transmitter of the New Delhi diplomatic post was used almost exclusively for sending cables from the recently established American air force command to the War Department. In his last few reports from New Delhi, Wilson described the mood as one of impatience.

When they learned of the Cripps offer, Nehru was profoundly distressed and Gandhi characterized it as a "post-dated cheque."[19] All of the Congress newspapers criticized the retention of control of defense and the non-accession option, which invited the division of the country. Within twenty-four hours of the optimistic Murray memorandum, the New Delhi office reported to Washington that the Congress' Working Committee would reject the plan.

Before the Congress gave any official reply, however, Lord Halifax was predicting the failure of the mission. In a conversation with Welles on April 1, Halifax blamed the Congress for the failure. He argued that, since the Congress realized it could not possibly reach an agreement with the Muslim League, it preferred to shift responsi-

[19] V. P. Menon, *The Transfer of Power in India* (Princeton: Princeton University Press, 1957), p. 126; telegram from New Delhi, March 17, 1942, *FRUS, 1942*, 1:619–21.

bility onto the British. The former viceroy assured Welles that the Japanese menace and favorable economic conditions would prevent any major disorders.[20]

On April 2 the Working Committee agreed to reject the plan on the grounds of the non-accession and defense provisions, but it also resolved to continue negotiations, particularly for an interim settlement. On April 3 arrangements were made for conferences between Nehru and General Archibald Wavell, commander in chief in India, to delineate a division of responsibility between an Indian defense minister and the commander in chief.

On April 3, in the midst of a crisis tinged with cautious optimism, Johnson arrived in New Delhi. Although he lacked diplomatic experience and any sophisticated knowledge of Indian politics, Johnson knew of Roosevelt's deep interest in the Indian situation and was aware of the president's messages to Churchill. He quickly assumed an active role in the delicate negotiations.

After meeting twice with Cripps and once with Wavell on April 4, Johnson cabled Roosevelt urging presidential intercession with Churchill to modify the Cripps plan. Roosevelt was then informed that Cripps was suggesting to Churchill three British options on the defense issue: first, to refuse any concessions; second, to grant India control of the Defense Ministry, provided that the Indians agreed not to interfere with imperial war policy; third, to convert the Defense Ministry into a War Ministry under the commander in chief and thereby turn the defense ministership into an innocuous position to be given to an Indian. Cripps opposed the first and preferred the second, but he feared that the British cabinet, commander in chief, and viceroy would oppose both the second and third choices. Cripps acknowledged to Johnson that, unless Roosevelt influenced Churchill to accept the second approach, the mission would fail. Welles brought Johnson's plea to Roosevelt's attention, but the president declined to intercede, commenting that this might only complicate the situation.[21]

While Roosevelt refused to act, his personal representative assumed

[20] Telegram from New Delhi, March 31, 1942, 845.01/140; telegram from New Delhi, April 1, 1942, 845.01/142; memorandum of conversation by Welles, April 1, 1942, *FRUS, 1942*, 1:623.

[21] Telegrams from New Delhi, April 2 and 4, 1942, *FRUS, 1942*, 1:624–27; telegram to New Delhi, April 5, 1942, *ibid.*, pp. 627–28.

the position of mediator among Cripps, Wavell, Lord Linlithgow, Azad, and Nehru. From the fifth to the tenth of April, Johnson worked incessantly to prevent the failure of the Cripps mission. On April 5 and 6 Johnson informed Congress leaders of the revisions that were being made in the defense formula. The approach would follow the third alternative outlined in Johnson's April 4 cable. The commander in chief would sit on the viceroy's executive council as war member, and as such would be subject to the control of the British government. An Indian would be designated defense minister, and would assume certain nonessential functions, such as public relations, army printing, the operation of canteens, and securing petroleum requirements. In addition, an Indian would serve in the British war cabinet, handling questions dealing with Indian defense, and another would serve on the U.N. Pacific War Council. Acknowledging that the plan would be rejected by the National Congress, Johnson secured a promise from Nehru that the rejection would not be formally delivered until the American representative had had an opportunity to confer with various leaders. While Cripps and the Government of India were formalizing this revision in the defense formula, the importance of the defense of India became immediate. On April 5 the Japanese bombed Colombo, and the next day air raids struck towns on the southwestern Indian coast.

The revised formula was offered by Cripps on April 7 and was immediately found unacceptable by the Congress' Working Committee. Johnson then assumed the initiative in seeking to secure a compromise defense plan. With Cripps's approval, he went to Wavell, who along with the viceroy had urged Churchill's rejection of the defense approach favored by Cripps. Johnson won Wavell's and Lord Linlithgow's backing for an enlargement of the Indian defense minister's responsibilities, after assuring them that this would not interfere with military operations. On the morning of August 8 Johnson carried this suggestion, which most importantly included giving the defense minister control of the Defense Co-ordination Department, to Nehru and Azad. The Working Committee suggested certain modifications, notably the use of the term "national government" in place of "viceroy's council." This explicitly suggested a responsible Indian government, leaving only certain military powers to the commander in chief. While

Cripps had used the phrase "national government" in some early conversations with the nationalist leaders, the official statements had referred to "viceroy's executive council," thereby implying a continuation of the ultimate authority of the viceroy. When Cripps formally presented the second revised defense plan on the afternoon of April 8, the term "executive council" was intact.

Johnson's maneuverings produced hopes for a settlement in Delhi and consternation in London. Roosevelt's intimate adviser, Harry Hopkins, arrived in London on April 8 to discuss military plans. The next morning he met Churchill, who questioned Johnson's authority to mediate. The prime minister reported that he had received word from Lord Linlithgow that Cripps had offered the revised defense formula without consulting the viceroy. Lord Linlithgow further advised that the original proposal would have been accepted had not Cripps and Johnson anticipated failure. The revised defense formula was to be considered by the British cabinet at noon. Hopkins assured Churchill that the sending of Johnson had nothing to do with the Cripps mission and that, indeed, Cripps was probably seeking to use Johnson, and indirectly Roosevelt's name, to work out a settlement. Hopkins added that Roosevelt had given him instructions to reiterate that he would not be drawn into the question except at Churchill's request and after assurances from both sides that his mediation would be accepted. When Hopkins finished, Churchill cabled Lord Linlithgow that Johnson was not acting as Roosevelt's personal representative in the negotiations.[22]

Churchill's refusal to accept the compromise formula brought an end to the negotiations. Meeting on the evening of April 9, Cripps astounded Nehru, Azad, and Johnson with the terse statement that the original defense offer would stand. The "Johnson formula" was withdrawn. An embittered Johnson cabled Roosevelt that "London wanted a Congress refusal."[23]

On April 11 the National Congress formally rejected the plan, with all other political groups except the Liberal party following suit. The

[22] Telegrams from New Delhi, April 7 and 9, 1942, *ibid.*, pp. 628–30; Hopkins to Roosevelt, April 9, 1942, *ibid.*, pp. 629–30; telegram from London, April 9, 1942, 845.01/152.

[23] Telegram from New Delhi, *FRUS, 1942,* 1:631–32.

Muslim League's objection was based on the uncertainty of non-accession, while the possibility of division produced the rejections of the Hindu Mahasabha and spokesmen for the Sikh community. As Cripps prepared to depart, a note of bitterness prevailed, with the long-time friend of Indian freedom speaking of the tyranny of the Congress and accusing Nehru of seeking Johnson's aid to secure what the Congress was incapable of gaining on its own.

Hopkins' assurances to Churchill have been viewed as the decisive factor in the failure of the Cripps mission.[24] Yet, had Hopkins upheld Johnson as Roosevelt's mediator, he would have taken an untenable position. Considering Churchill's rebuff of Roosevelt's personal efforts, it is unlikely that he would have accepted Johnson as having any authority to intervene in British-Indian relations. Hopkins, however, should have stood behind Johnson and challenged the accuracy of the viceroy's report. Johnson's report on the negotiations of April 7 and 8, however, was not received in Washington until the early afternoon of April 9, so that Hopkins was unaware of Johnson's view that he had the backing of the viceroy. At the least, Hopkins could have upheld Johnson by expressing confidence that the American representative would not be acting illegally. He could have requested time to check on Johnson's role, rather than blame Cripps for what Johnson had allegedly done.

Even if the "Johnson formula" had remained, however, the Congress' acceptance would still have been uncertain. Nehru said later that, before the April 9 meeting, chances of agreement were about seventy-five per cent. The defense question was part of the broader issue of whether India was to have a responsible wartime government. Congress leaders felt that Cripps had led them to believe they would secure a "national government," but that was more than the British were willing to give. The "Johnson formula" was a nominal change from the first defense plan, and even Churchill acknowledged that in his conversation with Hopkins. It was, however, a satisfactory resolution to the most important immediate question. A defense compromise might have led to negotiations and resolution of the broader question.

---

[24] M. S. Venkataramani and B. K. Shrivastava, "The United States and the Cripps Mission," *India Quarterly*, July, 1963, pp. 248–50.

Considering the limitations of the original offer and the attitudes of the British and the National Congress, failure was almost certain.

Only Roosevelt's direct intervention with Churchill could possibly have renewed negotiations. Roosevelt received conflicting interpretations on the breakdown from Churchill and Johnson. On the evening of April 10 Churchill cabled that word from Cripps indicated that the Congress' rejection was based on the failure to attain a national government and not merely on the defense issue. The prime minister quoted his reply to Cripps, which read in part:

You have done everything in human power and your tenacity, perseverance and resourcefulness have proved how great was the British desire to reach a settlement. You must not feel unduly discouraged or disappointed with the results. The effect throughout Britain and in the United States has been wholly beneficial. The fact that the break comes on the broadest issues and not on tangled formulas about defense is a great advantage.[25]

The next morning Roosevelt received Johnson's report on the futile compromise, with its condemnation of the British and the suggestion that Churchill and the viceroy had undermined Cripps. Earlier in the week, intervention had been urged not only by Johnson but in State Department memorandums prepared by Berle and Paul Alling of Near Eastern Affairs. While Roosevelt refused to comment on the Indian situation at his April 10 news conference, pressures were building for another appeal to Churchill.[26]

Abruptly on the afternoon of April 11, Roosevelt cabled Churchill, urging that negotiations be reopened and challenging the prime minister's interpretation of the failure:

. . . I most earnestly hope that you may find it possible to postpone Cripps's departure from India until one more final effort has been made to prevent a breakdown in negotiations.

I am sorry to say that I cannot agree with the point of view set forth in your message to me that public opinion in the United States believes that

---

[25] Churchill to Roosevelt, April 11, 1942, *FRUS, 1942*, 1:632–33.

[26] Telegram from New Delhi, April 11, 1942, *ibid.*, p. 632; Berle to Welles, April 2, 1942, 845.00/1288; transcript of Roosevelt press conference, April 10, 1942, Roosevelt Papers.

the negotiations have failed on broad general issues. The general impression here is quite the contrary. The feeling is almost universally held that the deadlock has been caused by the unwillingness of the British Government to concede to the Indians the right of self-government, notwithstanding the willingness of the Indians to entrust technical, military, and naval defense control to the competent British authorities. American public opinion cannot understand why, if the British Government is willing to permit the component parts of India to secede from the British Empire after the war, it is not willing to permit them to enjoy what is tantamount to self-government during the war. . . . I read that an agreement seemed very near last Thursday night. If he [Cripps] could be authorized by you to state that he was empowered by you personally to resume negotiations as at that point with the understanding that minor concessions would be made by both sides, it seems to me that an agreement might yet be found.

I still feel . . . that if the component groups in India could now be given the opportunity to set up a nationalist government similar in essence to our form of the government under the Articles of Confederation with the understanding that upon the termination of a period of trial and error they would then be enabled to determine upon their own form of constitution and, as you have already promised them, to determine their future relationship with the British Empire, a solution could probably be found.[27]

Roosevelt's intervention unfortunately came too late. Such pressure at the time Johnson was on the verge of working out a compromise plan would have been extremely difficult for Churchill to resist. Moreover, the president's naïve comparison of the Indian situation to the American colonies further undermined his proposal. If the State Department had been consulted, a more realistic suggestion could have been quickly formulated. Instead, as was frequently the case, Roosevelt relied on personal diplomacy, which often amounted to acting on whim.

Officially, Churchill responded to Roosevelt's appeal with a polite rejection, but his war memoir reflected outright scorn for Roosevelt's ideas. As far as Churchill was concerned, the mission had failed. Receiving the message in the early morning hours of April 12, the prime minister said he could decide such matters only with the approval of the cabinet, which could not be convened until the next day. Moreover, Cripps had already departed, and the positions of all sides were

[27] Roosevelt to Churchill, April 11, 1942, *FRUS, 1942,* 1:633–34.

matters of record. Churchill would bring the matter before the cabinet if Roosevelt requested it, but the prime minister obviously opposed reopening the negotiations. He closed: "Anything like a serious difference between you and me would break my heart and surely deeply injure both our countries at the height of this terrible struggle."[28]

In his war history Churchill forthrightly upheld British rule against what he regarded as Roosevelt's naïveté:

I was thankful that events had already made such an act of madness impossible. . . . The President's mind was back in the American War of Independence, and he thought of the Indian problem in terms of the thirteen colonies fighting George III at the end of the eighteenth century. I, on the other hand, was responsible for preserving the peace and safety of the Indian continent, sheltering nearly a fifth of the population of the globe. . . . Without the integrity of executive military control and the power to govern in the war area, hope and chance alike would perish. This was no time for a constitutional experiment with a "period of trial and error" to determine the "future relationship" of India to the British Empire. Nor was the issue one upon which the satisfying of public opinion in the United States could be a determining factor. We could not desert the Indian peoples by abandoning our responsibility and leaving them to anarchy and subjugation.[29]

Churchill and Roosevelt both referred to the importance of American opinion, which by the end of the negotiations reflected a lack of appreciation of the Congress' position. Yet Americans remained primarily interested in winning Indian support for the war and were unwilling to accept suggestions that the situation was beyond resolution. For the first twelve days of April, the Cripps negotiations had been front-page news in America. Some criticism of the Congress began with the favorable press reception of the Cripps offer and word that the Congress had refused to accept it. As the negotiations began, a series of articles on Nehru by the syndicated columnist Raymond Clapper presented the nationalist leader in an unfavorable light. Based on interviews with Nehru, who was in a melancholy mood at the time, Clapper's portrayal was that of a man suspicious of American assistance as the foreshadowing of exploitation, more concerned with as-

[28] Churchill to Roosevelt, April 12, 1942, *ibid.*, pp. 634–35.
[29] Churchill, *Hinge of Fate*, pp. 219–20.

certaining Britain's confession of past crimes than with meeting immediate problems, and a Hamlet uncertain of his own leadership. When on April 5 word reached India of the unfavorable American response to the Congress' initial reluctance, Nehru appealed to Americans to reserve judgment.

Reports of Johnson's arrival led to speculation that the United States might intervene. At his April 7 press conference, however, Roosevelt denied rumors that he would mediate. That evening, in a widely publicized speech in New York City, British Ambassador Lord Halifax warned that negotiations would likely fail because of the fundamental disunity of India and the inability of the National Congress to represent all Indian groups. The next day, when Johnson's role became more definitely known in the American and Indian press, reports spread that the National Congress had sought American intervention. Nehru, however, quickly denied the stories, stating that only Britain and India could resolve the problem.

After optimistic reports that a compromise had been negotiated, the collapse, rejection, and recriminations came as shock waves. The American press reflected impatience with both sides, but in a tone critical of the National Congress. The Congress' demands were questioned in newspapers throughout the country, as well as in *Time*, *Newsweek*, and *The Nation*. Even *The Christian Century* refused to accept the Congress' position on defense. While it had viewed the Cripps offer as fair, *The New Republic* upheld the Congress' reservations on defense and non-accession. Yet, to defenders and critics of the Congress, the need for a settlement remained obvious and resulted in repeated calls for Roosevelt's mediation or a U.S. guarantee of British promises. Few newspapers and journals accepted Churchill's position that a settlement had become impossible.[30]

[30] *New York Times*, April 5–13, 1942; *Toledo Blade*, March 31–April 12, 1942; *Pittsburgh Press*, March 31–April 12, 1942; *San Francisco News*, March 31 and April 1, 1942; *Chicago Sun*, April 4, 1942; *The Christian Science Monitor*, April 3, 1942; *The Nation*, April 18, 1942, pp. 447–48; *Time*, April 13, 1942, pp. 30–36; *ibid.*, April 20, 1942, pp. 41–42; *The New Republic*, April 13, 1942, pp. 478–79; *ibid.*, April 20, 1942, p. 524; *The Christian Century*, April 22, 1942, pp. 519–21; *Los Angeles Times*, April 2, 1942; transcript of Roosevelt press conference, April 7, 1942, Roosevelt Papers.

The Cripps failure left a deep scar on British relations with the National Congress, limiting, if not entirely precluding, chances for a reconciliation. In Britain most of the press and political leaders accepted the government's explanation that responsibility for the failure rested with the National Congress. In a parliamentary debate on April 28 and 29, some members of the Labour party challenged the government and called for the reopening of negotiations. Amery and Cripps argued that the maximum concessions possible had been offered and that they could not yield on Britain's obligations to defend India and to protect the minorities against Hindu domination. In India a despairing Congress condemned the British and gravitated again toward the leadership of Gandhi. Some leaders and newspapers expressed the view that the Cripps mission had been a cynical act to show world (particularly American) opinion the supposed impossibility of reaching an Indian settlement. Nehru defended Johnson against Cripps's charge that the Congress had sought American mediation, commenting that Johnson had rendered friendly assistance but had in no way been called upon to mediate. After Cripps returned to London he altered his position on Johnson's role to virtual agreement with that of Nehru.[31]

For three weeks Johnson sought to promote negotiations by using U.S. influence to support the Nehru-Azad wing of the National Congress. At Johnson's suggestion Nehru wrote a letter to Roosevelt which Johnson's office then cabled on April 13 to Washington. While he did not appeal for Roosevelt's aid, Nehru emphasized the military potential of a free India and the popular opposition to the Japanese. Having just read Churchill's April 12 communiqué, Roosevelt realized that further pressure on Churchill at that point would have resulted in an open break with his friend. Roosevelt's response to Nehru was brief and ignored the point raised by Nehru. As cabled by the State Department for relay to Nehru, it read:

The President greatly appreciates your letter dated April 12 which he had received through Colonel Johnson. He has been deeply gratified by the message which it contains. He feels sure that all of the people of India will make

31 Telegram from London, April 28, 1942, *FRUS, 1942*, 1:646–47; telegram from London, May 5, 1942, 845.01/190; *New York Times*, April 14, 23, and 27, 1942.

55

every possible effective effort to resist Japanese aggression in every part of India. To the utmost of its ability the Government of the United States will contribute towards that common cause.[32]

Johnson, however, remained determined to commit the United States to working with Nehru in his anticipated struggle with Gandhi. The All-India Congress Committee was to meet at Allahabad on April 29 and would consider Gandhi's call for non-violent resistance to the Japanese. Johnson believed that Nehru would oppose Gandhi and that Gandhi's program would be defeated in favor of moderation. Also, the chances for Nehru's triumph would be substantially improved if agreement with the British were likely on a compromise plan that had been endorsed by the United States. For ten days prior to the Allahabad session Johnson struggled to work out such a compromise and to gain Roosevelt's support. Johnson held a press conference in which he affirmed America's interest in India and extended Roosevelt's greetings to the peoples of India, an action which caused concern in the State Department because it implied a direct Roosevelt commitment to the Indian people.

On April 21 Johnson urged that Roosevelt call upon China and Britain to join in issuing a statement of Pacific war aims, including freedom for India and the determination to defend India. In the State Department the suggestion met with opposition from Wallace Murray and from the Division of Far Eastern Affairs. Murray observed the difficulty in getting British and Chinese approval before April 29, the broad implications of such a statement, and that a policy aiding Nehru would antagonize other elements. The Division of Far Eastern Affairs acknowledged that it had previously considered a clarification of Pacific war aims to be useful, but at the same time it accepted Murray's reservations.

Murray was unquestionably correct in noting the difficulty of getting approval prior to April 29, but, if the National Congress had known that the overtures had been made, this might have lessened the appeal of Gandhi's call. A firm commitment to Indian independence and to defend the country could hardly have been opposed by any Indian

---

[32] Roosevelt to Nehru (New Delhi), April 15, 1942, *FRUS, 1942*, 1:637; see also Nehru to Roosevelt (cabled from New Delhi), April 13, 1942, *ibid.*, pp. 635–37.

political group. In principle the British could not have rejected the plan, for it reaffirmed their pledge of dominion status after the war. The Johnson plan was, however, vague as to the interim arrangement in India; perhaps American guarantees would have allayed much of the Indians' suspicion of British wartime plans.

After sending his April 21 dispatch Johnson held extensive talks with Nehru seeking to arrange an interim settlement consistent with the Congress' position and the compromises that Cripps had seemed to favor. He was confident that such a temporary government could be set up, provided that Roosevelt urged its approval on Churchill. On April 27, however, the State Department cabled Johnson that a statement of Pacific war aims would not be made and further warned the personal representative against becoming too closely identified with any particular political group.[33]

While reflecting the best hope for the realization of U.S. interests, Johnson did seek to accomplish a great deal in a very short time. He also assumed that the spirit of negotiation still prevailed in London and in India. Churchill, having refused Roosevelt's April 11 appeal when there was a slight chance to retrieve the Cripps collapse, was unlikely to respond to any last-minute American overtures to prevent the Congress from following Gandhi—an act which would reinforce the logic of continued British rule.

At Allahabad, the Congress' Working Committee received Gandhi's recommendation urging non-cooperation and non-violent resistance. Nehru, as he had done so often, surrendered to Gandhi. The Working Committee approved a resolution condemning the indifference of the British to the defense of Burma and the repressive measures adopted in many areas of India. The Government of India immediately prohibited publication of the resolution. Finally the Congress approved the resolution drafted by Nehru, but, reflecting the ideas of Gandhi, it demanded freedom and called upon the people to adopt non-violent non-cooperation against any invaders.

Still not prepared to accept failure, Johnson made a final appeal to

[33] Telegrams from New Delhi, April 21 and 25, 1942, *ibid.*, pp. 638–39, 642; telegram to New Delhi, *ibid.*, pp. 644–45; memorandum, Division of Near Eastern Affairs, April 23, 1942, 123 Johnson, Louis/25; memorandum by Adviser on Political Relations (Murray), April 24, 1942, 845.01/175.

Roosevelt. Reiterating the position of Nehru and Azad during the Cripps negotiations, Johnson urged the transfer of the viceroy's executive committee into a national government appropriately represented by the Congress, the Muslim League, and other parties. The "Johnson formula" was again offered as a solution to the defense issue. As Johnson's plea reached Washington, another pessimistic report on the Indian situation was received from Clarence Gauss, U.S. ambassador to China, who had just visited India. Gauss saw India as inviting Japanese invasion. The people were suspicious of a government headed by the detached and depressed viceroy and a defense entrusted to a tired and old Wavell.

Although Hull resumed his duties as secretary of state on April 20, 1942, Welles continued to exercise responsibility for advising Roosevelt on Indian policy. After considering Johnson's suggestion of U.S. backing for a compromise interim arrangement, Welles recommended that it be rejected. Arguing that India was now primarily a military problem, Welles maintained that political discussions would only worsen communal tensions and cause further alienation between Indians and the British, thereby rendering the defense of the country more difficult. At Welles's suggestion, Roosevelt rejected Johnson's final plan.[34]

Within a day of receiving Roosevelt's reply, Johnson requested permission to return to the United States. The ostensible reason was poor health; Johnson had been suffering from a nasal dust infection since late April and had been hospitalized. The failure to attain a political settlement, which Johnson had regarded as his principal purpose, unquestionably hastened his return. After the State Department noted that Johnson's abrupt departure might be subject to misinterpretation in India and would enable the Axis powers to claim that America was abandoning India, Roosevelt urged Johnson to remain. On May

[34] Telegram from New Delhi, May 4, 1942, *FRUS, 1942*, 1:648–50; telegram to New Delhi, May 8, 1942, *ibid.*, p. 650; telegram from Chungking, May 5, 1942, *FRUS, 1942: China*, p. 38; memorandum by Adviser on Political Relations (Hornbeck), May 7, 1942, *ibid.*, pp. 40–41; telegram from New Delhi, April 29, 1942, 845.01/174; memorandum, Welles to Roosevelt, May 7, 1942, 845.01/207.

Judging from his memoirs, Hull seemed to approve Welles's recommendation; he wrote that the United States attempted all that any Indian nationalist could have expected (Cordell Hull, *Memoirs of Cordell Hull*, 2 vols. [New York: Macmillan, 1948], 2:1483).

11 Johnson underwent surgery in New Delhi, after which three doctors recommended that he return to America.

On May 16 Johnson departed from India, ending his forty-three day mission there. He never resumed his duties, and two months later he was appointed president of General Dyestuff Corporation. While Johnson failed to prevent the political stalemate, the fault did not rest with him. In the period between the collapse of the Cripps mission and the Allahabad session, he sought to bridge the gap between the indifferent British and the frustrated National Congress. A few others also were active, notably Chakravarty Rajagopalachari, in the attempt to gain Congress approval of the non-accession provision of the Cripps offer. In the course of these efforts Johnson and Nehru became friends, and Nehru visited the American diplomat when he was hospitalized.[35] Johnson's mission demonstrated America's interest in India, but it also illustrated the limitations of that involvement.

[35] Telegram from New Delhi, May 9, 1942, *FRUS, 1942*, 1:651; telegram to New Delhi, May 13, 1942, *ibid.*, p. 653; telegram from New Delhi, May 14, 1942, *ibid.*, p. 654; U.S. Army Medical Corps Report to Johnson, May 14, 1942, 123 Johnson, Louis/38; Johnson to Nehru, May 12, 1942, Jawaharlal Nehru, *A Bunch of Old Letters Written Mostly to Jawaharlal Nehru and Some Written by Him* (London: Asia Publishing House, 1960), p. 484; *New York Times*, July 11, 1942.

III

The "Quit India" Resolution and the August, 1942, Impasse

FROM MAY UNTIL AUGUST of 1942 India's position remained politically and militarily precarious. With a Japanese invasion seemingly imminent, the National Congress followed Gandhi into a desperate "Quit India" campaign to force the end of the British *raj*. Despite the lack of a high-ranking head of the U.S. diplomatic mission in New Delhi, American interest in India continued to run deep. Pressures on Roosevelt to intervene mounted as the nationalist and British actions foreshadowed an irrevocable impasse. By early August, when the National Congress adopted the "Quit India" resolution, Indian leaders, prominent State Department officials, and many American groups and individuals had concluded that only mediation by the United States could secure a settlement. The President's efforts, however, proved to be halfhearted. Instead, to the great consternation of many Indian leaders and Americans, Roosevelt acquiesced in the British policy.

To the United States, the Indian question had become entangled with the military effort. In the first six months of 1942, India became a base of American army operations. The security of India was vital to the preservation of Allied control over the Middle East. As Germany advanced across North Africa toward Suez and as Japan completed its conquest of Southeast Asia, the Allies were alarmed by the specter of an Axis military link in the Middle East.

Actually the Axis powers never agreed to concentrate on a drive toward unity. The conquest of Burma, accomplished with surprising ease by a relatively small number of Japanese infantry and armored units, completed Japanese prewar planning. A large-scale invasion of India would require more troops and improved overland communication. For months the Japanese had contemplated whether to continue their advance to the west or to expand farther into the central Pacific. On May 15 the Japanese informed the Germans that their next offensives would be against Midway and Hawaii. Imperial headquarters, however, ordered the Fifteenth Army to stabilize its position in Burma. While it could carry out offensive air raids, no specific operations into China or India were authorized.

The British and Americans were unaware of these decisions. Although the Japanese move toward Midway seemed to indicate concentration in that theater, an attack on India appeared highly probable. The Indian army, which by the spring had nearly one million men under arms, concentrated on the defense of Assam and Bengal, the eastern coast, and Ceylon.

Moreover, India was vital as a supply route to the Chinese, whose lines of transport and communication had been shattered by the Japanese conquests. In January the Chinese government requested that lend-lease material be used to construct a road from Assam to link up with the Burma Road. When Chiang Kai-shek visited India he secured Government of India approval for the construction of roads from both Ledo and Imphal. Karachi, more than one thousand miles from Assam, became the port of disembarkation for American men and supplies. Bombay and Calcutta, both preferable in terms of geographic proximity and railway facilities, were ruled out: in the first case by a hopelessly clogged port, and in the other by susceptibility to air raids. Besides the great distance, the Karachi-to-Assam line was further handicapped by the inadequacies of the Indian railway system, which lacked double track in many areas between Karachi and Delhi and also had stretches of meter gauge between Calcutta and Assam.

The construction of airbases and the planned road into China required large-scale lend-lease operations. Based on agreements of February and March, 1942, India supplied the American military stores with war munitions and many of the usual exports to America, particu-

61

larly jute. U.S. exports to India increased nine times over prewar levels; nearly all were lend-lease materials. In late May the Grady mission completed its investigation and recommended U.S. aid to India's technical and industrial development through the dispatch of technicians, production officials, and tools and equipment.

Finally the United States opened an outlet of the Office of War Information in New Delhi, with branches in Bombay, Calcutta, and Karachi. The propaganda agency avoided India's domestic problems, but through information libraries, newsletters, and films did promote the Allied war cause and, of course, a favorable view of America.[1]

Given the constant Japanese menace, American concern continued. While many newspapers and journals showed less interest after the Cripps failure, the consensus of press comment in May and June, 1942 shifted to the Congress' position. The Indian journalists Syud Hossain in *Free World* and Anup Singh in *Asia*, and the scholarly English spokesman for the Congress H. N. Brailsford in *The New Republic*, argued the Congress' case against the British offer. In *Pacific Affairs*, Michael Greenberg, a Cambridge University Fellow and member of the International Secretariat of the Institute of Pacific Relations, summarized the Congress and British positions but with an evident pro-Congress bias. In an article appearing in *American Mercury* and reprinted in *Reader's Digest*, Time-Life correspondent Allan Michie blamed both sides for the impasse yet emphasized Britain's long delay in seeking an accord. Observing that the Congress had been criticized in America, an article in *Time* detailed the nationalists' objections to the Cripps plan. An editorial in *The Christian Century* maintained that the United States had to clarify its anticolonial position, while *The New Republic* called for Roosevelt's intervention and for an American presence at renewed negotiations. In *Asia* the philosopher Bertrand Russell suggested that the deadlock could be resolved by a U.S. guarantee of postwar independence. Editorially and through Hossain's article, *Free World*, the organ of the Free World Association, urged U.S. intervention and guarantees of independence.

In a speech before the Free World Association, which included

---

[1] Charles F. Romanus and Riley Sutherland, *United States Army in World War II: China-Burma-India Theater*, vol. 1, *Stilwell's Mission to China* (Washington, D.C.: Office of the Chief of Military History, Department of the Army, 1953), pp. 76–77, 100–101, 148, 201–9, 232.

many Americans long active in liberal causes, Vice President Henry Wallace encouraged the hopes for further official involvement. Commenting on the frequently expressed statement that the "American Century" was beginning, Wallace emphasized America's obligation to end imperialism in all forms. In a typical reaction to the speech, *Amerasia* managing editor Philip Jaffe described Wallace as championing a "Pacific Charter."[2]

While most Indians continued to believe that only changes in London's attitude could resolve their difficulties, many looked to the United States for support. An editorial in the nationalist *Amrita Bazar Patrika* foresaw the United States pressuring Britain to seek a settlement and active American mediation in future negotiations. On May 29 the Indian press carried an open letter from the maharaja of Indore to Roosevelt, appealing for U.S. intervention. The British Embassy promptly reminded the State Department that the maharaja had acted illegally, since the princes lacked diplomatic authority. Moreover, the British minister in Washington, Sir Ronald Campbell, charged that the American consul in Bombay had been instrumental in publicizing the maharaja's letter. On June 8 Consul Howard Donovan admitted that, at the request of a friend, he had unwittingly delivered a sealed letter to the Reuters office in Bombay, but he said he had not known the contents of the letter until it was published in the *Times of India*.

A few days earlier, in a meeting with Sumner Welles, Walter White of the National Association for the Advancement of Colored People urged that Roosevelt call a Pacific conference to be attended by the president, Indian leaders, and Chiang Kai-shek. The United States was then to mediate the Indian problem through a commission which

2 Syud Hossain, "Why Cripps Failed in India," *Free World*, May, 1942, pp. 296–98; Anup Singh, "What Happened in India," *Asia*, June, 1942, pp. 341–43; H. N. Brailsford, "What Happened at Delhi?" *The New Republic*, June 1, 1942, pp. 760–61; *Time*, June 29, 1942, pp. 29–30; Michael Greenberg, "India's Independence and the War," *Pacific Affairs*, June, 1942, pp. 164–87; Allan A. Michie, "Many Indias: Land of Contrasts in Cultures, Peoples, Religions," *American Mercury*, June, 1942, pp. 722–27; abbreviated reprint of the preceding in *Reader's Digest*, June, 1942, pp. 71–74; *The Christian Century*, June 10, 1942, p. 749; *The New Republic*, May 11, 1942, pp. 619–20; *ibid.*, June 29, 1942, p. 877; *Free World*, 2 (1942):359; Bertrand Russell, "To End the Indian Deadlock," *Asia and the Americas*, June, 1942, pp. 338–40; Philip F. Jaffe, "A Charter for Asia," *Amerasia*, June, 1942, pp. 161–65.

would include one prominent American Negro. At the recommendation of Welles and other officials in the State Department, this impractical scheme was ignored.

At the State Department, post-mortems on the Cripps mission were presented by Girja Shankar Bajpai, Graham Spry, and Louis Johnson. The representative of the Government of India blamed the failure on Nehru and Rajagopalachari, who feared that an interim government might fail and sought to place responsibility for the deadlock on the British. In an interview on May 13 with Paul Alling, chief of the Division of Near Eastern Affairs, and in a brief meeting with Roosevelt two days later, Spry, a Canadian who had served as special assistant to Cripps, maintained that the Congress wanted to avoid political responsibility during the war. While voicing sympathy for British, Indian, and American interests, Spry implied that any further action on India would be futile. After his return and recuperation, Johnson visited the State Department on May 26 and held a lengthy discussion with Wallace Murray, W. Leonard Parker, Calvin Oakes, and Alling of the Division of Near Eastern Affairs. Still bitter from his Indian experience, Johnson reiterated his view that the British had sabotaged Cripps by failing to support the "Johnson formula" and other compromises accepted by Cripps. Johnson denounced the Muslim League as a creature of British rule and argued that the British had no intention of defending India. Johnson's audience doubted much of his case, particularly the view that a settlement was still possible considering the divergence in the British offer and the demands of the National Congress.[3]

[3] *Amrita Bazar Patrika* (Calcutta), May 19, 1942; telegram from Bombay, May 29, 1942, *Foreign Relations of the United States, 1942*, vol. 1, *General: The British Commonwealth, the Far East* (1960), pp. 665–66; memorandum of conversation by Welles, *ibid.*, pp. 666–67; telegram to Bombay, June 6, 1942, *ibid.*, p. 669; telegram from Bombay, June 8, 1942, *ibid.*; memorandum of conversation by Adviser on Political Relations (Murray), April 24, 1942, *ibid.*, pp. 639–43; memorandum of conversation by Alling, May 13, 1942, *ibid.*, pp. 651–53; memorandum of conversation by Oakes, May 26, 1942, *ibid.*, pp. 657–59; memorandum of conversation by Oakes, May 26, 1942, *ibid.*, pp. 660–62; Welles to Roosevelt, May 22, 1942, and memorandum for files, May 25, 1942, Box O.F. 93, Negroes, May, 1942, Roosevelt Papers, Franklin D. Roosevelt Library, Hyde Park, N.Y.; *New York Times*, May 16, 1942.

George Merrell, the ranking officer at New Delhi, and Donovan from Bombay reported extensively on the further deterioration of Indian politics. After conversing with several missionaries in southern and western India, Donovan drew Washington's attention to the widespread anti-Western sentiment. An apprehensive Merrell foresaw Gandhi launching a mass civil disobedience campaign which would render India useless in the war effort. When Nehru returned to Delhi after a two week retreat in the Kulu Valley, Lampton Berry of the mission staff met with him on May 24 and 25. Informed of the American interest in his response to Gandhi's anticipated campaign, Nehru declined to comment until after he had met with Gandhi. Yet Berry was convinced that Nehru favored following Gandhi. After his second meeting with Berry, Nehru requested that the New Delhi office cable a message to Johnson. Seeing the country on the verge of an internal crisis to which the British were indifferent, and knowing that Gandhi was increasingly determined, Nehru assured his American friend that the Congress' position would shortly be clarified.

After meeting with Gandhi, Nehru cabled Johnson that popular opinion was behind the "Quit India" campaign. Yet the mahatma assured Nehru that he wanted to avoid any embarrassment to the Allied cause and was anxious that American opinion understand his motives. While not openly disagreeing with Gandhi, Nehru worked behind the scenes during June and early July in an attempt to forestall Gandhi's campaign.[4]

Gandhi's concern with American opinion revealed an awareness that his recent statements had been unfavorably received in America. In late April, Americans had learned of Gandhi's disenchantment with the Allies in his widely reported denunciation of American troops in India:

Now we have promise of a never-ending stream of soldiers from America and possibly China. I must confess that I do not look upon this event with equanimity. Cannot a limitless number of soldiers be trained out of India's millions? Would they not make as good fighting material as any in the

[4] Telegram from Bombay, May 19, 1942, 845.00/1352; telegrams from New Delhi, May 21, May 25, and June 4, 1942, *FRUS, 1942*, 1:663–65, 667–69; telegram from New Delhi, May 26, 1942, 845.00/1371.

world? Then, why foreigners? We know what American aid means. It amounts in the end to American influence, if not American rule added to British.[5]

In his paper *Harijan* Gandhi issued statements that bewildered and upset Americans. He suggested that the British presence invited a Japanese attack and that withdrawal would probably remove the possibilities of invasion.[6] Answering the British contention that internal divisions made necessary the continuation of the British *raj*, Gandhi wrote: "My answer now is: 'Leave India to God. If that is too much, then leave her to anarchy.'"[7] In the same May 24 issue Gandhi questioned whether India felt moral sympathy for any of the Allies and criticized the United States for entering the war and misusing its resources.

I expressed my opinion some time ago that it is a wrong thing for America and unfortunate for world peace that America, instead of working—as she could have worked—for peace, identified herself with the war. . . . I do not know all the facts that determined America to throw herself into the caldron. But somehow or other, opinion has forced itself upon me that America could have remained out, and even now she can do so if she divests herself of the intoxication that her immense wealth has produced. . . . Both America and Britain lack the moral basis for engaging in this war, unless they put their own houses in order, while making a fixed determination to withdraw their influence and power both from Africa and Asia, and remove the color bar. They have no right to talk about protecting democracies and protecting civilization and human freedom until the canker of white supremacy is destroyed in its entirety.[8]

In June, when a few American journalists visited Gandhi, his views received greater attention. Cognizant of the limited but adverse reaction to his previous statements, Gandhi modified his position. Yet his intention to launch a civil disobedience campaign also became more evident and more than offset any good will achieved by his clarifications. At various times in early June, Louis Fischer, as well as repre-

5 *Harijan*, April 26, 1942.
6 *Ibid.*, May 3 and May 31, 1942.
7 *Ibid.*, May 24, 1942.
8 *Ibid.*

sentatives of International News Service, Time-Life, and Associated Press, visited Gandhi at Wardha. In response to Fischer's prodding, Gandhi conceded in the June 14 *Harijan* that an independent India would permit the Allies to have military bases. Instead of denouncing the United States, Gandhi said he expected American power to be exerted behind India's cause. Indeed, he suggested that the United States should make further assistance to Britain conditional upon India's being granted freedom. Most American press attention focused on his talk of a civil disobedience movement that would affect the world. Yet, even on that point, Gandhi was in a compromising mood. He asked the reporters to tell Roosevelt that he wished to be dissuaded from launching the campaign. In a letter to Chiang Kai-shek, Gandhi assured the Chinese leader that India would do nothing to encourage the Japanese. While his conciliatory mood was reported in many newspapers, editorials in several papers, including the *New York Times, The Christian Science Monitor,* and *New York Herald Tribune,* criticized the civil disobedience campaign as an attempt to force concessions from Britain and the United States at a time of crisis.[9]

Gandhi's clarifications were appreciated by the State Department. Prior to the June 14 assurance that India could be used as a military base, Washington had considered dispatching an envoy to meet with Gandhi and determine his views on that matter. The project had been vetoed by Alling in Near Eastern Affairs and Murray of Political Affairs because of their apprehension that any identification of the United States with Gandhi might complicate the situation and alienate other leaders. Since April, Alling had believed that Johnson's close association with Nehru had invited Gandhi's anti-American outbursts.

In New Delhi, Merrell interpreted Gandhi's statements as a final appeal to the United States and China for assistance. If no encouragement came, Gandhi would launch the campaign to end British rule. The New Delhi post kept open the Johnson-Nehru line of communi-

---

[9] *Ibid.,* June 14, 21, 28, and July 5, 1942; *Time,* May 25, 1942, pp. 32, 34; *ibid.,* June 29, 1942, p. 30; D. G. Tendulkar, *Mahatma: Life of Mohandas Karamchand Gandhi,* vol. 6 (Bombay: Jhaveri & Tendulkar, 1953), pp. 116–17, 141–43; telegram from New Delhi, June 21, 1942, *FRUS, 1942,* 1:674–76; *The Christian Science Monitor,* June 29 and July 6, 1942; *New York Times,* July 17, 1942; *Hindu,* June 29, 1942.

cation. Merrell cabled a message from Nehru to Johnson, reaffirming that Gandhi would accept the armed defense of a free India. When Johnson's reply warned that Gandhi was being misunderstood in America, Nehru acknowledged that fact but reiterated that India had to be freed in order to defend itself.[10]

Yet Gandhi was concerned with American opinion, and this ultimately led to a direct appeal to Roosevelt. On July 1 Gandhi forwarded a message to Fischer, who was then in Delhi, requesting that the American deliver it to Roosevelt. Gandhi also anticipated that Fischer would convey the Indian leader's willingness to be dissuaded from a civil disobedience campaign. After emphasizing Gandhi's affection for America and Britain, the message reiterated the views expressed in the recent issues of *Harijan*.

Dear Friend: I twice missed coming to your great country. I have the privilege of having numerous friends there both known and unknown to me. Many of my countrymen have received and are still receiving higher education in America. I know too that several have taken shelter there. I have profited greatly by the writings of Thoreau and Emerson. I say this to tell you how much I am connected with your country. Of Great Britain I need say nothing beyond mentioning that in spite of my intense dislike of British Rule, I have numerous personal friends in England whom I love as dearly as my own people. I had my legal education there. I have therefore nothing but good wishes for your country and Great Britain. You will therefore accept my word that my present proposal, that the British should unreservedly and without reference to the people of India immediately withdraw their rule, is prompted by the friendliest intention. I would like to turn into good will the ill will which, whatever may be said to the contrary, exists in India towards Great Britain and thus enable the millions of India to play their part in the present war. . . . I venture to think that the Allied declaration that the Allies are fighting to make the world safe for freedom of the individual and for democracy sounds hollow, so long as India and, for that matter, Africa are exploited by Great Britain, and America has the Negro

10 Memorandum, Alling to Murray, April 28, 1942, 845.20/106; memorandum, Alling to Murray, June 11, 1942, 845.01/196; telegram from New Delhi, June 15, 1942, *FRUS, 1942*, 1:672; telegram to New Delhi, June 18, 1942, *ibid.*, p. 674; telegram from New Delhi, 845.01/207; Nehru to Berry, June 23, 1942, Jawaharlal Nehru, *A Bunch of Old Letters Written Mostly to Jawaharlal Nehru and Some Written by Him* (London: Asia Publishing House, 1960), p. 491.

problem in her own home. But in order to avoid all complications, in my proposal, I have confined myself only to India. If India becomes free, the rest must follow, if it does not happen simultaneously.

In order to make my proposal fool-proof I have suggested that, if the Allies think it necessary, they may keep their troops, at their own expense in India, not for keeping internal order but for preventing Japanese aggression and defending China.[11]

Gandhi has been criticized for sending his message through Fischer rather than through the American mission in Delhi, since this delayed the reception of his message in the United States.[12] Considering that Fischer had persuasively presented American reservations to the civil disobedience campaign, however, Gandhi understandably communicated his message through Fischer rather than through a diplomatic post with which he had negligible contacts. Moreover, Gandhi characteristically authorized Fischer to pass judgment on his message and was relying on Fischer to present his case if he found it reasonable. He wrote to Fischer: "If it does not commend itself to you, you may tear it to pieces. . . . Tell your President I wish to be dissuaded."[13] In the end the message reached Roosevelt without appreciable delay. Because wartime travel restrictions might have delayed him, and because he was planning to remain in India, Fischer gave the letter to an American military officer who had travel priority. The State Department, of course, was fully informed of Gandhi's modifications. As Fischer subsequently acknowledged, he probably should have retained the letter and used it as the basis for securing an audience with Roosevelt, which might have enabled him to present Gandhi's case more effectively than was possible in the letter.[14]

Regardless of when Gandhi's message was received or the possibility of Fischer representing Gandhi, the adverse military situation rendered any action by Roosevelt virtually impossible. The Allied unity, which

[11] Gandhi to Roosevelt, July 1, 1942, *FRUS, 1942*, 1:677–78.

[12] M. S. Venkataramani and B. K. Shrivastava, "The United States and the 'Quit India' Demand," *India Quarterly*, April, 1964, p. 123.

[13] Louis Fischer, *The Life of Mahatma Gandhi* (New York: Harper & Bros., 1950), pp. 375–78.

[14] Louis Fischer, *The Great Challenge* (New York: Duell, Sloan & Pearce, 1946), pp. 169–70.

he always prized, seemed more imperative than ever at the high tide of the Axis advance. The American navy had thwarted the Japanese at the Battle of Midway, but the Pacific picture remained singularly bleak. Throughout June and July, Roosevelt was preoccupied with resolving the divergent Russian and British views concerning a second front in Europe. When Churchill and his military and political advisers visited Washington on June 21 for several days of conferences, the prime minister argued against the Russian demand for a diversionary attack on France and urged a campaign in North Africa. During the deliberations the Germans secured impressive gains, advancing to within one hundred miles of Alexandria and menacing the Suez Canal. The United States rushed assistance to the beleaguered British forces while Churchill hurried home to defend his government against criticisms in the House of Commons.

As the Working Committee of the National Congress assembled at Wardha in early July, its deliberations were far removed from the concern of the American government and public. After Gandhi outlined his "Quit India" demand, about half of the committee opposed a civil disobedience campaign, and Nehru attempted at length to discourage Gandhi. When Gandhi threatened to leave the Congress and lead an independent movement, however, the opposition collapsed. On July 14 the Working Committee adopted the "Quit India" resolution, which demanded Britain's withdrawal. To avoid embarrassing the Allies, the Congress formally offered to let Allied troops remain. It also stated that, if the demand were rejected, the Congress would utilize its nonviolent strength. The "Quit India" resolution was then submitted for consideration and final approval to the All-India Congress Committee scheduled to meet at Bombay on August 6.

While the resolution contained no open appeal to the United States, the day after its adoption Azad commented that it was implicitly addressed to America. Congress leaders hoped for U.S. pressure on Britain. Shortly before the Wardha meeting, Nehru had observed that American initiative would alter the political situation.[15]

Despite these hopes, however, the Wardha resolution met with an unfavorable response in America. In most newspapers Gandhi and the

[15] Michael Brecher, *Nehru: A Political Biography* (New York: Oxford University Press, 1959), pp. 284–85.

National Congress were condemned for inviting internal chaos and a Japanese invasion. Press coverage emphasized the demand for withdrawal and minimized the offer to support the Allies. Editorials in the *New York Times, New York Herald Tribune, Philadelphia Inquirer, Baltimore Sun, St. Louis Globe Democrat, The Christian Science Monitor,* and other papers joined in the chorus of criticism. Many of the criticisms were, however, tempered with calls for U.S. action. The *Chicago Sun* and *The Nation* regarded the "Quit India" demand as dangerous, but urged an American or U.N. guarantee of postwar independence and assistance in securing an interim national government.

As usual, unequivocal defense of the National Congress came from *The Christian Century,* where Oswald Garrison Villard scored American support of British imperialism, and *The New Republic,* whose editorial demanded British withdrawal. Both journals pressed for American or U.N. action. Kate Mitchell, in *Amerasia,* stood virtually alone in pointing out the evolution of Gandhi's position and its considerable modification since the Allahabad resolution in May. Neither *Time* nor *Newsweek* devoted much attention to these events, but the latter implicitly criticized the Congress by carrying accounts of the loyalty of the Indian Muslims and their opposition to a civil disobedience campaign.[16]

The adverse American press reaction surprised and disappointed Indian leaders. The *Hindu* of Madras lamented Americans' ignorance of Indian developments. In an interview with three foreign correspondents, Gandhi denied that implementation of the Wardha resolution would result in internal chaos but suggested that only outside pressure could produce a settlement:

So far as we are concerned, we have closed our hearts. As we have said in our resolution, all hopes have been dashed to pieces. The burden is shifted. But it is open to America, to Britain, to China and even to Russia, to plead

[16] Kate L. Mitchell, "Capital Notes: New Delhi," *Amerasia,* August, 1942, pp. 251–54; *New York Times,* July 18, 1942; *Chicago Sun,* July 21, 1942; *The Nation,* July 25, 1942, pp. 63–64; *Newsweek,* July 13, 1942, pp. 38, 41, and July 27, 1942, pp. 42–43; Oswald Garrison Villard, "Final Hour in India," *The Christian Century,* July 29, 1942, pp. 933–34; *The New Republic,* July 27, 1942, p. 100, August 3, 1942, p. 131, August 10, 1942, pp. 175–76; Venkataramani and Shrivastava, "The 'Quit India' Demand," pp. 128–30.

for India which is pining for freedom. And if an acceptable proposal is made, it would certainly be open to the Congress or any other party to entertain and accept it.[17]

The possibility of compromise through American efforts was presented to Washington by the ranking U.S. diplomatic officer in Delhi. In a cable of July 14 Merrell held that the Wardha resolution reflected moderation and that the Congress would accept a plan which followed the lines taken during the Cripps negotiations. As had been true of Johnson, Merrell adopted the view of the moderate elements in the National Congress, observing the reluctance of Azad, Nehru, and nationalist papers such as the *Bombay Chronicle* and *Lahore Tribune* to follow a civil disobedience campaign. In his message of July 16 Merrell played down the popular Muslim support for Jinnah's recent renewal of the Pakistani demand. On the basis of two conferences held between Berry and Nehru, Merrell reported the Indian leader's willingness to accept a pledge of independence and the establishment of a provisional national government. At a press conference on July 20 Azad elaborated on this possibility, calling for a U.S. or U.N. guarantee of postwar independence and mediation of an interim settlement.[18]

Encouraged by this move toward a possible settlement, on July 21 Merrell pressed the State Department to have Roosevelt issue such a guarantee. The president also was to submit a plan for an interim government which all principal parties would be obliged to accept in advance. Merrell suggested a plan similar to the Johnson scheme. Merrell preferred a unilateral rather than a U.N. effort, for Roosevelt enjoyed great prestige in India, and such action required more speed than would be forthcoming if the United Nations were called upon. Convinced that the plan would find general acceptance in the National Congress, Merrell envisioned Muslim League adoption as well, provided the British agreed. As he saw it, the British had no choice: "If it is unacceptable to the British at this stage of the proceedings, then they are more diehard, obtuse, and reactionary than even the Congress leaders suspect."[19]

[17] *Harijan*, July 26, 1942.
[18] Telegrams from New Delhi, July 14, 16, 17, and 18, 1942, *FRUS, 1942*, 1: 679–81, 683–89.
[19] Telegram from New Delhi, July 21, 1942, *ibid.*, pp. 691–94.

Merrell's plan received only passing attention in Washington. A memorandum drafted by the Division of Near Eastern Affairs and approved by its officers blocked further consideration, holding that the plan's fundamental weaknesses rendered its credibility questionable. An American guarantee would violate constitutional procedures and thus would lack legal backing. The alternative of a U.N. guarantee would be unacceptable to other Allies with imperial interests. Moreover, the British and Muslim League could hardly be expected to acquiesce. Merrell had ignored the league's insistence that any political settlement be preceded by resolution of the communal problem.[20]

Yet subsequent developments demonstrated the potential of the Merrell plan; in 1946 Jinnah accepted a division of the executive council which was identical to Merrell's suggestion (six Hindus, five Muslims, and three representatives of other groups). The viceroy forced this acceptance by tacitly threatening to withdraw British backing for the league.[21] An American guarantee, as the Near Eastern Affairs memorandum contended, would have been without precedent. Yet such a guarantee would not have posed insurmountable constitutional problems. Given the wide executive authority in foreign affairs which Roosevelt had assumed during the war, a presidential underwriting of Indian independence would likely have been acceptable to most Americans and probably could have gained the endorsement of a joint resolution of Congress. Public opinion polls in July indicated a high degree of awareness of the Indian situation and continued sympathy for the Indian demand. A cross-section of opinion sampled on July 29 revealed that 43 per cent favored the proposition that Great Britain should grant complete independence, while only 17 per cent opposed it (see Table II). The possibility of American involvement in internal difficulties was slight, for the British had promised postwar independence and would be primarily responsible for the details of withdrawal.

Yet the Roosevelt administration continued to avoid bringing any pressure to bear on Britain. To Roosevelt, military planning remained the priority. On July 16, as Merrell's initial reports on the Wardha resolution were being received, Roosevelt dispatched Hopkins, Chief

20 Memorandum, Near Eastern Affairs, July 27, 1942, 845.00/1566.
21 M. S. Venkataramani and B. K. Shrivastava, "America and the Indian Political Crisis," *International Studies*, July, 1964, pp. 11–12.

of Staff General George Marshall, and naval commander Admiral Ernest King to London where, together with European commander General Dwight D. Eisenhower, they engaged in heated deliberations with Britsh officers. Roosevelt did not take action on the Indian situation in the midst of these tenuous discussions, but he did urge all Americans and other peoples to heed an address delivered by Hull on the evening of July 23. Carried on the radio networks and immediately transmitted around the world, Hull's speech reflected an implicit tone of exasperation with the National Congress. After reviewing the U.N. effort, the secretary of state elaborated on American support for freedom movements: "It has been our policy in the past—and will remain our policy in the future—to use the full measure of our influence to support attainment of freedom by all peoples who, by their acts show themselves worthy of it and ready for it."[22] In his memoirs Hull conceded that he had India in mind when he delivered this address. While he was opposed to imperialism and more distrustful of the British than many of Roosevelt's advisers, Hull believed that colonial peoples had to be prepared for independence. Implicitly, willingness to support the Allied cause and to accept postponement of freedom had become a test of a colonial people's worthiness.[23]

Just four days later, Cripps broadcast a special message to America. Citing Gandhi's statement opposing American troops, Cripps denounced Gandhi as a naïve visionary who endangered the security of India and the U.N. cause. Following what was to become standard British propaganda, Cripps ignored Gandhi's subsequent qualifications as well as the position of Nehru and Azad. In a press conference at Allahabad, Nehru condemned the speech for its misrepresentations and distortions. Yet, to an American press that had been unreceptive to the Wardha resolution and had generally welcomed Hull's address, the Cripps message reinforced misgivings about the National Congress.[24]

[22] *Department of State Bulletin*, July 25, 1942, p. 642.

[23] Cordell Hull, *Memoirs of Cordell Hull*, 2 vols. (New York: Macmillan, 1948), 2:1484–85.

[24] Kurt L. Mattusch, "The American Public and India," *Amerasia*, Fall, 1942, p. 406; Jawaharlal Nehru, *Important Speeches of Jawaharlal Nehru: Being a Collection of Most Significant Speeches Delivered by Jawaharlal Nehru from 1922 to 1945*, ed. Jagat S. Bright, 2nd ed. rev. (Lahore: Indian Printing Works, 1946), pp. 234–35.

Although reluctant to upset Churchill, Roosevelt finally did act, but in an indirect and almost apologetic fashion. Coinciding with its dismissal of Merrell's plan, the Division of Near Eastern Affairs on July 25 adopted a modified plan by which the United States, through its New Delhi representative, would indicate to Nehru and Azad its inability to guarantee independence. However, the United States would agree to assist in negotiations if a sound basis for settlement developed, or, in other words, if Nehru and Azad agreed to bring the Muslim League into the picture. In the event that such conditions were met, the United States would dispatch a leading representative to sit in on negotiations. While a formal guarantee would be impossible, the United States, together with China and possibly the Soviet Union, might receive messages from Britain which affirmed the independence pledge, and these would constitute an acknowledgment of Britain's intentions. The memorandum offered no interim plans, nor did it specify a date for independence.[25]

While the Near Eastern Affairs proposal was being considered, a message from Chiang Kai-shek on July 25 brought the Indian situation directly to Roosevelt's attention. The Chinese government's interest in India had continued. In late June, Madame Chiang had advised Nehru to delay action until American policy became clear, assuring him that her husband would seek joint Chinese-American action. Prior to the Wardha resolution, Chiang remained inactive, although he did advise Nehru against actions that would embarrass the United Nations. The situation worsened, however, and Chiang cabled Roosevelt on July 25 that only the United States could secure a settlement and suggested the substance of the Merrell plan:

Your country is the leader in this war of right against might and Your Excellency's views have always received serious attention in Britain. Furthermore for a long time the Indian people have been expecting the United States to come out and take a stand on the side of justice and equality. . . . For the sake of our common victory the United Nations must seek to stabilize the Indian situation and to secure the Indian people's participation in the joint war effort. . . . The only way to make them reconsider their course of action is for the United Nations, and especially the United States which they have always admired, to come forth as third parties and offer them

25 Memorandum, Near Eastern Affairs, July 25, 1942, 845.00/1559.

sympathy and consolation. . . . Should however the situation be allowed to drift until an anti-British movement breaks out in India, any attempt on the part of the British to cope with the crisis by enforcing existing colonial laws by resorting to military and police force, will only help to spread disturbances and reactions. . . . On the other hand the wisest course and most enlightened policy for Britain to pursue would be to restore to India her complete freedom and thus to prevent Axis troops from setting foot on Indian soil. . . . Therefore I earnestly hope that the United States would advise both Britain and India in the name of justice and righteousness to seek a reasonable and satisfactory solution, for this affects vitally the welfare of mankind and has a direct bearing on the good faith and good name of the United Nations. The United States as the acknowledged leader of democracy has a natural and vital role to play in bringing about a successful solution of the problem.[26]

In a conversation with Welles on July 28, Chinese Ambassador T. V. Soong reiterated the Chinese position.[27] Caught between the sharply conflicting views of America's two closest allies, Roosevelt sided with the British after giving proper deference to the Chinese suggestion. Roosevelt then decided to forward Chiang's message to Churchill, but not as a means of pressing Chiang's views. Indeed, the president's covering cable requested Churchill's advice in replying to Chiang. Welles, who earlier had discouraged any interference, now pressed for the substance of the Near Eastern Affairs plan. Before dispatching the message to London on July 29, the under secretary warned that it would produce no beneficial results and urged American mediation:

I think I should add, however, that I do not believe the message now drafted will be productive of any useful results. All of the information we have in the Department of State confirms the views expressed by Chiang Kai-shek that a desperately serious situation is going to break out in India after the meeting of the Indian National Congress on August 6. This is a question of vital concern to our own military and naval interests in the Far East. It would seem to me that the services of the American Government and of the Chinese Government as friendly intermediaries between the Indian National

26 Chiang Kai-shek to Roosevelt, July 25, 1942, *FRUS, 1942*, 1:695–98; telegram from Chungking, July 7, 1942, *Foreign Relations of the United States, 1942: China* (1956), pp. 100–102; Madame Chiang Kai-shek to Nehru, June 26, 1942, and S. H. Shen to Nehru, July 8, 1942, Nehru, *A Bunch of Old Letters*, pp. 494–96.
27 Memorandum of conversation by Welles, July 28, 1942, *FRUS, 1942*, 1:698–99.

Congress and the British Government might serve in bringing about some satisfactory arrangement which would hold during the war period and could in any event, in view of the critical situation now existing, do no harm.[28]

The tone of Roosevelt's cable invited Churchill's most forthright rebuttal. The British reaction was definitively stated on July 30 by Churchill and Amery. While the contents of his message to Roosevelt remain classified, it can be safely conjectured that Churchill reaffirmed unequivocally that India was Britain's problem. In a conversation with the American ambassador, Amery left no doubt that Britain rejected the need for conciliation with the Congress. The secretary of state for India maintained that only the British could provide stability and that, if the Congress pursued its "Quit India" demand, the Government of India would arrest Congress leaders.[29]

Having made his gesture on behalf of Chiang Kai-shek, Roosevelt retreated. The July 25 Near Eastern Affairs plan was ignored. On August 1 Roosevelt replied to Gandhi's message, but avoided a direct response to Gandhi's plea. Instead, Roosevelt wrote of the need for Allied harmony and enclosed a copy of Hull's July 23 address.[30] At his August 4 press conference the president declined comment on Gandhi's reported call for the United States to force a British withdrawal. Behind the scenes, pressures continued but were ignored. Henry Grady, who had met Gandhi during the visit of the U.S. technical mission to India, urged a public statement guaranteeing postwar independence but asking Indian leaders to disavow immediate changes. The unofficial White House adviser, Robert Sherwood, also suggested a statement of Allied aims and American assurance of independence. Having failed to alter Roosevelt's course a few days earlier, Welles strenuously disapproved these proposals.[31]

[28] Welles to Roosevelt, July 29, 1942, *ibid.*, pp. 699–700; Roosevelt to Churchill, July 29, 1942, *ibid.*, p. 700.

[29] Telegram from London, July 30, 1942, *ibid.*, pp. 700–702. The U.S. Department of State Purport Book lists Churchill-Roosevelt message, July 30, 1942, 845.00/1542–1/5; it remains a classified British document.

[30] Roosevelt to Gandhi, August 1, 1942, enclosed in telegram to New Delhi, August 5, 1942, *FRUS, 1942*, 1:703.

[31] Grady to Roosevelt, August 5, 1942; Sherwood to Roosevelt, August 4, 1942; M. J. McDermott to Early, August 4, 1942, Box O.F. 48-H, India, 1942; and transcript of Roosevelt press conference, August 4, 1942; Roosevelt Papers.

Roosevelt's apparent resignation to a showdown paralleled the press's anticipation of the Bombay session. The "Quit India" demand continued to be viewed unfavorably, with much of the editorial comment substantially endorsing Hull's position that India had to fight the Japanese to earn its independence. Gandhi was frequently caricatured by cartoonists, typically as the skinny holy man in loin cloth and oversized glasses naïvely observing the Japanese wolf on the threshhold.[32] The ridicule of Gandhi increased after he was quoted as desiring to visit Japan, where he would plead China's case. The *Los Angeles Times* commented: "Surely even a man in a bed sheet would have enough sense to know the futility of such a plea."[33] Almost alone, the Hearst papers consistently defended Gandhi and the Congress. In contrast, the syndicated columnist Raymond Clapper returned to his portrayal of a Hamlet-like Nehru who lacked the fortitude and conviction to challenge Gandhi's disastrous course. In the *New York Times,* a letter from Bertrand Russell, long a supporter of Indian demands and a former president of the India League in England, condemned all those who supported Gandhi for aiding the Japanese. In the same paper, columnist Anne O'Hare McCormack held that the Congress lacked reasons to doubt Britain's motivation.

A group of Americans headed by Herbert Agar, editor of the *Louisville Courier-Journal,* publicly urged the National Congress to put aside its demand and support the United Nations. The committee included economist Alexander Sachs, writer Walter Millis, theologian Henry P. Van Deusen, Bishop Henry W. Hobson, and Christian Gauss, dean of the Princeton University Graduate School. In its message of August 6 the committee warned that civil disobedience would alienate American opinion.[34]

Meanwhile, Louis Fischer had returned to America and was attempting to counteract this trend in opinion. In an interview on August 6

[32] *New York Times,* August 5, 1942; *Pittsburgh Press,* August 6, 1942; *Toledo Blade,* August 6, 1942; *The Christian Science Monitor,* August 6, 1942; Walter C. Mackett, "Some Aspects of the Development of American Opinion on India, 1918–1947" (Ph.D. diss., University of Southern California, 1957), pp. 339–42.

[33] *Los Angeles Times,* August 6, 1942.

[34] *New York Times,* August 5 and 6, 1942; *San Francisco News,* August 7, 1942; *Los Angeles Examiner,* August 5–7, 1942.

he argued that the United Nations would be strengthened militarily if India gained freedom, for this would induce overwhelming popular support for the war. Fischer also sought desperately to secure an interview with Roosevelt. Upon his arrival Fischer telegraphed the White House, but on August 7 he was informed that a meeting was impossible. As soon as he received that denial, he again cabled Roosevelt, averring that Gandhi was amenable to mediation but that the British and the viceroy were content to preserve the status quo. Fischer closed: "I am convinced that the British authorities will do nothing. I am convinced that the right approach by you might save the situation. A terrible disaster may be impending in India."[35]

By August 7 Roosevelt had full knowledge of the impending disaster. Deputy Prime Minister Attlee sent a lengthy cable explaining the Government of India's controversial decision to seize and publish the records of the Congress Working Committee's Allahabad meeting. The purpose was to demonstrate the defeatist outlook of the Congress leadership and thus to force Indians to repudiate the Congress. As soon as the Congress adopted the "Quit India" resolution, Attlee reiterated Britain's intention to arrest the leaders, a step which Americans would agree was necessary. Since Attlee was known as a friend of Indian nationalism and was the leader of the Labour party, his message signified a closing of ranks behind Churchill. From New Delhi, Merrell reported that the publication of Congress documents had only succeeded in creating further antagonism between the government and the public and stood as another instance of failure to provide constructive leadership.[36]

At Bombay the National Congress' total disenchantment reached its climax. While he earlier and subsequently had reservations about the wisdom of the "Quit India" demand, Nehru moved for passage of the resolution calling for British withdrawal under threat of a mass non-violent struggle. The resolution affirmed that a free India would become a U.N. ally and offered a concession to the Muslim League by proposing a large measure of provincial autonomy in an independent

[35] Fischer to Roosevelt, August 5 and 7, 1942, PSF: India, 1942–43, Roosevelt Papers; *New York Times*, August 6, 1942.

[36] Attlee to Roosevelt, August 7, 1942, *FRUS, 1942*, 1:703–5; telegrams from New Delhi, August 8, 1942, *ibid.*, pp. 707–8.

Indian union. Adopted on August 8, the appeal, cast in terms of the Allies' military and ideological goals, called upon the United Nations for support:

The freedom of India must be the symbol of a prelude to the freedom of all other Asiatic peoples under foreign domination. Burma, Malaya, Indo-China, Indonesia, Iran and Iraq must also attain their complete freedom. It must be clearly understood that such of these countries as are under Japanese control now, must not subsequently be placed under the rule or control of any other colonial power. . . . The earnest appeal of the Working Committee to Great Britain and the United Nations has so far met with no response and the criticisms made in many foreign quarters have shown an ignorance of India's and of the world's need and sometimes even hostility to India's freedom. . . . The A.-I.C.C. would yet again at this last moment, in the interest of the world freedom, renew this appeal to Britain and the United Nations.[37]

Indian leaders hoped for U.S. action. Gandhi wrote in *Harijan* that, because America had made common cause with Britain, it could not escape responsibility for India. Azad planned appeals to Roosevelt, Chiang Kai-shek, and the Russian ambassador in London. On the morning of August 9 the Congress president arose at four o'clock and began to draft a letter to Roosevelt. Before finishing it, he took a brief rest. Shortly thereafter Azad was awakened and informed that the police had come to arrest him. On that morning all nationalist leaders were quickly arrested. As he met the police, Gandhi advised his followers to "do or die."

The hopes for American action had been dashed, for, in Washington, Roosevelt had in effect closed the door on India. Not until August 8 did he reply to Chiang's July 25 message. Roosevelt rejected the plea for intervention, stating the British position that such action would undermine authority. Roosevelt's only attempt to communicate with Indian leaders was to endorse a cable sent by the Philippine leader Manuel Quezon to Nehru and Gandhi which affirmed the

[37] *March of Events (Being the Case of the Indian National Congress), 1942–1945* (Bombay: Provincial Congress Committee, 1945), pp. 3–4; Brecher, *Nehru,* pp. 286–88.

American commitment to Asian freedom.[38] As word of the arrests reached Washington, Roosevelt formally acquiesced in the British policy. In a cable to Churchill he informed the prime minister of his response to Chiang. Expressing agreement with British policy, Roosevelt added that the Chinese petitions had to be given consideration to prevent Chiang from taking more aggressive action.

I have emphasized the fact that we would of course not wish to pursue any course which undermines the authority of the Government of India at this critical time. I have, however, told him that I would be glad to have him keep in close touch with me with regard to this and any other question which affect the vital interests of the United Nations because of my belief that it is wiser to have him feel that his suggestions sent to me receive friendly consideration.[39]

British suppression, reinforced by American indifference, produced an open revolt. As word of the arrests spread across the subcontinent, large numbers of people rose in frustrated anger. Mass demonstrations brought normal activities in several cities to a standstill. While initially peaceful, the spontaneous movement was accompanied by tension, and thus made violence inevitable. Riots, sabotage, and occasional atrocities brought the British *raj* its sternest challenge since 1857. American consuls kept the State Department informed of the growing disorder. Merrell underscored the fact that America's identification with Britain had brought the loss of much American prestige.

Even in the face of a revolt which the British had encouraged Americans to believe was impossible, American indifference continued. On August 11 Roosevelt replied to Fischer's urgent message of August 7 by informing Gandhi's unofficial emissary that White House sources of information on India were sufficient. Again temporizing with half-measures, Roosevelt approved a statement, proposed

[38] *Harijan*, August 9, 1942; Maulana Abul Kalam Azad, *India Wins Freedom: An Autobiographical Narrative* (Bombay: Orient Longmans, 1959), p. 84; V. P. Menon, *The Transfer of Power in India* (Princeton: Princeton University Press, 1957), p. 943; Roosevelt to Chiang Kai-shek, August 8, 1942, *FRUS, 1942,* 1:705–6; Roosevelt to Quezon, August 9, 1942, Box O.F. 48-H, India, 1942, Roosevelt Papers.
[39] Roosevelt to Churchill, August 9, 1942, Winston S. Churchill, *The Second World War: The Hinge of Fate* (Boston: Houghton Mifflin, 1950), p. 508.

by the State Department, affirming that American forces in India would avoid any involvement in the domestic disturbances. On August 11 Chiang Kai-shek, appalled at the arrests, made his final effort to induce American intervention. In a cable to Washington he appealed to Roosevelt as an author of the Atlantic Charter to take the steps necessary for resolution of the problem. Roosevelt's response on August 12 disavowed any intention of acting unless requested to do so by both the British and the nationalists, a reaction which assured the futility of Chiang's appeal.[40]

Although Roosevelt failed to act, he doubted the wisdom of Churchill's policy. When the crisis was discussed in cabinet meetings, Roosevelt expressed exasperation over the British attitude. At a session of the Pacific War Council on August 12 he reiterated that a solution would be found only through trial and error such as the United States had experienced in the 1780s. Ultimately, the preservation of Anglo-American unity proved the priority consideration. When Secretary of the Interior Harold Ickes pressed with Roosevelt the suggestion of an American guarantee of Indian independence, Roosevelt's reply revealed his dilemma: "You are right about India but it would be playing with fire if the British Empire were to tell me to mind my own business."[41]

The Bombay meeting, the arrests, rioting, and American acquiescence brought India back to the front pages of U.S. newspapers. As had been anticipated in prior editorial comments, the Congress resolution met with general criticism and the British suppression with approval. Yet many editorials—such as those in the *New York Times, San Francisco News,* and *Pittsburgh Press*—included pleas for British understanding and restraint. Walter Lippmann defended the British, offering the argument that the complex problems of India were not

[40] Amba Prasad, *The Indian Revolt of 1942* (Delhi: S. Chand & Co., 1958), pp. 59–80; telegrams from New Delhi, August 11, 1942, *FRUS, 1942,* 1:712–14; State Department press release, August 12, 1942, *ibid.,* pp. 720–21; Welles to Roosevelt, August 11, 1942, *ibid.,* pp. 714–15; Roosevelt to Chiang, August 12, 1942, *ibid.,* pp. 715–17; telegram from Bombay, August 11, 1942, 845.00/1433; telegram from New Delhi, August 12, 1942, 845.00/1432; telegram from New Delhi, August 15, 1942, 845.00/1460; Roosevelt to Fischer, August 11, 1942, PSF: India, 1942–43, Roosevelt Papers.

[41] Roosevelt to Ickes, August 12, 1942, PPF: 3650, Roosevelt Papers; Ickes to Roosevelt, August 10, 1942, *ibid.;* Hull, *Memoirs,* 2:1487–88.

receptive to quick solutions. On the other side the Scripps-Howard columnist W. P. Simms urged British acceptance of immediate independence.

Both sides were expressed in the journals, but the wisdom of British policy was more frequently questioned. The weekly coverage in *Newsweek*, an editorial in *Saturday Evening Post*, and an article by Mount Holyoke professor Alzada Comstock in *Current History* condemned Gandhi for playing into Japan's hands. *Commonweal*, an infrequent commentator on India, held that both sides were making serious mistakes. A sympathetic feature story on Nehru in *Time* charged that the American press had ignored the Indian viewpoint. Again defending the Congress' giving priority to independence rather than the war, *Time* concluded that, if the United Nations intended to build a better world, India was an ideal place in which to start.

The liberal journals upheld the Congress and called for American mediation of a settlement and a guarantee of British promises. Editorials in *Free World, The Christian Century, The New Republic,* and the previously equivocal *Nation* all urged Roosevelt to intervene. Articles by Lin Yutang in *The New Republic,* John Haynes Holmes in *The Christian Century,* and Louis Fischer in *The Nation* reinforced the editorials. Fischer's articles attracted much attention because he cited his conversations with Gandhi to substantiate the view of India's willingness to support the United Nations.[42]

Because public awareness of the Indian situation remained high and increased during early August, popular sympathy for the nationalist cause generally held firm. A cross-section examined by the American Institute of Public Opinion on August 13 revealed that 43 per cent still

[42] *New York Times*, August 11 and 13, 1942; *Pittsburgh Press*, August 12–14, 1942; *Los Angeles Times*, August 11–14, 1942; *The Christian Science Monitor*, August 12, 1942; Mackett, "American Opinion on India," pp. 343–50; *Newsweek*, August 17, 1942, pp. 13, 42, and 45, and August 31, 1942, pp. 41, 44; *Saturday Evening Post*, September 5, 1942, p. 100; *Time*, August 24, 1942, pp. 18–21; *Commonweal*, August 21, 1942, pp. 411–12; *Free World*, September, 1942, pp. 293–95; *The New Republic*, August 17, 1942, pp. 191–92; *ibid.*, August 24, 1942, p. 215; Lin Yutang, "India and the War for Freedom," *ibid.*, pp. 217–18; *The Christian Century*, August 12, 1942, p. 972, and August 19, 1942, p. 995; John Haynes Holmes, "The Hour Strikes in India," *ibid.*, pp. 1000–1002; Louis Fischer, "Gandhi's Rejected Offer," *The Nation*, August 22, 1942, pp. 145–47.

favored granting India complete independence (see Table II). The unfavorable reaction in most newspapers to the "Quit India" demand probably accounted for the increase in the percentage of those opposing independence (from 17 to 23). Among those favoring independence, fewer thought it should come immediately (a change from 55 per cent on July 29 to 46 per cent on August 13) and more thought it should be granted after the war (from 39 to 47 per cent).

Table II. American Public Opinion and India, July–August, 1942

Poll 1. Have you heard or read about plans to give India a greater amount of freedom from England?

	July, 1942	*August, 1942*
Yes	69%	74%
No	31	26

Poll 2. Should England grant India complete independence?

	July 29, 1942	*August 13, 1942*
Give complete independence	43%	43%
Give partial independence	5	2
Give dominion status	—	1
Make protectorate	—	1
Give when capable of governing themselves	—	1
Don't give	17	23
No opinion	34	29
Other answers	1	—

Poll 3. Of 43% samples in previous poll, should India be granted independence now or after the war?

	July 29, 1942	*August 13, 1942*
Now	55%	46%
After	39	47
Undecided	5	6
Other	1	1

Source: Prepared by Mildred Strunk, American Institute of Public Opinion, cited in *American Opinion, 1935–1946,* ed. Hadley Cantril (Princeton: Princeton University Press, 1951), p. 327.

As the American government's inaction and the seriousness of the crisis became evident, appeals for a change in policy were made to the State Department and the White House. Three prominent American missionaries in India appealed to Washington, one pressing for intervention and promulgation of a Pacific charter and the other two asking for authorization to assist as mediators.[43]

Labor groups brought pressure to bear on the government. At its annual convention the United Automobile Workers adopted a resolution calling for a settlement even if Roosevelt had to force British action. Similar resolutions were adopted by the Greater New York Industrial Council, which represented half a million Congress of Industrial Organization members, by the National Council of the National Maritime Union, and by a Congress of Industrial Organizations local in Chicago.

Long-time American spokesmen for Indian nationalism also pressed Roosevelt to intervene. In a conversation with Hull and in a letter to Roosevelt, the American Socialist party leader Norman Thomas warned that the president's historical reputation as a liberator rested on the resolution of the Indian crisis. A letter to the *New York Times* by Oswald Garrison Villard and a message by Pearl Buck to the Post War World Council urged intervention. Thomas, Villard, Holmes, Roger Baldwin, Harry Emerson Fosdick, John Flynn, and several others addressed an open appeal to Roosevelt to mediate in the establishment of a provisional government.

Strong demands also came, of course, from Indian nationalist groups. J. J. Singh, president of the India League of America, emerged as the chief spokesman for Indian nationalists in the United States. A Sikh who had immigrated in 1926 and had become a successful businessman in New York, Singh had expressed little interest in nationalism until the war. When he joined the India League in 1939, its membership was restricted to Indians and it did little to promote the nationalist cause. Under Singh's leadership, however, the league broadened its membership to include Americans, attracted considerable financial support, and championed the National Congress' position. As the

[43] At the request of the Research Guidance and Review Division, Historical Office, Department of State, the names of the missionaries and mission officials are not cited. The dates and file numbers of the correspondence are as follows: letter to Welles, July 26, 1942, 845.00/1450; letter to Welles, August 10, 1942, 845.00/1462; letter from Welles August 15, 1942, *ibid.*; letter to Welles, August 22, 1942, 845.00/1579; letter to Welles, August 25, 1942, 845.00/1561; letter to Hull, August 30, 1942, 845.00/1755.

August crisis worsened, Singh sought an interview with Roosevelt but was denied it. Singh called for vesting political responsibility in a reconstituted executive council comprised of popular Indian leaders. He believed that the defense issue could be resolved by establishing a joint Anglo-American-Chinese military council. In an emergency session on August 12 the India League appealed for Roosevelt's intervention. At a conference with Murray at the State Department on August 20 Singh reiterated his formula, which was similar to the plans of Johnson and Merrell.[44]

That same day Senator Robert Reynolds of North Carolina touched off a lengthy debate in the Senate when he urged that the United States aid in securing an Indian settlement as a means of proving the good faith of the United Nations. The few previous congressional actions on India had produced little reaction: on July 6 Congressman George O'Brien of Michigan had introduced a resolution providing for recognition of a national government; and on August 17 Senator Elbert Thomas of Utah had advocated U.N. action. Reynolds' comments, however, met with an immediate and unfavorable response. Majority leader Alben Barkley, Foreign Relations Committee Chairman Tom Connally, Walter George of Georgia, George Norris of Nebraska, Claude Pepper of Florida, and Scott Lucas of Illinois repudiated Reynolds for encouraging the enemy and causing Allied disunity. The speakers ignored the recent developments and treated India only as a problem in the Anglo-American alliance. Reynolds' comments even brought wrath from the pulpit. In his sermon the following Sunday, Bishop William Manning of the Cathedral of St. John the Divine in New York rebuked Reynolds for sabotaging the Allied cause.[45]

While Roosevelt proved unresponsive to public pressures, Hull

44 *New York Times*, August 7, 10, 13, and 18, 1942; Ferdinand Smith (Secretary, National Maritime Union of America) to Hull, August 13, 1942, 845.01/235; Walter Skiba (Chicago CIO Local 65) to Hull, August 22, 1942, 845.01/238; J. J. Singh to Roosevelt, August 7, 1942, Norman Thomas to Roosevelt, August 11, 1942, and Roosevelt to Thomas, August 25, 1942, Box O.F. 48-H, India, 1942, Roosevelt Papers; memorandum of conversation by Murray, August 20, 1942, 845.00/1543.

45 U.S. Congress, Senate, *Congressional Record*, 77th Cong., 2nd sess., 1942, 88, pt. 5:6003, 6857, 6887–95; *New York Times*, August 21 and 24, 1942.

surprisingly emerged as a vigorous critic of the British. Hull's irritation was triggered by Britain's equivocation on the Atlantic Charter—a point which again became evident in discussions concerning a joint announcement on the Charter's first anniversary. In a conference on August 8 the British minister Sir Ronald Campbell conveyed a message from Eden expressing the hope that any statement would be consistent with Churchill's September, 1941, qualifications. Hull promptly inquired whether the British would prepare a comprehensive statement detailing the conditions by which India would gain independence. The British ignored the request, and thus an innocuous anniversary statement was made on August 14. The next day, however, Hull did raise with Roosevelt the advantage to the Allied cause of such a clarification of British policy; he envisoned that it might serve to reopen negotiations. Although he had received no encouragement from the White House, on August 24 Hull questioned Halifax on the Atlantic Charter's universality. The British, however, made no attempt to accommodate Hull.[46]

Accordingly, when Fischer visited the State Department on August 27, he found the secretary attentive to his arguments, but utterly frustrated. As told in Fischer's account of the meeting,

He said: ". . . when I was a young fellow I raised a regiment to fight for Cuban independence. In 1933, against many odds, I championed recognition for Soviet Russia. We have introduced the Good Neighbor Policy in Latin America. I have favored equal rights for China. . . . But on the question of India, while the President is missing no opportunities, we cannot do much if the British are immovable. The other fellow may dig in his toes and say 'Here I stand even if everything else goes to pieces.' " He repeated this in several versions.[47]

As Hull spoke, the "other fellow's" policy was clarified. Through harsh repression the revolt was broken by the end of August. More than five hundred instances of the use of arms, nearly a thousand whippings, and a few machine gunnings from the air silenced politi-

[46] Memorandum of conversation by Hull, August 8, 1942, *FRUS, 1942*, 1:706–7; Hull to Roosevelt, August 15, 1942, *ibid.*, pp. 721–22; memorandum of conversation by Hull, August 24, 1942, *ibid.*, pp. 726–27; Hull, *Memoirs*, 2:1485.
[47] Fischer, *The Great Challenge*, pp. 170–71.

cally conscious Indians. According to the official records, casualties from August 9 to August 30 totaled 1,028 killed and 3,125 seriously injured. A nationalist description of the revolt puts the casualties much higher (at least 7,000). Most important, about 100,000 nationalists were arrested within a few months, many for the duration of the war.[48]

On September 10 a triumphant Churchill addressed a cheering Parliament on his Indian policy. After reiterating the Cripps offer as the definitive British policy, the prime minister launched into a criticism of the National Congress:

The Indian National Congress does not represent all India. It does not represent the majority of the people of India. It does not even represent the Hindu masses. It is a political organization built around a party machine and sustained by certain manufacturing and financial interests. Outside that party and fundamentally opposed to it are 90 million Muslims in British India . . . 50 millions depressed classes or untouchables . . . and 95 million subjects of Princes. . . . In all there are 235 millions in these large groupings alone out of the 390 millions in all India. This takes no account of the large elements among Hindus, Sikhs, and Christians in British India who deplore the present policy of the Congress Party. . . . The Congress Party has now abandoned the policy in many respects of non-violence which Mr. Gandhi has so long inculcated in theory and has come into the open as a revolutionary movement. . . . It is fortunate indeed the Congress Party has no influence whatever with the martial races on whom the defence of India, apart from the British forces, depends. Many of these races are divided by unbridgeable religious gulfs from the Hindu Congress and would never consent to be ruled by them nor shall ever be against their will so subjugated. . . . The Congress conspiracy against communications is breaking down. Acts of pillage and arson are being repressed and punished with an incredibly small loss of life. Less than 500 persons have been killed. . . . I therefore, feel entitled to report to the House that the situation in India at this moment gives no occasion for undue despondency or alarm.[49]

The impasse was complete.

[48] Amba Prasad, *Indian Revolt*, pp. 59–93; Brecher, *Nehru*, pp. 288–90.
[49] *New York Times*, September 11, 1942.

IV

The William Phillips Mission

CHURCHILL'S ADDRESS TO PARLIAMENT underlined the fact that a resolution of the Indian deadlock would be possible only through American pressure and mediation. At a time when most Americans believed that a compromising spirit was needed, the prime minister implicitly closed the door on negotiations until the end of the war. Churchill's verbal assault on the Indian National Congress revealed his hardened imperial outlook. In the press and within the State Department the reaction to Churchill's position was negative. As ensuing developments verified Britain's intransigence, President Roosevelt reasserted his interest in the Indian situation. In December the respected diplomat William Phillips was designated the president's "personal representative" to India. The Phillips mission rekindled Indian hopes for American intervention. Like Louis Johnson before him, Phillips urged Roosevelt to assume a positive role on behalf of the nationalists.

After a brief lull in press attention to India, Churchill's speech again aroused public concern. The response of the liberal journals was predictable, with *The Nation, The New Republic, The Christian Century, Free World,* and *Far Eastern Survey* all chastising Churchill. Viewing the comments as those expected of a subaltern fifty years earlier, *Time* answered Churchill's charges against the National Congress. *Newsweek* saw the speech as a "hands-off" warning to America and China. Raymond Clapper, while continuing to regard the Congress as troublesome, criticized Churchill for failing to prove the sincerity of Britain's Atlantic Charter promises. Newspaper editorial comment echoed this sentiment; the *New York Times* expressed deep disappointment and called for a change in British policy.

In the aftermath of the Churchill address, calls for American intervention were renewed throughout the fall of 1942. Many individuals, groups, and journals—some of which had previously been silent or critical of the National Congress—championed U.S. action. *The Nation* continued to present the National Congress' case. Articles by Fischer placed responsibility for the Cripps failure on the British, and Gandhi's letter to Chiang Kai-shek was published as proof of his anti-Axis conviction. Over the radio and in letters to several journals, Bertrand Russell, who in August had disapproved of the Congress' policy, urged U.N. intervention to work out a wartime settlement. In *The Christian Century*, E. Stanley Jones called on Roosevelt to insist that the Atlantic Charter be implemented in India. This sentiment was also expressed in resolutions of the India League of America and in the editorials of *The Christian Century* and *India News*. Between the lines, *Time* accounts on India belied its pro-Congress sympathy. An appeal from the imprisoned Gandhi somehow eluded censors and reached America. In it Gandhi reminded the United States that, having made common cause with the British, it had assumed responsibility for Britain's policy in India.

In the *Saturday Evening Post*, Edgar Snow, renowned for his reports on China, found Indians generally united behind Gandhi and maintained that American action was needed. Editorially the *Saturday Evening Post* urged that pressure be brought to bear on the British, and *Time* noted Snow's conclusions, with apparent approval. A number of labor unions, including the New Jersey American Federation of Labor and several locals of the United Automobile Workers and the United Electrical, Radio, and Machine Workers, called upon Roosevelt to intervene or mediate. From England, and to a lesser extent from Canada, various liberal and labor groups advocated American or U.N. mediation.[1]

[1] *Free World*, December, 1942, pp. 221–24, and January, 1943, pp. 63–69; *The Christian Century*, September 23, 1942, pp. 1139–40, and October 21, 1942, pp. 1278–79; E. Stanley Jones, "Two Americas: Two Britains," *ibid.*, October 14, 1942, pp. 1250–52; *The Nation*, September 19, 1942, pp. 224–25; Louis Fischer, "Why Cripps Failed," *ibid.*,

In his reports from India, *New York Times* correspondent Herbert Matthews described the mounting dissatisfaction with the United States. On the basis of conversations with business and political leaders, including representatives of the Hindu Mahasabha, moderates Sir Tej Bahadur Sapru and Rajagopalachari, Matthews drew attention to the Indian belief, even among moderates and those cooperating with the Government of India, that the United States was becoming attached to British imperialism. From India, appeals to Roosevelt for intervention came from the Hindu Mahasabha and the Muslim premier of Bengal, Abdul Kasem Huq.

The most striking appeal to Roosevelt was a full-page petition signed by fifty-seven Americans in the *New York Times* of September 28. It called for Roosevelt and Chiang Kai-shek to insist upon a reopening of negotiations. The signers included: writers Pearl Buck, Clare Boothe Luce, Louis Bromfield, Dorothy Canfield Fisher, Fannie Hurst, William Shirer, and Upton Sinclair; editors and publishers Bruce Bliven of *The New Republic*, C. Halliwell Duell and Freda

---

September 19, 1942, pp. 230–34, and September 26, 1942, pp. 255–59; *Far Eastern Survey*, September 21, 1942, pp. 1954–60; *Time*, September 21, 1942, pp. 28 and 33, September 28, 1942, pp. 6 and 8, October 5, 1942, pp. 30–31, and October 12, 1942, pp. 25–26; *Newsweek*, September 21, 1942, p. 38; Edgar Snow, "Must Britain Give Up India?" *Saturday Evening Post*, September 12, 1942, pp. 9–10 and 109–111, and October 31, 1942, p. 100; *Asia and the Americas*, February, 1943, pp. 98–100; *India News*, July–September, 1942, pp. 2–3, and October, 1942, p. 1; *India Today*, September, 1942, pp. 1–2, and October, 1942, p. 1; *New York Times*, September 23, October 12, and November 3, 1942; Walter C. Mackett, "Some Aspects of the Development of American Opinion on India, 1918–1947" (Ph.D. diss., University of Southern California, 1957), pp. 353–56.

William Levine (Local 51 UAW-CIO, Detroit) to Roosevelt, November 2, 1942; J. Zeller (Local 7 UAW, Detroit) to Roosevelt, October 27, 1942; Thomas De-Lorenzo (UAW, Long Island) to Roosevelt, October 25, 1942; A. Verderame (Local 713 UAW, Bloomfield, N.J.) to Roosevelt, November 2, 1942; all on file in Box O.F. 48-H, India, 1942, Roosevelt Papers, Franklin D. Roosevelt Library, Hyde Park, N.Y.; Frank Neidl (Local 103, United Electrical, Radio and Machine Workers, Camden, N.J.) to Roosevelt, November 19, 1942, 845.00/1733.

In addition to the various labor groups urging Roosevelt to act, the President received similar appeals from such obscure and innocuous groups as the West Side Knitting Circle, New York City, and the New Haven V for Victory Club; see Box O.F. 48-H, India, 1942, Roosevelt Papers.

Kirchwey of *The Nation,* Paul Kellogg of *Survey Graphic,* Richard Walsh of *Asia* and John Day Company; academicians Tyler Dennett, William Hocking, Max Lerner, and Frederick Schuman; Walter White of the NAACP; Roger Baldwin of the American Civil Liberties Union; and a few labor and religious leaders. In October the Fellowship of Reconciliation and a newly founded American Round Table endorsed the call for Roosevelt to mediate.

While most of the press comment favored some American effort, in several journals an air of uncertainty prevailed which reflected the adverse reactions to both the "Quit India" resolution and the subsequent British policy. The October 12 issue of *Life,* for example, included an account of the August "Hindu Rebellion" which in picture and text presented the National Congress in terms that were compatible with Churchill's sentiments. Gandhi was depicted as arriving in Bombay in a Packard accompanied by a "Cotton King," and the Congress was presented as an upper-class Hindu group whose leader was a "handpicked" Muslim. In the same issue, however, the editors addressed an open letter to the British people warning that Americans were entitled to expect some positive action toward an Indian settlement. In one of its rare accounts on India, *Collier's* focused on disturbances in Bengal in order to depict Indians as hopelessly caught up in fighting among themselves.[2]

As outside pressures increased, the Roosevelt administration became more aware of British policy. In early September the Government of India's suppression was brought directly to Washington's attention when Merrell was not permitted to deliver Roosevelt's message to the imprisoned Gandhi; it was thus thought that government authorities could not be depended upon to carry the letter. The Government of India also refused to forward the Roosevelt-endorsed message of Quezon to Gandhi and Nehru. Merrell kept the State Department informed of the hostile reaction to Churchill's speech in the Indian press, including the pro-British *Times of India* and *Statesman,* as well as of that in the nationalist papers.

[2] *New York Times,* September 6, 23, 28, and 29, October 5, 8, 9, and 29, and November 12, 1942; *Life,* October 12, 1942, pp. 34, 36–37; *Collier's,* December 12, 1942, pp. 48, 50–51.

On September 15 Roosevelt was again confronted by the Indian question. Senator George Norris informed the president that he was being pressured to introduce a resolution calling for American action on the Indian question, but said that he wanted to avoid any move which would harm the war effort. The same day Roosevelt received through Halifax a statement by Amery which revealed Britain's assumption that the Cripps offer had been the final possible basis for a settlement during the war. In the course of defending the Cripps offer and dissecting Roosevelt's attempts to draw parallels between India and the American colonies, Amery again conveyed the official attitude that the Indian question was Britain's problem. On September 17 Roosevelt asked Norris to defer any resolutions for fear of an Anglo-American rupture. But on September 17 Roosevelt did have Hull suggest to Halifax that conciliatory speeches by British leaders would be more useful. In his conversations with Hull the British ambassador gave the impression of agreement, claiming that he had advised London and Delhi to follow a more moderate approach.[3]

The impressions of three American journalists also received White House or State Department attention. Administrative Assistant Lauchlin Currie placed on Roosevelt's desk the Matthews dispatch of September 30, underlining the passage that, while Indians had not anticipated American intervention, they viewed the United States as becoming attached to British imperialism. Fischer submitted to the State Department a plan for a provisional settlement based on U.N. guarantees. Murray found this to be reasonable but dependent upon the willingness of the British to part with power. Upon his return from India, Snow advised the State Department that a settlement was impossible as long as Churchill remained in power or his authority on India went unchallenged.

[3] Telegrams from New Delhi, September 3 and 5, 1942, *Foreign Relations of the United States, 1942*, vol. 1, *General: The British Commonwealth, the Far East* (1960), pp. 728–31; memorandum of conversation by Hull, September 17, 1942, *ibid.*, pp. 733–34; memorandum of conversation by Welles, September 24, 1942, *ibid.*, pp. 734–35; telegram from New Delhi, September 15, 1942, 845.00/1601; Norris to Roosevelt, September 15, 1942, and Roosevelt to Norris, September 17, 1942, 845.00/1631; copy of letter from Amery to Eden, September 1, 1942, given to Hull by Halifax, September 15, 1942, PSF: India, 1942–43, Roosevelt Papers; Louis Fischer, *The Great Challenge* (New York: Duell, Sloan & Pearce, 1946), p. 167.

Indian officials in America reinforced the trend of dissatisfaction with British policy. Indian Agent General Bajpai emerged as a bit independent of the British Embassy. In conversations with Murray, he related that Indians believed Roosevelt had failed to replace Johnson in deference to the British, who resented "personal representatives" in India. In a meeting with Berle on October 8 the industrialist K. C. Mahindra of an Indian Supply Mission added his estimate that Indians saw Americans agreeing with the British policy of suppression and suggested that the United States could no longer ignore the international implications of the Indian problem.[4]

The address of Wendell Willkie on the evening of October 26 capped the pressures on Roosevelt. Having completed a world-wide tour in part to demonstrate bipartisan support of Roosevelt's postwar plans, the Republican presidential candidate of 1940 spoke to an American radio audience of thirty-six million. Willkie took the occasion to voice criticism of Roosevelt's inaction on India. While he had not stopped in India, because of State Department concern that a visit might be misinterpreted by both the British and the Indians, Willkie had gathered discontent over the Indian impasse from other Allied leaders, principally Chiang Kai-shek. Willkie spoke directly of the seeming inconsistency between ideology and practice.

We are also punching holes in our reservoir of good will every day by our failure to define clearly our war aims. Besides giving our Allies in Asia and Eastern Europe something to fight with, we have to give them assurances of what we are fighting for. . . . Many of them have read the Atlantic Charter. Rightly or wrongly, they are not satisfied. They ask: what about a Pacific Charter? What about a World Charter? . . . Many of them also asked the question which has become almost a symbol all through Asia: what about India? Now I did not go to India and I do not propose to discuss that tangled question tonight. But it has one aspect, in the East, which I should

---

[4] Currie to Roosevelt, October 2, 1942, Box O.F. 48-H, India, 1942, Roosevelt Papers; Fischer to Welles, September 27, 1942, 845.00/1653; memorandum by Murray, October 9, 1942, 845.00/1672; Currie to Murray, enclosing memorandum by Snow, October 21, 1942, 845.00/10–1242; memorandum by Murray, October 29, 1942, 845.00/1714; memorandum of conversation by Murray, October 13, 1942, *FRUS, 1942*, 1:740–42; memorandum of conversation by Berle, October 8, 1942, *ibid.*, pp. 737–38.

report to you. From Cairo on, it confronted me at every point. The wisest man in China said to me:

"When the aspirations of India for freedom were put aside to some future unguaranteed date, it was not Great Britain that suffered in public esteem in the Far East. It was the United States." . . . He was telling me, and through me, you, that by our silence on India we have already drawn heavily on our reservoir of good will in the East. People of the East who would like to count on us are doubtful. They cannot ascertain from our government's wishy-washy attitude toward the problem of India what we are likely to feel at the end of the war about all the other hundreds of millions of Eastern peoples. They cannot tell from our vague and vacillating talk whether we really do stand for freedom, or what we mean by freedom.[5]

Willkie's speech forced Roosevelt to clarify the U.S. position and to end months of procrastination on designating a "personal representative." At a press conference on October 27 the president affirmed that the Atlantic Charter applied to all the world. On that day also Hull told reporters that the United States was waiting for opportunities to give the fullest possible attention to India. Although Walter Lippmann and a few editorials still critical of the National Congress regarded Willkie's argument as encouraging the transfer of power to an unreliable leadership, most of the press comment on it was favorable. With the tide of opinion inclining toward a more active role in India, Roosevelt on October 31 cabled Phillips in London, asking him to become the "President's personal representative" to India.[6]

The appointment of Phillips, made public six weeks later, ended months of uncertainty as to whether the vacancy caused by Johnson's departure would be filled. During the summer the designation of Phillips had been suggested by Murray, Merrell, and Hull. Yet, since Phillips had just been appointed to represent the Office of Strategic Services in London, it seemed unlikely that Roosevelt would be willing to shift him to Delhi. As an alternative, Murray had suggested the former ambassador to Japan, Joseph Grew. Roosevelt's delay reflected his uncertainty as to the proper role of the United States in the Indian

[5] *New York Times*, October 27, 1942.
[6] *Ibid.*, October 28, 1942; *San Francisco News*, October 27, 1942; *Amerasia*, November, 1942, pp. 415–18; William Phillips, *Ventures in Diplomacy* (Boston: Beacon Press, 1952), pp. 343–44.

question. The British and Indian representatives in Washington offered differing views of the American role. The British preferred that the post remain vacant, but, in October, Halifax pressed his government's determination that, if a successor to Johnson were to be named, the United States should discourage talk and hope of American mediation. In his conversations with American officials, however, Bajpai repeatedly urged them to fill the position.

Phillips did offer more prestige to the Delhi post than Johnson. He was intimately associated with Roosevelt and carried impressive diplomatic credentials. Born in 1878 into a prominent Boston family, Phillips had held a variety of diplomatic posts since 1903. He had worked in England, China, the Netherlands, and Canada and as an assistant secretary of state under Wilson; for Roosevelt, Phillips served as under secretary of state and later as ambassador to Italy. His appointment to the Delhi post underlined the importance that Roosevelt attached to India. At the same time, the State Department and the White House anticipated that Phillips, by contrast with Johnson, would be cautious and inclined to favor a non-intervention policy. Like many American officials with his background, Phillips was an Anglophile. He seemed ideal for Roosevelt's purposes, which were to demonstrate America's interest in India and to support non-intervention.[7]

In the interim between Phillips' acceptance on November 4 and his departure for Delhi on December 28, the scope of his mission gradually crystallized. Because Phillips lacked any familiarity with the Indian situation, Welles and Murray suggested that Roosevelt call him to Washington for full discussions. Instead, Roosevelt instructed Phillips to proceed directly to New Delhi, although he authorized him to discuss the Indian question with British officials. Hull's instructions of November 20 advised Phillips to provide any possible assistance in

[7] Murray to Welles, June 17, 1942, 845.00/1421; Murray to Welles, July 22, 1942, 845.00/1422; telegram from New Delhi, July 22, 1942, 845.00/1384; memorandum of conversation by Alling, September 4, 1942, *FRUS, 1942*, 1:728–29; memorandum of conversation by Hull, October 2, 1942, *ibid.*, p. 736; Cordell Hull, *Memoirs of Cordell Hull*, 2 vols. (New York: Macmillan, 1948), 2:1491; Phillips, *Ventures in Diplomacy*, pp. 3–342; Murray to Stettinius, October 25, 1943, 845.00/9–943; Breckenridge Long, *The War Diary of Breckenridge Long: Selections from the Years 1939–1944*, ed. Fred L. Israel (Lincoln: University of Nebraska Press, 1966), pp. 260, 299–300, 311.

resolving the Indian impasse, but to avoid taking sides. While no tenure was indicated in the appointment, the American government regarded the Phillips mission as a short-term effort to exert whatever influence it could. Phillips conceived of his role as one of gaining the confidence of various groups and becoming a center around which some problems might be resolved. Although the British initially objected to the title "personal representative," preferring the less imposing "commissioner," they demurred in return for American assurances that Phillips would not be presented as a mediator.[8] At his press conference of December 11 Roosevelt allayed British apprehensions:

He [Phillips] is going to serve, as they call it in the State Department, "near the Government of India"— . . . And there is no truth in rumors that he will carry any—Mr. Phillips will carry any special plan or formula for the solution of the Indian problem. He will perform the regular duties of an American diplomatic representative abroad. And that's all there is to that.[9]

In London, Phillips was encouraged by press comment and by his meetings with government officials. The *Times* and *Manchester Guardian* praised the appointment of an experienced and competent diplomat. Eden expressed the hope that Phillips would convey the complexities of the Indian situation to the American government. At a luncheon meeting with Phillips on December 16, Churchill held forth on India for more than an hour, criticizing Willkie's remarks and affirming Britain's sincerity and willingness to negotiate on the basis of the Cripps offer. A few days later the prime minister sent Phillips a copy of *Twenty-One Days in India*, a rare book which had been recommended to Churchill before his journey to India as a subaltern. In the accompanying letter Churchill acknowledged that the world described in the book had long since disappeared, but he noted that it served as a useful introduction to the Indian scene.

---

[8] Telegram from London, November 4, 123 P 54/525; Phillips to Roosevelt, November 4, 1942, PSF and OSS, Roosevelt Papers; Murray to Welles, November 7, 1942, 123 P 54/525; memorandum by Murray, November 10, 1942, 123 P 54/529; Roosevelt to Phillips, December 8, 1942, 123 P 54/537; telegram to London, November 20, 1942, *FRUS, 1942*, 1:746–48.

[9] Transcript of Roosevelt press conference, December 11, 1942, Roosevelt Papers.

Considering Phillips' ignorance of India and the one-sided impressions he gathered from British officials, a briefing at the State Department would have helped prepare him for the mission. He certainly would have profited from conversations with Berle, Welles, Bajpai, and representatives of the Division of Near Eastern Affairs. On November 30 the Indian agent general discussed with Berle the shortcomings of the reactionary rule that was descending on his country. On December 17 the viceroy delivered a speech in Calcutta which seemed to Merrell and other observers to indicate a shift in British policy from acknowledging the possibility of Pakistan to seeking to maintain unity. Merrell viewed the speech as a British attempt to sabotage the efforts of moderates to reconcile the Muslim League with other Indian groups in the interest of presenting a united front to the British. Earlier reports from the Delhi mission had observed that Jinnah feared the American government's pressure on the British might lead to a settlement unfavorable to the Muslim League. Familiarity with the trend of the Delhi reports and State Department opinion regarding India unquestionably would have fortified Phillips, for his first month in India proved to be a period of learning what he could well have secured from a few days at the State Department.[10]

When Phillips arrived in India on January 8, 1943, he encountered an Indian mood of despair over the political situation which in turn led to a combination of optimism and skepticism in the reactions to his appointment. American assurances of the universality of the Atlantic Charter had been overshadowed by Churchill's November address affirming his intent not to preside over the liquidation of the British Empire. Gandhi's message to America had produced no manifest results. News of the Phillips mission understandably met with a mixed response. The nationalist *Amrita Bazar Patrika* commented that, since Johnson had been unable to alter British or American policy, any accomplishment by Phillips was unlikely. The Muslim

[10] Phillips, *Ventures in Diplomacy*, pp. 344–47; telegram from London, December 19, 1942, *Foreign Relations of the United States, 1943*, vol. 4, *The Near East and Africa* (1964), pp. 178–80; Mackett, "American Opinion on India," pp. 372–73; telegram from New Delhi, November 4, 1942, 845.00/1696; memorandum of conversation by Berle, November 30, 1942, 845.00/1722; telegram from New Delhi, December 19, 1942, 845.00/1750.

League's *Dawn* predicted that the United States would avoid any hint of intervention. Elsewhere the appointment was favorably received, with the *Times of India, Leader,* and *National Call* viewing the Phillips mission as an indication of renewed American interest.

At the Delhi airport Phillips was received by the aide-de-camp of the viceroy and other lesser officials, as well as by representatives of the press. Phillips told reporters that the purpose of his visit was to learn about India. When a correspondent asked about his impressions of the country, Phillips replied that he had been flying high and had seen little of India. This inspired a cartoon in the Indian press which depicted Phillips peering down at India from a plane; spread below and concealing the subcontinent was a cloud held in place by two cherubs with the faces of Amery and the viceroy. Despite this, the initial Indian reaction to the American envoy was generally favorable. The *Hindustan Times,* edited by Gandhi's son and owned by the Birla family, extended a warm welcome on behalf of the people of India, chiding the Government of India for its failure to send top-level representation to greet Phillips. Welcomes combined with warnings not to expect dramatic results came from the British-owned *Statesman,* as well as from *Dawn, National Call,* and other papers.[11]

During his first month in India Phillips enjoyed a diplomatic honeymoon. His mission met with the approval of the Government of India and of at least the vocal segment of Indian opinion. The viceroy encouraged him to tour the country and to meet representative Indian leaders. The press and various Indian spokesmen were impressed by Phillips' obvious determination to become acquainted with all facets of the Indian situation. This honeymoon was a by-product of the political inertia that enabled Phillips to avoid definitions of U.S. policy. In addition, Phillips' cordial relations with the government were facilitated by his reluctance to request permission to visit the imprisoned Congress leaders. Yet Phillips' initial communiqués to Washington revealed a lack of sympathy for the position of the Government of India. Despite a ceremonious dinner in his honor at the

[11] Telegram from New Delhi, December 22, 1942, 123 P 54/554; *Hindustan Times,* January 10, 1943; memorandum of conversation by Berle, January 20, 1943, 123 P 54/588; Phillips, *Ventures in Diplomacy,* pp. 347–49; *India Today,* November, 1942, p. 4.

99

viceroy's palace, Phillips was unimpressed by the austere and intransigent Lord Linlithgow. Commander in Chief General Wavell and General Claude Auchinleck ("exiled" after he incurred Churchill's displeasure) both impressed Phillips, largely because of their implicit, if not stated, disapproval of British policy. Phillips quickly found that all Indian groups were distrustful of the British and that the suppression of the National Congress was increasing the strength of the Muslim League.[12]

On February 10, when Gandhi began a twenty-one-day fast, the United States was again directly confronted by the political impasse. From the palace of the Aga Khan near Poona, where he had been imprisoned since August, Gandhi had initiated correspondence with the viceroy on December 31, threatening a fast in protest of the prolonged incarceration of the Congress leaders. The viceroy still blamed Gandhi for the August disturbances and called upon him to renounce the "Quit India" resolution. The positions of the Government of India and the National Congress remained irreconcilable, however, and Gandhi commenced the fast on the six-month anniversary of the arrests.

On the eve of the fast, Phillips returned to Delhi from a week's tour of the Punjab and promptly met with Lord Linlithgow. Phillips finally requested permission to visit Gandhi during a southern tour which had been planned sometime before the intended fast became known. The viceroy, however, could now more easily deny the request. Because government officials were to be prohibited from meeting with Gandhi during the fast, Lord Linlithgow held that a visit by Phillips would be inappropriate. Yet, throughout the last hours before the fast, the government kept Phillips informed of the final efforts being made to forestall the fast. To Phillips, the government's inflexibility was incomprehensible. On the first day of the fast, his attitude toward the British crystallized. After meeting with two members of the Birla family and Devadas Gandhi, Phillips wrote to Washington: "Reluc-

[12] Telegram from New Delhi, January 14, 1942, 845.00/1767; letter from New Delhi, January 22, 1943, *FRUS, 1943*, 4:180–82; letter from New Delhi, January 27, 1943, *ibid.*, pp. 184–85; telegram from Delhi, January 25, 1943, 845.00/1771; letter from New Delhi, January 26, 1943, 845.00/1786; Phillips, *Ventures in Diplomacy*, pp. 349–51.

tantly I am coming to the conclusion that the Viceroy, presumably responsive to Churchill, is not in sympathy with any change in Britain's relationship to India."[13]

During the first week of the fast, pressures on Phillips to intercede increased. The American envoy's silence was criticized in the Indian press. By February 16 Gandhi's condition was reported as deteriorating. Even Indians loyal to the government questioned his treatment. Three Indians on the viceroy's executive council resigned in protest against the policy. In the central legislature a debate on the fast began. As the possibility of Gandhi's death became widely known, the government was bombarded with requests to free him.

On February 16, when Herbert Matthews and other reliable sources confirmed the severity of Gandhi's condition, Phillips cabled the State Department requesting permission to express American concern to the viceroy. Phillips realized this would probably not change British policy, but he hoped it would at least correct the impression of American acquiescence in that policy. In Washington that same day, Hull again urged moderation in a conversation with Halifax, but Halifax offered no hope for any change in policy. The State Department then authorized Phillips to intercede with the viceroy.

On February 18, in the midst of reports that Gandhi was failing, Phillips confronted the viceroy, but the effort proved futile; Lord Linlithgow was intractable, determined to maintain the prestige and power of the government. An incredulous Phillips learned that the British preferred Gandhi's likely death and the resulting unrest, which presumably could be handled, to the weakening of the government should Gandhi intimidate it.[14]

Because the viceroy refused to permit any press release on Phillips' visit, the president's representative remained in the vulnerable position of seeming to be indifferent. On February 19 Rajagopalachari

[13] Telegram from New Delhi, February 10, 1943, *FRUS, 1943*, 4:187; telegrams from New Delhi, February 8 and 9, 1943, *ibid.*, pp. 185–86; Phillips, *Ventures in Diplomacy*, pp. 352–59.

[14] Letter from New Delhi, February 11, 1943, *FRUS, 1943*, 4:188–91; telegrams from New Delhi, February 12, 16, and 18, 1943, *ibid.*, pp. 191–96; memorandum of conversation by Hull, February 16, 1943, *ibid.*, pp. 194–95; telegram to New Delhi, February 17, 1943, *ibid.*, p. 195.

warned Phillips of the necessity to clarify the U.S. position. A group of leaders from various Indian communities met in Delhi and, through their spokesman Sapru, issued a plea for Gandhi's release, but censors prevented its publication in India or transmission overseas. Convinced that the British were inviting a revolution, and frustrated by his inability to persuade Linlithgow, Phillips urged that Britain be pressured through Halifax.

Despite the prospect of Gandhi's death and all its ramifications, the United States again followed British policy. Halifax called at the State Department on February 20 and immediately disarmed Hull by warning that, should Phillips make any public references to Gandhi's fast, he would cause serious problems. The ambassador did, however, receive with equanimity Hull's argument that Gandhi should not be permitted to die. Nevertheless, on February 21 Phillips issued a statement that the United States was discussing the Indian crisis with the British. The next day Churchill warned the United States against any intervention. Halifax conveyed Churchill's message, which stated Britain's determination to meet the challenge of Gandhi's fast and again warned of great embarrassment between the two allies should the United States intervene. Welles presented the message to Roosevelt, who again shied away from confronting Churchill on India. The president indicated that the United States would avoid any involvement. The State Department thus concerned itself only with preparing a statement to be issued in the event of Gandhi's death.[15]

Roosevelt thus failed to challenge the British in a policy that could have caused the Allied war effort serious harm. Besides giving rise to serious disturbances in India, the death of Gandhi would have undermined the integrity of the United Nations. Despite the severity of the situation, however, intervention was ruled out for reasons other than the desirability of avoiding an open break with Britain. During the winter of 1942/43, the Allies had turned the tide with their victories in North Africa, at Stalingrad, and in the Pacific. The 1942 coalition

[15] Telegrams from New Delhi, February 19 and 20, 1943, *ibid.*, pp. 196–98; memorandum of conversation by Hull, February 20, 1943, *ibid.*, pp. 199–200; telegram to New Delhi, February 25, 1943, *ibid.*, pp. 203–4; Hull, *Memoirs*, 2:1492–93; memorandum, Near Eastern Affairs, February 19, 1943, 845.00/1790; Berle to Hull, February 22, 1943, 845.00/1848.

of embattled Allies had been transformed into one of almost certain victors, although the final victory seemed a long way off. In the interim the dependence of Britain on the United States had lessened. Much of Roosevelt's coercive potential of 1942 had passed.

Intervention would have been facilitated had it gained public support, but Americans were largely ignorant of the crisis. The Government of India had censored news from India to the point that little about the fast, Gandhi's physical condition, or the ramifications of his possible death reached the outside world. Indeed, early in the fast, foreign correspondents had been informed by the government that they could not present Gandhi or the National Congress in a favorable light. Coincidental with this censorship in India, the British had mounted a considerable propaganda campaign in the United States which was intended to erase the earlier pronationalist sentiment. Because the imperial view was being presented by British spokesmen in America and was reflected in the few dispatches from India, the public was unresponsive to suggestions of intervention. Nominal press comment followed the official interpretation that Gandhi was seeking to intimidate the government and that he really represented a small minority of Indians. Some public attention was gained by Ralph Templin and J. Holmes Smith, two of the missionaries expelled from India three years earlier, when they picketed the British Embassy.

Many groups and individuals, however, brought pressure to bear on Roosevelt. Through their leader V. K. Krishna Menon, Indians residing in London cabled Roosevelt to intervene. A large number of Americans long interested in Indian nationalism—including Pearl Buck, E. Stanley Jones, Harry Emerson Fosdick, John Haynes Holmes, Richard Walsh, and Reinhold Neibuhr—petitioned the White House. A group of African students led by Kwame Nkrumah, who was later to head the government of Ghana, also petitioned Roosevelt. Another group of fifty-six Americans pressed their demand for intervention by means of a sympathetic fast.[16]

[16] Telegram from New Delhi, February 17, 1943, 845.00/1790; telegram, Committee of India Congressmen, London, to Roosevelt, February 21, 1943, 845.00/1831; telegram, V. K. Krishna Menon to Roosevelt, February 21, 1943, *ibid.*; telegram, E. Stanley Jones to Roosevelt, February 21, 1943, Box O.F. 48-H, India, 1943, Roosevelt

While hoping for some action from Washington, Phillips remained incapable of providing the mediating influence that many Indians sought. He was besieged by cables and callers from all parts of India asking that the United States do something to relieve the deadlock, but the president's personal representative could only acknowledge the requests. On February 22 Rajagopalachari asked Phillips to carry a message from Gandhi's friends at Poona to the viceroy, but Phillips declined for fear of adverse British reaction. A few days later Phillips had to ignore Sapru's call for intervention to secure Gandhi's release. Indian disillusionment with the United States intensified as reports carried by the British-owned Reuters wire service told of American indifference to Gandhi's fast.

At Poona, Gandhi's condition worsened. Crowds gathered outside the palace, while close friends and family came to the bedside of the failing leader. Numerous efforts by Britons and Indians to intercede with the government were rebuffed. But, to the amazement of observers, Gandhi survived. On March 2 he ended the fast, although his condition remained critical for a few more days.

With the completion of the fast the minimal American public attention it had engendered abruptly ended. A few regarded the fast as a failure in that the viceroy had held firm against Gandhi's demands. The incident was viewed by many as an indication of the decline of the National Congress and as an enhancement of the British and the Muslim League. Britain's adamant refusal to negotiate was criticized

---

Papers; F. N. Nkrumah, President, and other officers, African Students' Association of the U.S. and Canada, to Roosevelt, February 21, 1943, 845.01/254.

Kwame Nkrumah, *The Autobiography of Kwame Nkrumah* (Edinburgh: Thomas Nelson & Sons, 1957), pp. 43–44. While in the United States, Nkrumah frequently signed his name "Francis N." or "F. Nwia-Kofi" Nkrumah, which accounts for the F. N. Nkrumah signature on this 1943 petition. This practice is evident in the letters cited in Bankole Timothy, *Kwame Nkrumah: His Rise to Power* (London: George Allen & Unwin, 1955), pp. 26–31.

Telegrams from New Delhi, February 13 and 15, 1943, *FRUS, 1943*, 4:192–93; telegram to New Delhi, February 20, 1943, *ibid.*, p. 198; *Los Angeles Times*, February 22 and 24, 1943; *Pittsburgh Press*, February 10, 24, and 25, 1943; *Toledo Blade*, February 11 and March 3, 1943; *India Today*, April, 1943, p. 2; *Newsweek*, February 22, 1943, pp. 45–46; *New York Times*, February 21 and 25, 1943; *The Christian Century*, March 3, 1943, p. 251.

in *Time*, however, and even in some of the journals that had defended the viceroy's stand during the fast.[17]

While the prevalent American mood was again tending to dismiss India, Phillips was proposing a bold move to Roosevelt. On March 3 the envoy urged that Roosevelt, with the approval of the British, invite the leaders of all Indian groups to meet at a conference presided over by an American and possibly including representatives from China and the Soviet Union. At the conference Britain would offer assurances of its willingness to transfer power at a certain date and to cooperate in a provisional government. American leadership was deemed vital, however, since Indians were no longer willing to accept British promises.

After submitting this plan Phillips embarked on a visit to the southern and central regions of the subcontinent. The tour served to lessen the impression, left by the fast episode, of American indifference. In Bombay he met with V. D. Savarkar, president of the Hindu Mahasabha, as well as with other political and business leaders. From Bombay, Phillips traveled to Hyderabad, whose fabulously wealthy Nizam entertained him. In Madras, Phillips met with Rajagopalachari, whom the ambassador admired for his willingness to seek a reconciliation with the British. The moderate spokesman also persuaded Phillips that, if Gandhi and Jinnah were permitted to talk, they could resolve the differences between their two groups. From Madras the American journeyed to the states of Travancore, Mysore, and Bangalore, as well as to Cape Comorin. In the course of his meetings with the princes, Phillips developed an awareness of their justifiable interest in any political settlement.

Upon his return to Delhi on April 1, Phillips still had not received any reaction from Washington to his March 3 suggestion, and, once in the capital, he again experienced frustration with the government.

---

[17] Telegram from New Delhi, February 22, 1943, *FRUS, 1943*, 4:200–201; letter from New Delhi, February 23, 1943, *ibid.*, pp. 201–3; letter from Bombay, February 16, 1943, 845.00/1869; telegram to New Delhi, March 5, 1943, 845.00/1790; Phillips, *Ventures in Diplomacy*, pp. 359–62; *Times of India*, February 15, 1943; *Bombay Chronicle*, February 13, 1943; *Pittsburgh Press*, March 6, 1943; *Toledo Blade*, March 4, 1943; Mackett, "American Opinion on India," pp. 380–81; *Newsweek*, March 15, 1943, pp. 48, 50; *Time*, March 15, 1943, p. 27.

On April 2 the viceroy rejected the moderate leaders' proposal for permission to confer with Gandhi; Phillips had regarded this as a possible break-through in the stalemate. Moreover, Lord Linlithgow accompanied his decision with a reiteration of the position that Gandhi had to repudiate the August resolution and assume responsibility for the disturbances. Also on that day, Phillips cabled Roosevelt for authority again to request permission to see Gandhi and Nehru. While he realized that rejection was almost inevitable, Phillips was convinced that, if he could invoke the backing of Washington, his petition would at least be strengthened.[18]

Phillips' efforts to induce a change in American policy failed. Roosevelt found the March 3 letter "amazingly radical for a man like Bill."[19] While not endorsing it, on March 19 the president instructed Hopkins to reveal its contents to British Foreign Minister Anthony Eden, who was then in Washington. This overture, of course, lacked any force, and thus the British could ignore it. As was frequently the case, the State Department lacked knowledge of the president's action. In fact, a lengthy memorandum of March 31 by Wallace Murray endorsed Phillips' suggestion, agreeing that it would uphold American integrity among Asian peoples.

The ambassador's April 2 plea also was supported by Murray, but was blunted at higher levels. Murray drafted a reply in which he authorized Phillips to indicate that the State Department wished that the envoy could visit Gandhi and Nehru. In submitting the draft to Welles, Murray argued that this minimal effort could help place the United States in the position of seeking to uphold the Atlantic Charter. Welles, however, prevailed upon Hull to hold the message, maintaining that upon Phillips' return the United States should review its Indian policy. Accordingly, the Murray draft was not sent. On April 14 Hull sent a message to Phillips explaining that State Department

[18] Letter from New Delhi, March 3, 1943, *FRUS, 1943*, 4:205–7; telegram from Bombay, March 11, 1943, *ibid.*, p. 208; telegrams from New Delhi, April 2 and 3, 1943, *ibid.*, pp. 210–12; letter from Madras, March 19, 1943, 123 P 54/591; Phillips, *Ventures in Diplomacy*, pp. 364–72.

[19] Roosevelt to Hopkins, March 19, 1943, *F.D.R.: His Personal Letters*, ed. Elliott Roosevelt, vol. 2 (New York: Duell, Sloan & Pearce, 1950), p. 1414.

backing would be inappropriate but that the request could be made on a "personal basis."[20]

During the interlude between his request and its denial, Phillips did meet one important leader with no difficulty. On the evening of April 6 Jinnah accepted an invitation to meet Phillips at the American mission. For nearly four hours Jinnah and Phillips discussed the Pakistani question. When Phillips questioned the economic and political viability of an independent Muslim state, Jinnah insisted that Pakistan was practicable and indeed the only solution to the communal problem; he also held to the Muslim League's demand for equal terms with the National Congress in any interim government. While finding Jinnah to be courteous, charming, and brilliant, Phillips remained skeptical of the Pakistani scheme.[21]

Shortly before he finally received a reply to his April 2 appeal, Phillips encountered another minor irritant. On April 11 Sumner Welles responded publicly to a letter written a few days earlier by Harvard professor Ralph Barton Perry requesting that the State Department explain its policies in several areas, including India. After affirming the United States' interest and willingness to help in reaching a solution to the Indian problem, Welles denied that intervention in India was the test of the government's dedication to liberalism: "But to make active intervention in the Indian situation a test of liberalism, as some have done, presupposes a definition of liberalism which, I must confess, is beyond my comprehension."[22]

The Reuters dispatch of the under secretary's position omitted the reference to the government's willingness to assist, which meant that most papers headlined the story as a denial of any American interest. Some of the Congress papers, such as the *Hindustan Times* and *Tribune,* received complete reports from their correspondents and focused on the assurance of America's interest. Several editorials, including the pro-Congress *National Call,* which relied on the Reuters dispatch, criticized apparent American indifference. The Muslim

[20] Memorandum, Murray to Welles, April 6, 1943, *FRUS, 1943,* 4:212; memorandum, Welles to Hull, April 6, 1943, *ibid.,* p. 213; memorandum, Murray to Welles and Hull, March 31, 1943, 845.00/1916; Phillips, *Ventures in Diplomacy,* p. 381.

[21] Telegram from New Delhi, April 7, 1943, *FRUS, 1943,* 4:213–14.

[22] *New York Times,* April 11, 1943.

League's *Dawn* took the occasion to reiterate its opposition to any intervention, undoubtedly reflecting its realization of the official American hostility to the Pakistani demand. While much of the nationalist press was critical of the United States, the *Hindustan Times* affirmed that Indians should seek to resolve their differences with the British on their own, and without external assistance.[23]

As the reaction to the Welles letter subsided, it became known that the Phillips mission was about to end. Phillips' departure in the spring was consistent with the original intent, a brief mission; indeed, on February 15 Roosevelt had instructed Phillips to return in April or May. Before leaving India, Phillips repeatedly pressed again with Hull and Roosevelt the degree to which Indians looked to the United States. Attending a meeting of Indian newspaper editors on April 19, Phillips found editors representing all parts of the country and all political persuasions telling him that the United States should move to break the deadlock. For instance, the editor of the Associated Press of India, who regarded Gandhi and the Congress as unduly stubborn, expressed the desperate Indian hope for American action. In a lengthy letter to Roosevelt after this session, Phillips recounted his dismay over the British attitude and India's disillusionment with Britain and increasingly with the United States.

Yet, as far as his own mission was concerned, Phillips realized that to Indians the critical test of success was whether he would visit Gandhi and Nehru. The Indian editors' meeting had left no doubt of that criterion. Editorials in the *Hindustan Times* and *Amrita Bazar Patrika* typified the sentiment that his mission had proved futile. Despite the lack of State Department backing, Phillips decided to request permission for a meeting with the leaders. He took the opportunity afforded by a two-day visit with the viceroy at his Himalayan retreat at Dehra Dun; there Phillips found Lord Linlithgow to be

[23] Telegram from New Delhi, April 13, 1943, 845.00/1917; *Dawn*, April 13, 1943; *Hindustan Times*, April 13, 1943; *New York Times*, April 14, 1943.

The State Department did contact the Reuters agency about its transmission of the Welles letter. Reuters stated that the omission resulted from an editorial oversight (memorandum, Division of Current Information to Welles, May 3, 1943, 845.00/1917).

more relaxed and easier to approach than he had been in Delhi. Despite the accommodating atmosphere, the viceroy denied Phillips' request. Contrary to the previous denial, however, the viceroy did permit Phillips to publicize the request.[24]

On April 25 Phillips gave a farewell cocktail party for the press. He read a brief statement acknowledging the press's assistance and added: "I should like to have met and talked with Gandhi and Nehru. I asked permission and was told by the proper authorities that they were unable to grant the necessary facilities."[25]

By revealing the government's rejection of his request, Phillips placed responsibility for the shortcomings of his mission on the British. He left a favorable impression which was cast in Indian eyes as American interest denied the opportunity to help break the impasse. The Government of India was criticized in journals across the subcontinent, including the *Free Press Journal* of Bombay, *Tribune* (Lahore), *Amrita Bazar Patrika* (Calcutta), *Bombay Chronicle*, *Leader* (Allahabad), *Hitavada* (Nagpur), and *National Call* (Delhi). The *Hindustan Times* typified the editorial sentiment: "The refusal may be an exhibition of strength of sorts, but it is equally an exhibition before the world of the ineptitude of the men controlling our destiny at a critical period in our history."[26] Only the *Indian Social Reformer* called attention to the apparent unwillingness of the U.S. government to back Phillips, and thus leveled criticism at Washington as well as at the British *raj*. In America, Phillips' inability to meet with the nationalists aroused little concern. The revelation at his press conference was reported in the newspapers and in *Time* and *Newsweek*, but the only notable commentary consisted of *The Christian Century*'s

---

24 Telegram to New Delhi, February 16, 1943, *FRUS, 1943*, 4:194; telegrams from New Delhi, April 11 and 19, 1943, *ibid.*, pp. 214–17; letter from New Delhi, April 19, 1943, *ibid.*, pp. 217–20; Phillips, *Ventures in Diplomacy*, pp. 375–83; *Hindustan Times*, April 11 and 25, 1943; *Amrita Bazar Patrika* (Calcutta), April 22, 1943.

25 *New York Times*, April 26, 1943.

26 *Hindustan Times*, April 27, 1943; *ibid.*, April 23, 25, and 28, 1943; *National Call*, April 27, 1943; *Statesman* (New Delhi), April 27, 1943; *Tribune*, April 28, 1943; *Free Press Journal*, April 27, 1943; *Amrita Bazar Patrika*, April 28, 1943; *Bombay Chronicle*, April 28, 1943; *Leader*, May 3, 1943; *Hitavada*, April 30, 1943; *Sunday Standard* (Bombay), May 2, 1943.

anti-British stand and a letter addressed to the *New York Times* by Anup Singh, Roger Baldwin, and Frances Gunther.[27]

Immediately upon his return to the United States, Phillips reported to Roosevelt. The conversation proved unsatisfactory to Phillips, however, for Roosevelt was in a talkative mood and left the envoy little opportunity to convey his sense of urgency about India. Accordingly, after their meeting, Phillips wrote his recommendations to the president.

Assuming that India is bound to be an important base for our future operations against Burma and Japan, it would seem to me of highest importance that we should have around us a sympathetic India rather than an indifferent and possibly a hostile India. . . . While India is broken politically into various parties and groups, all have one object in common, eventual freedom and independence from British domination. . . . Words are of no avail. They only aggravate the situation. It is time for the British to act. . . . I feel strongly, Mr. President, that in view of our military position in India we should have a voice in these matters. It is not right for the British to say "this is none of your business" when we alone presumably will have the major part to play in the future struggle with Japan. If we do nothing and merely accept the British point of view that conditions in India are none of our business then we must be prepared for various serious consequences in the internal situation in India which may develop as a result of despair and misery and anti-white sentiments of hundreds of millions of subject people.[28]

Yet Roosevelt continued to be reluctant to confront the Indian question. At his press conference of May 14 he conveyed an air of indifference, commenting that he had nothing to say about India after his meeting with Phillips and that he "supposed" Phillips would return to India.[29]

Roosevelt did ask Phillips to present his views to Churchill, who was then in Washington. As Phillips suspected, Roosevelt preferred to avoid antagonizing Churchill on this touchy subject. Perhaps the president also was seeking to give Phillips a taste of what the United States

[27] *Indian Social Reformer*, May 1, 1943; *New York Times*, April 28, 1943; *The Christian Century*, May 5, 1943, p. 533; *Newsweek*, May 3, 1943, p. 46; *Time*, April 26, 1943, p. 32; *ibid.*, May 3, 1943, p. 36.

[28] Phillips to Roosevelt, May 14, 1943, *FRUS, 1943*, 4:220–22; Phillips, *Ventures in Diplomacy*, pp. 386–89.

[29] Transcript of Roosevelt Press Conference, May 14, 1943, Roosevelt Papers.

encountered in attempting to alter British policy. With these factors in the background, Phillips met the prime minister at the British Embassy on May 23. He argued that distrust of the British could be offset only by an immediate transfer of power to a representative interim government, with military affairs remaining in British hands. Churchill could have responded that this was substantially the Cripps offer, but instead he warned that a British withdrawal would result in a bloodbath born of communal warfare. As Phillips recalled the meeting:

It was hopeless to argue. I closed the interview by reminding him that I was not suggesting that the British should pull out of India then, that I was referring only to the desirability of encouraging the two dominant parties to get together and that, in my opinion, the present was the opportunity to do so.

The Prime Minister accompanied me to the head of the stairs and repeated once more his certainty of a "bloodbath." I was puzzled by his attitude. Never had I mentioned the sudden withdrawal of British power and yet he insisted upon assuming that was my proposal. It was only too clear that he had a complex about India from which he would not and could not be shaken.[30]

After his visit to the British Embassy, Phillips lunched at the White House and reported to Roosevelt on his disappointing conversation with Churchill. A short time later Phillips was again invited to the White House for dinner, after which he and the president talked at length about whether Phillips should return to India. Phillips favored returning only if he could assist in reaching a settlement, yet his encounter with Churchill had demonstrated the unlikelihood of negotiations. In fact, Roosevelt seemed resigned to the continuation of the Indian impasse and indicated that he intended to appoint Phillips ambassador to Canada.

Phillips, however, was reluctant to accept the Canadian position, fearing that such an appointment would be interpreted in India as an indication of American retreat. Indeed, in reporting on Phillips' meetings with Churchill and Roosevelt, the Indian press already was expressing disappointment in Phillips' apparent inability to change policies. A story in *Dawn* focused on the envoy's failure to impress

[30] Phillips, *Ventures in Diplomacy*, pp. 389–90.

111

American officials, while *Hitavada* · speculated on the course of a conversation between Phillips and Churchill in which the prime minister constantly referred to his experiences in India and refused to acknowledge the current situation.[31]

Instead of abandoning his interest in India and going to Ottawa, Phillips continued to urge that Roosevelt in some way secure the reopening of negotiations. On July 1 Phillips presented his views to the Senate Foreign Relations Committee, where Senators La Follette, Vandenberg, and Connally strongly backed his argument that the United States was entitled to a voice in resolving the Indian question. By that time the Indian press had become concerned over whether Phillips would return. During the summer months the American mission at Delhi explained that Phillips had departed for the hot season, implying that he would return in late September.

Phillips, of course, did not want to return unless he could be useful. In July he requested and was given a leave from official duties until he could resume his post in Delhi. In September, however, he was sent to London on a special mission. Phillips continued to perform a variety of diplomatic assignments while still technically the president's "personal representative" to India until Roosevelt, on March 17, 1945, finally accepted the resignation that had been offered almost two years earlier.[32]

Phillips' anomalous status reflected Roosevelt's uncertainty about Indian policy. To have accepted Phillips' resignation earlier would have increased Indian criticism, but to have dispatched Phillips to India would have rekindled Indian hopes and invited difficulties with the British. To the surprise of Roosevelt and the State Department, Phillips had lent support to the voices of Johnson, Berle, Merrell, and others urging American intervention. To the chagrin of these men, however, the Phillips mission failed to alter American policy.

[31] *Ibid.*, pp. 390–92; telegram from New Delhi, May 27, 1943, *FRUS, 1943*, 4:223–24; *Hitavada*, May 28, 1943; telegram from Bombay, May 31, 1943, 845.00/1993; Phillips to Roosevelt, May 31, 1943, PSF: India, 1942–43, Roosevelt Papers.

[32] Telegrams from New Delhi, July 2 and September 8, 1943, *FRUS, 1943*, 4:225–26; telegram to New Delhi, *ibid.*, pp. 226–27; *New York Times*, September 15, 1943; Arthur H. Vandenberg, Jr., and Joe Alex Morris, eds., *The Private Papers of Senator Vandenberg* (Boston: Houghton Mifflin, 1952), pp. 52–53.

V

Imperialists against Nationalists:
The Propaganda Battle

THE ACTIVITIES OF imperialist and nationalist representatives to influence American opinion reached a crescendo at the time of the Phillips mission. The extensive propaganda campaigns undertaken by the British and by sympathizers with the Indian National Congress played a significant role in shaping public attitudes. Through speeches, books, pamphlets, and articles they sought American support. By focusing on both sides' spokesmen, outlets, and arguments, these propaganda efforts can be appreciated and an estimation of their influence can be made.

THE BRITISH APPROACH

In the six months following Pearl Harbor the British were comparatively inactive. By the summer and fall of 1942, however, the pronationalist sentiment in America had begun to arouse British concern. While some believed the Cripps mission had been sufficient to prove British sincerity to American skeptics, others maintained that the American anti-imperialist tradition left Britain in an unfavorable light. A perceptive observer of the American scene, D. W. Brogan toured the United States in early 1942 and found that British stock was lower than at anytime since the beginning of the European war; he noted that Britain's imperial policy was the principal cause. Brogan suggested that the British had to be skillful in defending their Indian policy:

British imperialism is defensible in American terms, but the defense requires skill, candour, and a knowledge of what Americans dislike in our imperial attitude. It is not much use defending the Indian princes with warmth to a republican people. Mere honesty in government will not strike the average American as the whole duty of the political man. If his feelings have been ruffled by English supercilious manner, he is likely to have a fellow-feeling for the Indians who have to put up with those manners far more often than he has.[1]

Several British columnists expressed concern with the anti-British tone in the American press, even after the "Quit India" campaign. Sir Alfred Watson, former editor of the *Statesman* of Calcutta and Indian correspondent for the London *Times*, wrote in *Great Britain and the East* that Britain had to launch an extensive propaganda effort in America. As he phrased it: "What is wanted is not propaganda in the usual sense of the word, but a spreading of incontrovertible facts about the past and present relations of Indians and Englishmen in the East and a vindication of our position there. . . . America should be made to grasp the truth. It will not be easy to overcome the ingrained prejudice of the past."[2]

In late 1942 the British began an extensive effort to influence American opinion. Minister of Information Branden Bracken visited the United States and at a press conference accused nationalist agitators of harming the cause of the United Nations as well as that of Indian constitutional development.[3] The British Information Services accelerated its publication and distribution of articles, pamphlets, and books defending British rule. Many pro-British speakers toured the United States. Several books favorable to the British cause were written by recent visitors to India. It is impossible to distinguish official from

[1] D. W. Brogan, "Transatlantic Strains," *Spectator*, July 3, 1942, pp. 8–9.
[2] Sir Alfred Watson, "American Anxiety about India," *Great Britain and the East*, October 3, 1942, pp. 11–12; *idem*, "India Problems in the U.S.A.," *ibid.*, October 10, 1942, pp. 11–12.
[3] *New York Times*, August 28, 1943.

nonofficial efforts, but the distinction seems unimportant. The significant matter is the nature and impact of the propaganda.

The British campaign centered on the assumption of British expertise on India. The chief spokesmen of the imperial line were, in effect, presented as "Indian hands" by virtue of their service in India, extensive study, or travel on the subcontinent. Drawing heavily on his reputation as an enlightened viceroy, Lord Halifax emerged as the best-known and most effective imperial apologist. Many others with official experience were also active, including: Lord Hailey, who had spent forty years in the government and had been governor of the Punjab and later of the United Provinces; Henry Hodson, reforms commissioner of the Government of India in 1941–42; Sir Frederick Whyte, president of the Indian Legislative Assembly from 1920 to 1925; Sir Robert Holland, a member of the Indian civil service from 1895 to 1931; and Sir Frederick Puckle, a member of the Indian civil service since 1919 and secretary of the Department of Information and Broadcasting from 1941 to 1943 before going to America as an adviser on Indian Affairs at the British Embassy. As secretary of state for India and Burma, and because of his previous experience in colonial administration, Amery was also imputed to speak with authority on India. H. S. L. Polak, who had worked in India for forty years in business and newspaper enterprises, served as an experienced "Indian hand," but without official ties.

The insights of visitors to India were also utilized to defend the British position. Francis Charles Yeats-Brown, who had served briefly in the Indian army prior to World War I and subsequently had traveled extensively in India, had several years earlier written *Lives of a Bengal Lancer*, which became a popular novel and movie in America. During the war Yeats-Brown returned to India and wrote *Pageant India*. He was also a colorful lecturer. As something of a mystic, and under the tutelage of a guru, Yeats-Brown frequently concluded speeches with a demonstration of yoga by standing on his head for prolonged periods. A retired American diplomat, Post Wheeler, had also become a popular author who based his writing on his travels. After leaving the foreign service in 1934, he had authored such books as *Albanian Wonder Tales, The Golden Legend of Ethiopia, India and Some Historic Parallels,* and *Hathoo of the Elephants.* On the

115

basis of two years of travel throughout India during the war, Wheeler wrote *India against the Storm*. Beverley Nichols, a popular fiction writer, followed the same pattern; his strongly pro-British *Verdict on India* appeared after he toured India. Peter Muir's visit to India in 1942 quickly led to another defense of British policy. Reginald Coupland, the Oxford historian of colonialism and Indian constitutional development, provided a scholarly justification for imperial policy. In India when Cripps arrived, he remained with the mission and compiled a brief examination of the negotiations which supported the British position.[4]

The British Ministry of Information and the Washington embassy also utilized Indian defenders of the *raj*. T. A. Raman, an Indian journalist stationed in London, became an outspoken critic of Gandhi. In his pro-British speeches and articles, Bajpai lent to the imperial cause the prestige of his position as the Indian "representative" to the United States. Sir Firoz Khan Noon and Sir Ramaswami Mudaliar, both members of the viceroy's executive council, spoke to audiences throughout America in 1942 and 1943. The former president of the Muslim League and a member of the Legislative Assembly, Sir Muhammad Zafrullah Khan, along with Noon, was presented as a voice of Muslim support of the British. Begum Shah Nawaz, who had been a leader among Muslim women, was seen as a representative of that group's identity with the Government of India. Serving as an adviser to Amery, Sir Samuel Ebenzer Runganadhan spoke on behalf of the Indian Christian community.

Finally, British policy was endorsed by three American scholars. The well-known historians James Truslow Adams and Allan Nevins stressed the complicated nature of the Indian situation and chastised Americans for passing judgment on British efforts. Lennox Mills, a political scientist at the University of Minnesota who had written con-

---

[4] Reginald Coupland, *The Cripps Mission* (New York: Oxford University Press, 1942); Ramsey Muir, *This Is India* (New York: Doubleday, Doran & Co., 1943); Beverley Nichols, *Verdict on India* (New York: Harcourt, Brace & Co., 1944); Post Wheeler, *India against the Storm* (New York: Books Inc., 1944); F. Yeats-Brown, *Pageant of India* (Philadelphia: Macrae Smith Co., 1942).

siderably on British colonial policies, strongly defended the imperial view.

Spokesmen for the British appeared on platforms across the country. Halifax visited every state, speaking as often as ten times daily. His impressive appearance, his willingness to answer questions, and his firsthand familiarity with India made him an ideal ambassador. Moreover, he was aided by the general American sympathy for Britain's war effort. In handling questions dealing with India, Halifax cited his own experiences and frequently pointed out errors in popular concepts of India, thus leading many listeners to conclude that Americans lacked sufficient familiarity with India to pass judgment on British policy. On occasion the die-hard imperialism of Churchill embarrassed Halifax, but otherwise the prime minister had such a wholly favorable image in America that his outbursts on India caused the ambassador little concern. Halifax cultivated friendships among American writers, most notably with Walter Lippmann, whose articles became critical of the National Congress and apologetic for the British. The Ministry of Information also sent many other speakers to America, including Mudaliar, Bajpai, Noon, Raman, Polak, Begum Shah Nawaz, Zafrullah Khan, and Sir Samuel and Lady Runganadhan.[5]

In addition to supporting speakers, the Ministry of Information also distributed pamphlets, made available reprints of speeches and articles, and produced the monthly *Britain* (titled *Bulletins from Britain* until November, 1942), which carried many articles defending India policy. In some cases individuals became unintended imperial apologists. For instance, the widely known American missionary Sam Higginbottom had written a book in 1922 in which he listed some of

[5] Earl of Birkenhead, *Halifax: The Story of Lord Halifax* (London: Hamish Hamilton, 1965), pp. 533–45; Lord Halifax, "For the Unity of Free Peoples" (Speech delivered in Baltimore, December 7, 1942), *Britain*, January, 1943, pp. 27–30; Lord Halifax, "India: Britain Has No Fear of the Verdict" (Address before National Geographic Society, Washington, D.C., January 28, 1944), *Vital Speeches of the Day*, March 15, 1944, pp. 341–45; Sir Ramaswami Mudaliar, "America, India and the War," *Asiatic Review*, July, 1943, pp. 225–35; Henry S. L. Polak, "America, Britain and India," *ibid.*, pp. 268–83; *idem*, "America and India," *Spectator*, July 16, 1943, pp. 56–57; Lennox A. Mills, "Indian Deadlock," *Amerasia*, Summer, 1943, pp. 206–15; Allan Nevins, "Can We Understand Each Other?" *New York Times*, October 25, 1942; *ibid.*, August 17, 1942, and June 15, 1943.

the benefits of British rule. Although he was no longer in sympathy with the British position, that portion of his book was reprinted and distributed by the British Information Services.

The imperial viewpoint was also expressed in newspapers and journals. After the Cripps failure the British made an effort to present their position in popular and scholarly journals. By virtue of their backgrounds, Lord Hailey, Hodson, and Puckle had easy access to *Foreign Affairs,* Holland to the *Yale Review,* Coupland to *Pacific Affairs,* and Bajpai to the *Annals of the American Academy.*

Finally, the imperialist position was presented in several well-written and influential books. In the wake of the Cripps mission, defense of British policy came from *India and Freedom,* a collection of speeches and documents with a foreword by Amery. Within four months of Cripps's return, Coupland's account of the mission was published. In *What Does Gandhi Want?* Raman used Gandhi's quotes to vilify the nationalist leader. Yeats-Brown wrote his *Pageant India.* In 1943 Muir's *This Is India,* Raman's *Report on India,* and Whyte's *India: A Bird's Eye View* appeared on the American market. The following year Wheeler and Nichols added their efforts. These presentations of the British view varied considerably in tone and caliber. The arguments of Coupland, Lord Hailey, Hodson, and Holland were reasonably fair and balanced. At the other extreme, Yeats-Brown, Nichols, and Wheeler produced diatribes against Indian culture and politics and particularly against the National Congress.

The British position rested on several arguments. Most of the detailed works began with a description of Indian culture which stressed its diversity. This disunity was frequently conveyed by an imposing presentation of numbers. For instance, *Bulletins from Britain* once listed "Fifteen Facts about India." These included: 68 per cent of the Indians were Hindus, 22 per cent were Muslims, and the remainder belonged to many small religions; India was a land of twenty-four major languages, or the equivalent of the total number on the European continent; 295,000,000 of the 388,000,000 Indians lived in British India, while the remainder were scattered throughout the more than five hundred native states. These figures were utilized to illustrate the difficulty, if not impossibility, of treating India as a single nation.

Discussions of Indian culture also led to diatribes against Hinduism. By stressing the caste division of society, hundreds of gods, the humiliation of the untouchables, and "backward" practices and beliefs, the British spokesmen played on the popular American misconceptions of Hinduism. Again, the criticisms of Hinduism reinforced the notions of disunity and implicitly asked whether adherents to such a religion were competent to govern themselves. Nichols provided the most devastating verbal assault on Hindu culture, attacking not only its religious practices but its art and music as well.[6]

British rule had, however, benefited India, bringing improved communication and transportation, the introduction of Western education and democratic institutions, and a stabilizing influence. Proud of their achievements, the British acted with a sense of responsibility toward India and its "peoples" (invariably plural). The British had prepared India for self-government, as attested by the acts of 1909, 1919, and 1935, the predominance of Indians in the civil service, and the appointment of Indians to high offices, including five more to the viceroy's executive council in 1942. The Cripps offer was the final step in the British plan to grant independence under peaceful conditions. Representing this "enlightened *raj*" viewpoint, an article in *Britain* bore the sarcastic title "If This Be Tyranny."

British efforts to provide constitutional advance faltered, however, because of the Indians' inability to agree among themselves. In some statements on the rejection of the Cripps offer, responsibility was placed on the failure of the National Congress, Muslim League, and other groups to resolve their communal differences. The National Congress, however, was usually held to be largely, if not solely, at fault. Besides dismissing the Congress' claim that it represented all

---

[6] Muir, *This Is India*, pp. 1–15; *Bulletins from Britain*, April 15, 1942, p. 16, and August 26, 1942, p. 16; Nichols, *Verdict on India*, pp. 3–166; Wheeler, *India against the Storm*, pp. 20–75; Sir Frederick Whyte, *India: A Bird's Eye View* (New York: Oxford University Press, 1943), pp. 5–53.

An important exception to the criticisms of Indian culture came in the writings of T. A. Raman, who upheld the ideal of a united India while vigorously disagreeing with the policies of Gandhi and the National Congress. See his *Report on India* (New York: Oxford University Press, 1943), pp. 1–17, 192–94.

Indians, some British apologists—notably Coupland—suggested that its leaders feared real power.[7]

Invariably the Congress emerged as the villain in the Indian melodrama. Its refusal to cooperate in the war effort cast doubt on its commitment to the defeat of fascism. The "Quit India" campaign had invited military disaster for the Allies. Moreover, the Congress itself was depicted as fascist, with its dictatorial leadership, domination by a single race (Hindus), its standard uniform of dhoti and Gandhi cap, and its veneration of Gandhi, which was similar to that of Hitler. The case for equating the Congress with nazi ideology and practice was presented in greatest detail in the books by Wheeler and Nichols, but even without such an extreme interpretation the Congress was seen as a Hindu organization seeking to impose Hindu domination.

In some writings and speeches the criticism focused on Gandhi rather than on the entire Congress. The other Congress leaders may have been reasonable, but unfortunately they were without influence, and so the views of Nehru and Azad and their disagreements with Gandhi were ignored. As a Hindu proclaiming sympathy for independence, Raman developed most fully the anti-Gandhi angle. Drawing on Gandhi's writings in *Harijan*, Raman depicted him as being sympathetic to fascism, ungrateful for American assistance, and willing to permit a Japanese invasion. Gandhi emerged as a dreamer out of touch with the harsh facts of the war, one who foolishly adhered to non-violence even in resisting the Japanese.[8]

---

[7] W. J. Hinton, "If This Be Tyranny," *Britain*, December, 1942, pp. 5–8; E. P. Moon, "Plain Talk about India," *ibid.*, November, 1944, pp. 45–48; Sir Alfred Puckle,"As the British Look at India," *ibid.*, March, 1945, pp. 28–31; *Bulletins from Britain*, March 25, 1942, pp. 7–10, and July 29, 1942, p. 4; Lord Hailey, "India in the Modern World: A British View," *Foreign Affairs*, April, 1943, pp. 401–11; H. V. Hodson, "Responsibilities in India," *ibid.*, July, 1943, pp. 733–42; Sir Robert Holland, "A British View of India's Problems," *Yale Review*, March, 1942, pp. 569–87; Alan Moorehead, "When Cripps Went to India: Gandhi, Nehru, Jinnah, Cripps, Linlithgow in Action," *Harper's Magazine*, May, 1943, pp. 607–19; Raman, *Report on India*, pp. 54–124, 149–69; Yeats-Brown, *Pageant of India*, pp. 236–52.

[8] T. A. Raman, *What Does Gandhi Want?* (New York: Oxford University Press, 1942), pp. v–x, 3–33, 57–99, *et passim; idem, Report on India*, pp. 169–74; *idem*, "Understanding Mahatma Gandhi," *American Mercury*, April, 1943, pp. 434–40;

Against the pretensions of the Congress the British assumed a paternalistic attitude toward the Muslims, untouchables, princes, and other minority groups. Generally the Muslim League was seen as a thriving and expanding party which represented overwhelming Muslim opinion. The Muslims' traditional loyalty to the British *raj* and their important role in the army illustrated the fact that a large minority repudiated the extreme demands of the Congress. The Pakistani demand was understandable to them, although judgment on its merits was seldom passed except by Raman, who condemned it, and Nichols and Muir, who condoned partition.

In the British view, the untouchables also needed protection against domination by the high-caste Congress. Britain regarded Ambedkar as the voice of all untouchables; it ignored Gandhi's efforts on their behalf. In addition, the imperial attitude was that the princes, whose governments would be subject to extinction should the Congress come to power, required external assistance. Generally the native rulers were looked upon as enlightened and, in the oft-quoted words of Lord Curzon nearly half a century earlier, as a force in the preservation of Indian culture and society. Maud Diver's *Royal India*, published in 1942, reinforced this argument. Based on a study of the fifteen principal states, Diver concluded that the princes provided the best government in India.[9]

Finally, despite the fact that the National Congress refused to support the war, the British knew that most Indians were wholeheartedly behind the Allies. Indian industry was producing arms, munitions, clothing, and other supplies. An Indian industrialist writing in

---

idem, "Essentials of an Indian Settlement," *Far Eastern Survey,* October 5, 1942, pp. 205–11; Reginald Coupland, "Indian Deadlock," *Pacific Affairs,* March, 1944, pp. 26–37; S. M. Ahmed, "America's Interest in Indian Crisis," *Great Britain and the East,* June 13, 1942, p. 10; *idem,* "America, Gandhi and the War," *ibid.,* September 5, 1942, pp. 24–25; Muir, *This Is India,* pp. 10–14, 42–49, 216–24; Wheeler, *India against the Storm,* pp. 7–19, 94–350; Nichols, *Verdict on India,* pp. 179–203; *Bulletins from Britain,* August 12, 1942, pp. 11–12, and August 19, 1942, pp. 4–6.

9 Raman, *Report on India,* pp. 141–45; *idem,* "Essentials of an Indian Settlement"; Muir, *This Is India,* pp. 21–33, 109–16; Nichols, *Verdict on India,* pp. 204–26, 280–95; Maud Diver, *Royal India: A Descriptive and Historical Study of India's Fifteen Principal States and Their Rulers* (New York: D. Appleton-Century Co., 1942), pp. 1–25 *et passim.*

Britain claimed that all workers realized their destiny was tied to an Allied victory. The best proof of support was the fact that, at two million men, the Indian army was the largest volunteer army in the world. Moreover, the Indians had fought with distinction in the Middle Eastern and Italian campaigns. According to Amery in *Britain*, no army could achieve such a record unless its men believed in the cause for which they were fighting.[10]

THE NATIONALIST APPROACH

The nationalist position was presented in a less integrated manner. Under J. J. Singh's direction the India League of America remained the chief voice of the Congress, producing its monthly *India Today* as well as pamphlets and broadsides.[11] Many influential Americans served as its officers or on its advisory board, including Richard Walsh, Louis Fischer, Albert Einstein, Henry Luce, Philip Murray, and Walter White. In late 1943 a group of Indians organized the National Committee for India's Freedom, establishing its headquarters in Washington. The Committee's purpose was to present the Congress' position to the American capital. Unlike the League, the National Committee was restricted to Indians, yet it had close ties with the League, for its leadership was drawn largely from the ranks of Indians long active in the older organization, including the Committee's chairman Syud Hossain, vice-chairmen Haridas Muzumdar and Krishnalal Shridharani, and secretary-treasurer Anup Singh. In 1944 Singh began editing the Committee's monthly, *Voice of India*.

Besides these two major groups, a few individual Indians also were active. For several months in 1941 P. G. Krishnayya of New York had

[10] H. G. Misra, "India in War and After," *Britain*, May, 1944, pp. 40–44; L. S. Amery, "Three Indian Divisions," *ibid.*, December, 1944, pp. 29–31; Charles J. Rollo, "India's Modern Army," *ibid.*, May, 1945, pp. 28–31; D. F. Karaka, "India's Best Ambassador," *ibid.*, August, 1945, pp. 13–16; *Bulletins from Britain*, July 22, 1942, p. 15, August 26, 1942, p. 16, and September 9, 1942, p. 16; *India at War* (New York: British Information Services, 1943), pp. 1–30; Raman, *Report on India*, pp. 198–214.

[11] Among the pamphlets and broadsides published by the India League were the following: Anup Singh, *India: Her Position in a Changing World* (*ca.* 1942); *idem, Storm over India* (*ca.* 1942); Jawaharlal Nehru, *Can Indians Get Together?* (*ca.* 1942); Frances Gunther, *Britain without India* (*ca.* 1943); *idem, If India Loses, We Lose* (*ca.* 1943); Taraknath Das, *India and World Crisis* (*ca.* 1942); *idem, The Atlantic Charter and India* (*ca.* 1943).

published *India and the USA*, but publication of the journal was suspended the month before Pearl Harbor. In early 1944 Krishnayya revived his enterprise under the title *Orient and the U.S.A.* Another largely one-man operation was that of Lal Singh. Singh, a native of British Guiana but of Indian parents, had gone to India in 1924, where he joined the Congress. In San Francisco in 1942 he began editing the monthly *India News*, which represented the left-wing of the National Congress. The Muslim League had no voice in America until 1944, when Mubarak Ali Khan, who had long been active in seeking to secure American citizenship for Indian nationals, began editing the *New India Bulletin*. Like many Indian Muslims, Khan had initially been disposed toward the National Congress but had gravitated toward the Muslim League and acceptance of the Pakistani ideal.

The ability of the Indian groups to present their cause was limited by Britain's suppression of the National Congress. As India ceased to be of front-page concern in America, the nationalists had difficulty sustaining interest in their demands. Moreover, the arrests in India deprived them of well-known speakers from India. A collection of Nehru's writings entitled *Unity of India*, edited by Krishna Menon, was published in 1942. After the August arrests, John Day Company published Gandhi's *My Appeal to the British*, a collection of his writings and correspondence with the government.

This limitation was offset, however, by the pronationalist sentiment of certain American journals and the efforts of a few Americans to support the nationalist cause. *The Christian Century, The Nation, The New Republic, Asia and the Americas, Amerasia, Far Eastern Survey, Free World,* and *Time* consistently presented the Congress' viewpoint. Of the Americans who worked on behalf of the nationalists, Louis Fischer was the most prolific and influential. In speeches, articles, and books, he argued in clear and unequivocal terms. *A Week with Gandhi*, published shortly after Fischer's visit in 1942, presented the controversial leader as a responsible antifascist who was willing to compromise his ideals in the light of existing conditions. The following year Fischer cited in *Empire* the postwar implications of American policy in India. John Gunther's widely read *Inside Asia* included a large section on India, which, while presenting all sides of the controversy, was generally favorable to the nationalists. Gunther's wife, Frances, wrote extensively on behalf of the Congress and in her 1944

123

book, *Revolution in India,* bitterly denounced British policy. In many articles and in her thorough and influential *India without Fable,* Kate Mitchell argued from the National Congress' viewpoint. In speeches and in a collection of her writings entitled *American Unity and Asia,* Pearl Buck lent her prestige to the nationalist cause. Professors Ralph Barton Perry of Harvard and Frederick Schuman of Williams also championed the Congress.[12]

In addition to their American champions, the nationalists were supported by three English writers. H. N. Brailsford, who had close ties with leaders of the Congress, defended its policies in articles and in *Subject India.* John Hoyland, who taught in India for fifteen years, offered *Indian Crisis.* A revised edition of Gertrude Emerson Sen's 1930 landmark study, *Voiceless India,* affirmed the mass appeal of the Congress.

Naturally, Indians were also writing in America. Publications by B. Shiva Rao, Taraknath Das, and Anup Singh appeared. Shridharani followed his successful *My India, My America* with *Warning to the West.* Muzumdar, who had written extensively about Gandhi, sought to relate India to the Allied cause in his ponderous *The United Nations of the World.* In 1944 Kumar Goshal climaxed a nationalist interpretation of Indian history with a plea for the Congress' cause in *The People of India.* R. Palme Dutt's *The Problem of India,* a Marxist interpretation, was directed to the British people but was also produced in a special American edition by International Publishers.

Finally, America's interest in the nationalist cause was emphasized in three books dealing with the United States in Asia. Professor George Taylor of the University of Washington argued in *America in the New Pacific* that only the United States could provide the necessary mediation and guarantees for an Indian settlement. Harry P. Howard's *America's Role in Asia* and Leland Stowe's *They Shall Not*

---

[12] John Gunther, *Inside Asia,* 2nd ed. rev. (New York: Harper & Bros., 1942), pp. 364–506; Frances Gunther, *Revolution in India* (New York: Island Press, 1944); Kate L. Mitchell, *India without Fable* (New York: Alfred A. Knopf, 1942); Louis Fischer, *A Week with Gandhi* (New York: Duell, Sloan & Pearce, 1942); *idem, Empire* (New York: Duell, Sloan & Pearce, 1943); M. K. Gandhi, *My Appeal to the British,* ed. Anand T. Hingorani (New York: John Day Co., 1942); Pearl S. Buck, *American Unity and Asia* (New York: John Day Co., 1942).

Sleep pointed to the need for the United States to become identified with Asian nationalism.[13]

The nationalists challenged all of the arguments advanced by the British apologists. They proclaimed that India was culturally united and that communal divisions were a product of Britain's "divide and rule" tactic. The National Congress, as the oldest and by far the most influential of the nationalist groups, represented Indian aspirations. Its membership was drawn from all castes and religions, including many Muslims (most notably Congress president Azad). Its strength had been evidenced in the provincial elections of 1937, in which the Congress won in eight of the eleven provinces. The Congress had also run strongly in predominantly Muslim areas; indeed, the Muslim League received less than 5 per cent of the Muslim vote. Whatever strength the Muslim League enjoyed was the result of its support by the British. The princes were a legacy of an autocratic past, owing their power only to the British. In extolling the Congress, some spokesmen sought to distinguish between Gandhi and Nehru, taking into consideration the unfavorable image of Gandhi recently projected in America. They described Nehru, whose writings had been well received, as the principal voice of India. Yet Nehru's support of Gandhi in 1942 made this distinction difficult and resulted in the efforts of Fischer, Mitchell, Anup Singh, and others to reaffirm Gandhi's basic commitment to independence and his opposition to the Axis.

From these premises the nationalists maintained that India was prepared for the independence which a reactionary British government refused to grant. Indeed, freedom was usually envisioned as a panacea for internal economic, communal, social, and linguistic problems. At

13 H. N. Brailsford, *Subject India* (New York: John Day Co., 1943); John Hoyland, *Indian Crisis: The Background* (New York: Macmillan, 1943); Gertrude Emerson Sen, *Voiceless India*, 2nd ed. rev. (New York: John Day Co., 1944); Haridas T. Muzumdar, *The United Nations of the World: A Treatise on How to Win the Peace* (New York: Universal Publishing Co., 1942); Kumar Goshal, *The People of India* (New York: Sheridan House, 1944); R. Palme Dutt, *The Problem of India* (New York: International Publishers, 1943); Minoo Masani, *Our India* (New York: Oxford University Press, 1942); Krishnalal Shridharani, *Warning to the West* (New York: Duell, Sloan & Pearce, 1942); George E. Taylor, *America in the New Pacific* (New York: Macmillan, 1942); Harry P. Howard, *America's Role in Asia* (New York: Howell, Soskin Publishers, 1943); Leland Stowe, *They Shall Not Sleep* (New York: Alfred A. Knopf, 1944).

the very least, independence would produce wholehearted Indian participation in the war effort, a participation much more popular and extensive than the mercenary army was providing. The Cripps mission had been insufficient because it fell short of the demand for control of the government. The mission had been considered a grandstand play for the Americans' benefit. Considerable nationalist effort was directed toward demonstrating the shortsightedness of the British. To offset the effect of censorship, the India League of America produced several pamphlets illustrating the unrest of August, 1942, and the manner in which the British suppressed opposition.

Finally, the nationalists believed that, by the promise of the Atlantic Charter, the United States was obligated to make certain that India achieved its freedom. The extent to which Indians expected U.S. assistance was emphasized. Kate Mitchell referred to Azad's statement that the "Quit India" resolution was addressed to the United States and other countries. Fischer reported that Gandhi was wondering whether the Four Freedoms included the "freedom to be free." In Fischer's works Gandhi was seen as waiting for American intervention in the summer of 1942. Frances Gunther added that, before his arrest, Nehru had planned to record a message to Americans explaining the Indian demand and tacitly asking for American support. Indian nationalists believed that the United States should affirm the universality of its promises by issuing a Pacific Charter. Only American mediation, intervention, or guarantees could end the deadlock.[14]

[14] India League of America pamphlets: *Basic Facts about India* (New York, *ca.* 1943), pp. 1–30; and *What Happened after Gandhi's Arrest* (New York, 1942), pp. 1–7. See also Mitchell, *India without Fable*, pp. 34–218, 288–96; Goshal, *The People of India*, pp. 167–324 *et passim*; Fischer, *A Week with Gandhi*, pp. 30–39, 58–59, 85–86; Brailsford, *Subject India*, pp. 207–15 *et passim*; F. Gunther, *Revolution in India*, pp. 41–46, 77–91, *et passim*; Buck, *American Unity and Asia*, pp. 43–55, 74–95; Hoyland, *Indian Crisis*, pp. 86–100 *et passim*; Shridharani, *Warning to the West*, pp. 253–74; Syud Hossain, "India and America," *Survey Graphic*, November, 1942, pp. 529–32; Paresh Nath, "Pakistan: Is It God's Gift to the British Empire?" *Asia and the Americas*, October, 1943, pp. 567–70.

The nationalist arguments were also expressed in editorials and articles in the issues of *India Today*, 2–8 (1942–47); *Voice of India*, 1–3 (1944–47); *India and the USA*, 1 (1941); *The Orient and U.S.A.*, 2 (1944); and *India News*, 1–4 (1941–44). The Muslim League's position was presented in *New India Bulletin*, 1944–47.

THE OUTCOME

Naturally, each side in the propaganda battle resented the activities of the other. As discussed earlier, concern over the nationalist impact aroused the British in 1942 to emphasize their cause. In March, 1943, Halifax raised with Hull the question of nationalist agitation, particularly that arising from Gandhi's fast. Presumably referring to Roosevelt's avoidance of any public comment on the Indian situation, the secretary assured Halifax that the United States had attempted to reduce anti-British sentiment. On the other side *India Today* and speakers at rallies organized by the India League criticized Bajpai, Noon, Raman, and other "Indian stooges" of the imperial regime. In the Indian press, including the *Free Press Journal, Indian Social Reformer*, and *Hindustan Times*, the British were charged with spending lavishly to propagate lies in America. The nationalist resentment culminated in N. G. Jog's *Judge or Judas?*, a vitriolic attack on pro-British spokesmen, particularly Raman and Nichols. Alone among American political leaders, New York congressman Emanuel Celler, long interested in the nationalist cause and in the status of Indian aliens in America, condemned Britain's propaganda activities.[15]

In this struggle for the American mind the British emerged victorious. They were aided by the course of the war in the sense that, after the Allies assumed the initiative in 1943, the need for Indian participation declined. The political inactivity in India lessened public concern and seemingly affirmed Britain's contention that after the August, 1942, crisis only the British could provide stability. Following the considerable interest in India expressed during the spring and summer of 1942, a misunderstanding of the actions of the National Congress led many Americans to accept the view that India was a hopelessly complicated political problem. A cartoonist in *The New Yorker* captured the American attitude in a scene depicting two fashionable ladies at tea. One was saying, "It makes me so mad when

---

[15] Kurt R. Mattusch, "The American Public and India," *Amerasia*, Fall, 1942, pp. 397–408; *Hindustan Times*, July 22, 1944; *Indian Social Reformer*, September 9, 1944; *India Today*, February, 1945, p. 4, and January, 1945, p. 4; Cordell Hull, *Memoirs of Cordell Hull*, 2 vols. (New York: Macmillan, 1948), 2:1493; N. G. Jog, *Judge or Judas?* (Bombay: Thacker & Co., 1945), pp. 1–41; Chaman Lal, *British Propaganda in America* (Allahabad: Kitab Mahal, 1945), pp. 36–50 *et passim*.

127

I think how long I've been patient with India."[16] To such a mentality the British arguments had a strong appeal.

The skillfully organized propaganda found its way into influential sources, including popular magazines such as *Harpers, Reader's Digest, Fortune,* and the Scripps-Howard Sunday supplement *This Week.* For instance, the large audience of *Reader's Digest* was introduced to a condensed version of *Verdict on India.* The British view was also notably, if subtly, reinforced on the American screen. A half-dozen short-subject documentaries on India were produced by motion picture companies. While the films did present the subcontinent more realistically than had earlier Hollywood efforts, they generally relied on the long-popular theme of mysterious India. For instance, a March of Time release, "India in Crisis," linked the political demands of 1942 to the most superstitious and least understood elements of Indian culture. India was pictured as a phenomenon beyond understanding, with emphasis being placed on religious rites, caste taboos, and fakirs. As a British sympathizer with the Congress described it, "The film appears to be a somewhat self-conscious contribution from our American allies calculated to leave its audiences asking 'what can the British be expected to do, faced with such a teeming eruption of sub-humans?' "[17]

On the other hand, the nationalists had difficulty sustaining enthusiasm for a cause whose realization the events of 1942 had indefinitely postponed. While the British were reaching a public whose attitudes were uncertain, the nationalists were restricted largely to preaching to the converted.

A public opinion poll of April, 1943, revealed a shift from the earlier pronationalist sentiment. While 62 per cent of the Americans polled believed that India should receive its independence, only 19 per cent favored immediate independence. Disillusionment with Indian nationalists and acceptance of the British position were underscored in the finding that nearly half of the sample (47 per cent) believed independence should come after the war and 43 per cent accepted the suggestion that the United States should leave the prob-

[16] *The New Yorker* cartoon was reprinted in *Amerasia,* June, 1942, p. 165.
[17] Edgar Anstey, "The Cinema: 'March of Time,' " *Spectator,* July 10, 1942, p. 35.

lem to Britain. Only one-fifth believed the United States should help India achieve its freedom (Table III).

Table III. American Public Opinion and India, April, 1943

Do you think Britain should give the people of India their independence?

Give independence	62%
Don't give independence	19
Don't know whether should be given independence	19

The 62 per cent of the sample who favored independence were asked: now or after war?

Give now	19%
After war	40
Don't know when	3

Do you think we ought to help see that India gets her independence or should we leave that up to Britain? This was asked of the 62 per cent favoring independence and an additional 7 per cent who favored independence after the war (this 7 per cent being from the 19 per cent who opposed independence but in a second question said they favored it after the war).

We should help	22%
Leave to Britain	43
Don't know	4

Source: Prepared by Mildred Strunk, National Opinion Research Center, April 6, 1943, cited in *American Opinion, 1935–1946*, ed. Hadley Cantril (Princeton: Princeton University Press, 1951), p. 327.

The conditions that favored the British in the spring of 1943 and led to this sample of American opinion became more accentuated in subsequent months. Political inactivity, the course of the war, and the lack of a high-ranking American diplomat after Phillips' departure lessened public concern. To the disinterested or to those seeking an easy solution after the confusing events of 1942, the imperial argument appealed and indeed caught hold.

VI

American Opportunities and Inaction, 1943–1945

FROM THE DEPARTURE OF PHILLIPS until the end of the European war in May, 1945, the United States maintained a more distant role in Indian developments. Phillips was not followed by another high-ranking diplomat, a fact which symbolized President Roosevelt's inclination to forget about India. During this period, however, Roosevelt revealed a strong interest in resisting imperialism in other areas. Coinciding with the lessening of his concern about India, Roosevelt became preoccupied with preventing a resumption of French authority in Indochina at the end of the war, and he also worked for guarantees of self-determination among the peoples of Eastern Europe. At the Teheran Conference of November, 1943, the president and Russian premier Joseph Stalin talked at length and agreed on the desirability of ending European imperialism in Asia.[1] Perhaps this shift of emphasis represented an acknowledgment that, owing to Churchill's intransigence, assisting India was beyond America's capability; certainly it seemed easier to keep the French from returning to power in Indochina than to force the British out of their entrenched position in India. Yet Roosevelt's course of action failed to comprehend the con-

[1] Minutes of Roosevelt-Stalin meeting, November 28, 1943, *Foreign Relations of the United States: The Conferences at Cairo and Teheran, 1943* (1961), p. 485.

tinuing importance of India as the symbolic test of the Allied pledge to uphold self-determination; it also neglected to take into account the effect upon Indo-American relations of an American retreat from the problem.

Although Roosevelt preferred to ignore India, India still haunted the United States. From the summer of 1943 to the spring of 1945, nationalism confronted the American public and government on several levels: the Bengal famine, which many Indians blamed partly on the United States, from whom assistance was expected; the presence of large numbers of American forces on Indian soil, and the inevitable political ramifications; the modest political reawakening that led to renewed hopes of American encouragement for independence; the publication of Phillips' anti-British views, which produced a congressional storm and forced Roosevelt into at least a tacit agreement; the movement to secure American immigration and naturalization privileges for Indians; and the mission of Mrs. Vijayalakshmi Pandit to represent India at the United Nations Conference. While none of these offered the possibility of significantly altering British-Indian relations, they did provide an opportunity for the improvement of American relations with disillusioned Indian nationalists.

Caused by wartime dislocations as well as by climatic factors, the Bengal famine took a frightening toll: between 1,500,000 and 3,000,000 persons died of starvation. The food supply began diminishing in 1942 when the rice imports from Burma were lost after the Japanese conquest. The stationing of American and British troops in India, with a heavy concentration in the northeast, resulted in an additional drain on the available food supply. Then, in October, 1942, a cyclone struck Bengal, causing widespread death, disease, and destruction of crops. Neither the provincial nor the central government moved sufficiently to meet these conditions, and thus they worsened steadily to the point that by the summer of 1943 India was experiencing its worst famine of the twentieth century.

Although the Government of India attempted to minimize the extent of the suffering, the famine did come to official American attention in August, 1943. Syed Badrudduja, the mayor of Calcutta, cabled Roosevelt, urging that the president and Churchill "in the name of

starving humanity . . . arrange immediate shipment of food grains."[2]
Within a few days the American representatives on the British-American Combined Food Board suggested to their colleagues that a special allotment of rice be designated for India. The British, however, maintained that grains could be imported from Australia whenever over-burdened shipping facilities permitted. State Department officials viewed the British position as an indication of Britain's determination to prevent American involvement. Moreover, the ability of the United States to act unilaterally was negated, not only by traditional deference to the British on Indian policy, but also by the wartime arrangement by which shipping between the United States and India operated under British control.

William Phillips, still technically the president's representative to India, and George Merrell, the ranking American diplomat at New Delhi, were unwilling to accept this deference to the British. Before leaving for London to become political adviser to General Eisenhower, Phillips on September 9 told Roosevelt that the famine intensified political unrest which was directed at the United States as much as at Britain. Warning against the appearance of indifference, Merrell suggested that the State Department issue a statement explaining the extent to which food shipments to Russia, England, and North Africa were straining American resources but also assuring that the United States would collaborate with the British in aiding the victims of the famine. Fearing that such a statement might encourage hopes for assistance which could not be delivered, because of the British attitude, the State Department rejected Merrell's plan.[3]

While the State Department and the White House failed to move, J. J. Singh and the India League of America spearheaded a campaign to bring the famine to public attention. Singh wrote an eleven-page pamphlet, *Famine in India*, which he circulated among the press,

[2] Badrudduja to Roosevelt, August 23, 1943, cited in a State Department telegram to Calcutta, September 4, 1943, *Foreign Relations of the United States, 1943*, vol. 4, *The Near East and Africa* (1964), pp. 299–300.

[3] Memorandum, Adviser on Political Relations (Murray) to Chief, War Commodities Division (Cissel), August 28, 1943, *ibid.*, pp. 297–99; Phillips to Roosevelt, September 9, 1943, *ibid.*, pp. 300–301; telegram from New Delhi, September 25, 1943, *ibid.*, pp. 301–2; telegram to New Delhi, October 9, 1943, *ibid.*, pp. 304–5; telegram to New Delhi, October 13, 1943, *ibid.*, pp. 306–7.

members of Congress, and State Department officials. After describing the extent of the disaster, Singh charged the British with indifference and called for massive American assistance. In addition, Singh sent appeals to the president and later to the first lady. While the petitions to official Washington met with a meager response, much of the press did pick up Singh's criticism of the British. The two leading weeklies, *Time* and *Newsweek*, as well as *The Christian Century* and *The New Republic*, charged the British with poor planning and mismanagement. *The New Republic* called for assistance through the United Nations. On November 5 the Joint Congress of Industrial Organizations–American Federation of Labor War Relief Committee allocated $100,000 to assist the famine victims.[4]

To Singh and interested Americans, the launching of the U.N. Relief and Rehabilitation Administration in November, 1943, provided the opportunity to assist India. Intended to aid nations devastated by the war, UNRRA was formally organized at a conference in Atlantic City attended by representatives of forty-four nations. Singh appealed to Assistant Secretary of State Dean Acheson, who had been instrumental in the drafting of the UNRRA agreement, and to Herbert Lehman, the new organization's director general. The India League's president argued that because the Bengali famine had been primarily caused and aggravated by the war, its victims were entitled to relief from UNRRA; but, at a press conference, British representative Colonel John J. Llewellin refused to concede that the famine had been caused by the war and claimed that nothing needed to be done to aid India. Singh received strong sympathy from the delegates of several Asian and Latin American nations, who indicated a willingness to assist, provided the request was made by the Indian delegate Bajpai. As always, however, Bajpai was tied to imperial policy and thus failed to raise the question. With Acheson acquiescing in Llewellin's position, the Bengali famine received no official consideration. British and

4 Singh to F. Roosevelt, September 29, 1943, and Singh to E. Roosevelt, November 2, 1943, Box O.F. 48-H, India, 1943, Roosevelt Papers, Franklin D. Roosevelt Library, Hyde Park, N.Y.; Anup Singh, *Famine in India* (New York: India League of America, 1943), pp. 1–11; *The New Republic*, September 15, 1943, p. 669; *Newsweek*, October 4, 1943, pp. 38, 40, and October 18, 1943, pp. 32, 35; *The Christian Century*, November 3, 1943, pp. 1261–62; *India Today*, October, 1943, pp. 1–2; *India News*, December, 1943, pp. 1–4.

American policy at the Atlantic City conference was scored in several Indian and American newspapers, and by *Time, The Christian Century,* and *The New Republic.* In his *PM* and in *The Nation,* I. F. Stone charged the British with distorting the facts by claiming that inadequate shipping made relief operations impossible. He observed that many ships carried only partial cargoes to Indian ports and that the large American shipping operation to Australia could be utilized to carry Australian wheat to India.[5] *India Today,* the journal of Singh's India League, commented bitterly: "India will survive this famine, as she survived famines in the past. But the memory of the hundreds of thousands who died because no help came from their allies, will be a ghost not quickly laid."[6]

Indeed, the UNRRA's failure to help India led to U.S. congressional action authorizing assistance to the famine's victims. After a visit from Singh, Congressman Karl Mundt, a member of the House Committee on Foreign Affairs, brought the issue to congressional attention. In hearings on a bill to appropriate funds for UNRRA, Mundt questioned Acheson about the exclusion of India, but refused to accept Acheson's interpretation that UNRRA operations were restricted to areas directly devastated by military operations. After a lengthy floor discussion in the House on December 21, Mundt introduced an amendment to the appropriations bill which would permit UNRRA assistance to India. The amendment received strong backing in the press and was overwhelmingly adopted by the House, the Senate, and the Council of UNRRA. One technicality remained, however, which could not be eliminated by American action: a government had to request UNRRA assistance. The Government of India which ironically gave some $30,000,000 to UNRRA, never made the request.[7]

[5] I. F. Stone, "The Indian Skeleton at Atlantic City," *The Nation,* December 11, 1943, pp. 686–87; Norman Angell, "The Indian Famine," *Far Eastern Survey,* January 12, 1944, pp. 7–10; *Amerasia,* January 7, 1944, p. 3; *The New Republic,* December 20, 1943, p. 868; *Time,* December 6, 1943, pp. 16–17; *The Christian Century,* December 15, 1943, p. 1461.

[6] *India Today,* December, 1943, p. 4.

[7] U.S. Congress, House, *Congressional Record,* 78th Cong., 1st sess., 1943, 89, pt. 8:10909–92.

Because direct official assistance was impossible, private American efforts were undertaken in 1944. The American Friends Service Committee provided leadership. The various groups concerned about the famine agreed that the Friends would act as the purchasing and distributing agent for all relief work in India. Following a quick visit to Bengal, the Committee's director, James Vail, began relief distributions in May, 1944. In the offices of Richard Walsh, editor of *Asia and the Americas*, the India Famine Relief Committee was organized to solicit financial support. Technically the funds were channeled through the British War Relief Society. The appeal of the India Famine Relief Committee received strong support from the India League, *The Christian Century*, Pearl Buck, I. F. Stone, and indirectly from the British journalist Michael Brown in his book *India Need Not Starve*. The Committee raised more than $100,000 during 1944. In addition to this private backing, the National War Fund provided $100,000 per month through August, 1944. The Friends Service Committee was able to provide food and vitamins, and dispatched relief teams into rural Bengal.[8]

With the curtailing of National War Fund allocations, however, a more extensive private campaign became necessary; as a result, American Relief for India was organized in 1945. The new group, which replaced the Famine Relief Committee, appealed openly as an American enterprise. Headed by Henry Grady as chairman and Phillips as a vice chairman, and with its directors including Henry Luce and Sumner Welles, American Relief for India launched its fund-raising campaign in the spring of 1945. At a time when Americans were besieged with requests to assist devastated areas, American Relief for India solicited some $200,000. In Bengal the American Friends Service Committee expanded its activities. Working in close cooperation with Christian missions, as well as with Indian charitable groups and government officials, the Committee channeled its energies (as conditions permitted) from relief to rehabilitation. In short, it helped to coordi-

---

[8] American Friends Service Committee, *A Report on Friends' Famine Relief in India, 1945* (Philadelphia, 1946), pp. 1–7; James G. Vail, "In the Indian Famine Area," *Asia and the Americas*, August, 1944, p. 349; *The Christian Century*, May 10, 1944, pp. 588–90, and November 22, 1944, p. 1339; Michael Brown, *India Need Not Starve* (Bombay: Longmans, Green & Co., 1944), pp. 110–90.

nate the revival of Bengal by distributing multi-vitamin tablets and massive cholera inoculations, reconstructing villages and opening industrial training centers, and by encouraging the formation of agricultural and industrial cooperatives.[9]

Private American relief to Bengal helped to offset much of the disenchantment caused by Roosevelt's failure to act. The president's apparent indifference is difficult to understand unless one considers it in the light of wartime exigencies. American subservience to the British in UNRRA followed Roosevelt's policy of not upsetting Churchill about India. Apparently this acquiescence prevailed not only on political questions but also in matters of human suffering. In 1944 Churchill did ask the American navy to assist in shipping wheat from Australia to India, but, when the Joint Chiefs of Staff objected to diverting any shipping from military operations, Roosevelt refused even that limited assistance. The National War Fund's backing of the Indian relief program was ended on the assumption that the Fund's resources could be used more effectively in Eastern Europe. The need to cultivate friendly relations with the Indian people, a point frequently mentioned by the supporters of American Relief for India, seemed to matter little to Roosevelt.[10]

Americans were also drawn toward India by the war. Within a year after the attack on Pearl Harbor the United States had developed a considerable military presence in India. The Ledo Road, which linked Assam with the old Burma Road, was built under the direction of Americans and with manpower largely from Negro engineering forces, Chinese troops, and Indian laborers. From air bases in Assam the air force supplied China in the famous "hump" operation across the Himalayas. To meet the urgent demands of China, new bases were constructed in 1943. Also, Calcutta replaced Karachi as the principal American base. The strain on the port and railway facilities of Bengal

[9] American Friends Service Committee, *Report on Friends' Famine Relief*, pp. 8–21; *New York Times*, April 18, 1945.

[10] Paraphrase of Churchill-Roosevelt message, April 29, 1944, in letter from Halifax to Hull, May 1, 1944, *Foreign Relations of the United States, 1944*, vol. 5, *The Near East, South Asia and Africa, the Far East* (1965) pp. 271–72; Hull to Roosevelt, May 31, 1944, *ibid.*, pp. 272–73.

and Assam led to American military supervision of transportation operations.

By October, 1943, when the construction of the Ledo Road was first revealed, Americans had become aware of India as an important center of the campaign against Japan. Popular magazines carried many accounts of the extremes of the GI's experience in India, ranging from those in the cities who had personal valets and much money to spend to engineers in remote Assam engaged in difficult and dangerous work.

The easy-going GI was generally popular among the Indians, who found the Americans more engaging than the usually austere and distant British troops. Yet many Indians blamed the economic devastation of Bengal on the military, for it had been brought on not only by the increased demands on food supplies but also by the spiraling prices caused by the purchasing power of the Americans. Others resented the military presence, seeing in it a collaboration of the United States with Britain to suppress the National Congress. Finally, racial prejudice manifested itself in a few publicized and bitterly resented verbal assaults on Indians by GIs.[11]

After receiving persistent reports from military and diplomatic posts in India warning that the American effort was misunderstood, on February 1, 1944, Roosevelt, acting on his own initiative, issued a statement affirming that the sole purpose of the army was to defeat Japan.[12] While Roosevelt's assurance was welcomed in India, it eliminated only part of the suspicions that arose from Anglo-American collaboration.

Three days later the Japanese launched an attack on Assam, thus arousing American concern that a large-scale invasion of India was beginning. The leaders of the Japanese Fifteenth Army hoped this attack would lead Tokyo to authorize expanded operations in India,

[11] *Statesman* (New Delhi), January 10, 1943; *Life*, November 30, 1942, pp. 16, 18, and January 18, 1943, pp. 11–12, 14, 16; *Newsweek*, January 4, 1943, pp. 21–23; *The Nation*, March 4, 1944, pp. 275–76, and April 15, 1944, pp. 442–43; *Saturday Evening Post*, February 12, 1944, pp. 18–19, 85–88.

[12] Roosevelt to Hull, January 17, 1944, and Hull to Roosevelt, January 19, 1944, Box O.F. 48-H, India, 1944, Roosevelt Papers; *Department of State Bulletin*, February 5, 1944, p. 145.

but Imperial General Headquarters and Allied intelligence recognized that Japan lacked the facilities for much activity other than raiding. Yet the thrust of February, 1944, succeeded in blockading Imphal, a key Allied communication center. In late June the Allies broke the blockade, and the remnants of the Japanese army retreated into Burma. Of the 155,000 men who had invaded India, the Japanese sustained 90 percent casualties (65,000 killed and 75,000 wounded).

In late 1943 India began stirring politically, and the Roosevelt administration was forced to reconsider some of its policies. The renewed activity centered on two British decisions: the appointment of General Wavell as viceroy and the unconditional release of Gandhi. Diplomats, politicians, and correspondents speculated whether these actions foreshadowed changes in Britain's position. The pronationalist elements in America again pressed for official action. Their premise that some move was necessary to offset Indian disappointment with America was substantiated by diplomatic reports from India.

Wavell's elevation to the viceroyalty led to much press and diplomatic analysis. Opinions as to the meaning, if any, of replacing Linlithgow varied sharply. Several journalists viewed the appointment as an indication of moderation from the hard line Linlithgow had represented. From London, Ambassador Winant suggested that the Churchill government was seeking to improve Anglo-American relations by replacing a viceroy who embodied the old-style imperialism with a modest, unassuming military man who reflected the strategic importance of India. Phillips continued to take an active interest in India and met with Wavell in London shortly before the viceroy-designate left for India. Reiterating America's willingness to assist in resolving the deadlock, Phillips indicated his desire to return to Delhi should such an opportunity occur. While Wavell appeared reticent to seek outside aid, Phillips wrote to Roosevelt that he did seem much more flexible than his predecessor.

In India, however, the American diplomatic mission reported that Indians viewed Wavell as the embodiment of Churchill's policies. After a final interview with Linlithgow, Merrell reported the retiring viceroy's observation that the *raj* would remain for another fifty years because it would take that long for Indians to learn to govern themselves. Both Merrell and the political officer at Delhi, Lampton Berry, warned that mounting despair was leading to disillusionment with the United States. The American public had little knowledge of this mood and indeed was being led by British propaganda to assume that India was devoting all its energies to the war effort.[13]

In America, nationalist groups and their supporters capitalized on the modest interest aroused by the Wavell appointment. Throughout late 1943 and early 1944 they became more vocal and demanding. The publication of Wendell Willkie's *One World* during the summer of 1943 aided their cause, for the Republican leader restated the position taken in his October, 1942, address—namely, that the United States suffered throughout Asia for its failure to assist Indian freedom. On the first anniversary of the arrests of the Congress leaders, nationalist sympathizers picketed before the White House. At a large India League rally in New York on August 10, Congresswoman Clare Boothe Luce delivered a widely publicized, fiery address castigating Churchill and Roosevelt. The American Round Table on India called for following Wavell's appointment with the establishment of a provisional popular government. H. N. Brailsford urged that the principal Allies should issue a Pacific Charter and immediately carry its promise into effect in India. The support of American labor groups for the nationalists reached its peak, with both the United Automobile Workers and the Congress of Industrial Organizations adopting resolutions calling on Roosevelt to make representations to the British to secure the release of the Congress leaders and a resumption of negotiations. In speeches and articles the respected missionary E. Stanley Jones continued to champion the Congress' demand for independence.[14]

[13] Walter C. Mackett, "Some Aspects of the Development of American Opinion on India, 1918–1947" (Ph.D. diss., University of Southern California, 1957), p. 393; telegram from London, September 20, 1943, *FRUS, 1943*, 4:227–28; Phillips to Roosevelt, September 30, 1943, *ibid.*, pp. 228–29; telegram from New Delhi, October 8, 1943, *ibid.*, pp. 230–31; telegram from New Delhi, October 18, 1943, *ibid.*, p. 231; telegram from New Delhi, October 28, 1943, 845.00/2161.

[14] Wendell Willkie, *One World* (New York: Simon & Schuster, 1943), pp. 183–84; *New York Times*, August 9, 10, September 27, and October 6, 1943; *India News*, December, 1943, p. 3; H. N. Brailsford, "An Englishman's Plea for India Now," *Asia and the Americas*, September, 1943, pp. 546–48; E. Stanley Jones, "Gandhi and the Christian Missions," *The Christian Century*, May 3, 1944, pp. 553–55.

In the early months of 1944 Indian discontent was evidenced in the actions of groups normally neutral or loyal to the *raj*. Besides the usual criticisms of the government in the nationalist journals, the Muslim League press and several moderate newspapers charged the British with procrastination in seeking a settlement. At its meeting in late January the National Christian Council of India adopted a resolution calling for cooperation with the British Council of Churches in seeking the release of prisoners and reopening negotiations. In March the Indian Legislative Assembly, usually subservient to the viceroy, passed a resolution censoring the government for its imprisonment without trial of thousands of nationalists.[15]

The release of Gandhi and the ailing leader's overture for discussions with Wavell and Jinnah renewed the hopes for negotiations. Merrell in Delhi and Phillips in London continued to view developments from far different perspectives. In his reports Merrell remained skeptical of any change in British policy, suggesting that the freeing of Gandhi might have been motivated by a desire either to avoid the embarrassment of having him die while imprisoned or to bolster the National Congress in order to counterbalance the recent gains made by the Muslim League. While Merrell believed that Wavell personally hoped to establish a rapport with Gandhi, the viceroy was in fact the pawn of London. Wavell's rejection of a meeting with Gandhi reflected his inability to act independently. From London, however, an enthusiastic Phillips saw a Gandhi-Jinnah reconciliation as the key to a settlement.[16] Indeed, Phillips wished to assist in that movement. He wrote to Washington on May 17: "The two men have it in their hands to reach an accord which the British will find hard to ignore and sometimes I wish I were there to do what I could to pull them together and so help create a team which might automatically develop into a self-governing dominion."[17]

Phillips' optimism was shared by the liberal press in America. Articles by Brailsford, Jones, and Fischer and editorials in *The Nation*,

[15] Telegram from New Delhi, January 21, 1944, 845.00/2202; letter from New Delhi, March 17, 1944, 845.00/2232.

[16] Telegram from New Delhi, May 6, 1944, 845.00/2256; telegram from New Delhi, June 30, 1944, 845.00/6-3044.

[17] Phillips to Murray, May 17, 1944, 845.00/5-1744.

The New Republic, and *The Christian Century* took their cue from Gandhi, urging that his reconciling spirit be followed by negotiations. Wavell's rejection met with criticism from these journals as well as from the left wing press in England and nationalist and moderate newspapers in India. British policy also came under some strong denunciations in a debate in the House of Commons.[18]

It seemed to many pronationalist elements that U.S. policy was changing during this summer of cautious optimism. They were encouraged by statements of Vice President Henry Wallace and Secretary of State Hull. In a pamphlet, *Our Job in the Pacific,* written for the Institute of Pacific Relations, Wallace held that the United States was obliged to assist in enlarging the growth of free Asia and the lessening of imperialism. In a qualification ignored by *India Today* and other nationalist sources, Wallace carefully added that America should not underwrite declarations of independence. At a press conference in early June, Hull stated essentially the same position; his remarks were interpreted by reporters as a reaffirmation of interest in India.[19]

Despite these promises of change, Roosevelt continued to pursue the type of policy which avoided antagonism of the British. His determination to follow a line of least resistance was evident in his ignoring Phillips' suggestions and his resolution of the means by which his August, 1942, letter should be delivered to Gandhi. After Gandhi's release the State Department raised with the White House the disposition of Roosevelt's message, which had been returned because of Gandhi's arrest. According to Hull's analysis, Roosevelt had three alternatives: the letter could be retained, which might lead Gandhi to charge Roosevelt with ignoring his appeal of July 1, 1942; the message could be delivered with an explanation of its delay; or Roosevelt could draft an updated response, which might encourage Gandhi to correspond further. Roosevelt chose the second option, which avoided

[18] *New York Times,* August 8 and 19, 1944; Louis Fischer, "Gandhi's New Strategy," *The Nation,* July 29, 1944, pp. 123–24; *ibid.,* August 12, 1944, p. 170; *The Christian Century,* July 26, 1944, p. 868; H. N. Brailsford, "What Hope for India," *The New Republic,* July 24, 1944, pp. 181–83.

[19] Henry Wallace, *Our Job in the Pacific* (New York: Institute of Pacific Relations, 1944); *Department of State Bulletin,* June 3, 1944, pp. 1–2; *New York Times,* June 16, 1944; *India Today,* June, 1944, pp. 1–2.

the risks of offending Gandhi and of inviting additional messages. The delivery of the twenty-two-month-old letter served no purpose aside from its politeness and perhaps its tacit indication that Roosevelt's active interest had ended in 1942. The Roosevelt-Gandhi exchange was not yet a dead issue, however. On July 6 columnist Drew Pearson featured an account of the incident. While his story aroused only mild interest in America, it was interpreted by Indians as an indication of American subservience to the British; the nationalists held that, if the United States had insisted on its delivery in 1942, the Government of India would have been obliged to comply.[20]

Roosevelt also refused to consider the possibility of allowing Phillips to return to India. In his May 17 message Phillips had all but requested permission to resume his India mission. On July 22 Phillips cabled another message to Roosevelt, urging the president to raise the Indian question directly with Churchill. Recalling his previous encounters with the prime minister on this issue, Roosevelt refused to give the suggestion serious consideration.[21]

Within a few days, however, Roosevelt was forced into an embarrassing position in his dealings with the British, Indian nationalists, and American liberals. On July 25 Pearson published excerpts from the Phillips-Roosevelt communiqué of May 14, 1943, in which Phillips had urged the president to use his influence to secure British promises for an announcement of a definite date for postwar independence and the establishment of an interim representative coalition government.

Who had passed this information to Pearson? The columnist, of course, never revealed his source; in a memoir written twelve years later, Pearson did acknowledge that the informant had been a State Department official who believed that the policy suggested by Phillips would have inspired Indian cooperation in the war effort. Roosevelt believed that the guilty party was Welles, who had resigned as under secretary in the fall of 1943 under pressure from Hull and in the midst of scurrilous rumors. In response to an indignant letter from

[20] Telegram from New Delhi, May 19, 1944, *FRUS, 1944*, 5:234–35; Hull to Roosevelt, June 2, 1944, *ibid.*, pp. 235–36; telegram to New Delhi, July 7, 1944, *ibid.*, p. 236; telegram from New Delhi, July 10, 1944, *ibid.*, p. 237; letter, Bombay to New Delhi, July 10, 1944, 845.00/7–1044.

[21] Telegram from London, July 22, 1944, *FRUS, 1944*, 5:237–38.

Caroline Phillips, the wife of the diplomat, Roosevelt, in a letter of August 30, 1944, reasoned that Welles, a friend of Pearson, had likely revealed Phillips' recommendations. As Roosevelt pointed out, Phillips had sent copies of his May 17, 1943, letter to the president, the State Department, and Welles. State Department officials maintained there had been no leak from their files. This, Roosevelt admitted to Caroline Phillips, did not necessarily prove anything, but, by a process of elimination, he believed Welles was most likely responsible. Other circumstantial evidence also pointed to Welles. First, the views of Phillips closely paralleled the thinking of Welles, who, as revealed in his own syndicated column, had become increasingly concerned with the problem raised by nationalism in Asia.[22] Further, passing classified correspondence to Pearson would have been in character for Welles; during his years as under secretary he had delighted in acting independently of State Department channels and routine.

Regardless of the informant, the British response was immediate and definite. On the day of publication Sir Ronald Campbell, the British minister in Washington, gained assurances from Berle that the State Department had not authorized and indeed regretted Pearson's action. The consternation of the Foreign Office caused Phillips to withdraw his July 22 suggestion, but the United States refused Britain's request for an official disavowal of the Phillips position. In a conversation on August 8 with Under Secretary Edward Stettinius, Campbell asked that Roosevelt or Hull disassociate the United States from the disparaging remarks made by Phillips about the Indian army, the role of Britain against Japan, and Churchill's qualification of the Atlantic Charter. In a memorandum to Roosevelt the next day, however, Hull observed that, since much of the State Department shared Phillips' views, it would be unwarranted in disavowing Phillips' position. Roosevelt concurred, leaving the implication of agreement with Phillips. After eighteen days of American silence Halifax pressed the

[22] Drew Pearson, "Confessions of an S.O.B.," *Saturday Evening Post*, November 3, 1956, pp. 88, 90; Caroline Phillips to Roosevelt, August 26, 1944, and Roosevelt to Caroline Phillips, August 30, 1944, PSF: Phillips, Roosevelt Papers; *India Today*, June, 1944, pp. 1–2.

point with Stettinius, but again the British failed to gain the desired assurances.[23]

While the Pearson story was virtually ignored in the American press, it received attention in India. The Indian response varied considerably, from reaffirming suspicions of Anglo-American collaboration to foreseeing fresh American approaches to the British. In some papers, including the *Hindustan Times*, editors speculated that Roosevelt would now insist that the Atlantic Charter be applied to India. In the *Bombay Sentinel* and *Bombay Chronicle*, Roosevelt's failure to act on the recommendations in Phillips' letter confirmed the view of American subservience to the British. The communist *People's War* underscored Phillips' condemnation of British imperialism.[24]

As the ramifications of the July 25 column were passing, on August 28 Pearson initiated a second and more significant phase of the controversy. Pearson now reported that Phillips had been declared *persona non grata*. He quoted a recent message from Eden to Campbell in which the Foreign Secretary had commented that India was worth a thousand Phillipses. Moreover, Pearson offered an accurate account of Campbell's presentations of July 25 to Berle. Again Campbell promptly met with Berle, who learned that the reference to Eden's message had been substantially correct. Berle acknowledged, however, that the charge that the British had demanded the recall of Phillips was incorrect. On August 18 the State Department had announced Phillips' resignation; pressing family problems had been given as the reason. If Phillips had been declared *persona non grata*, Berle and Ambassador Winant were ignorant of that fact. On August 29 Winant cabled Hull that neither Churchill nor Eden had ever raised with him objections to Phillips and that Phillips himself had mentioned to Winant his determination to return to America for personal reasons. As the Pearson report made its way onto the wire services and Congress began to

---

[23] Memorandum of conversation by Berle, July 27, 1944, *FRUS, 1944*, 5:239; telegram from London, July 28, 1944, *ibid.*, pp. 239–40; telegram to London, July 28, 1944, *ibid.*, pp. 240–41; memorandum of conversation by Stettinius, August 8, 1944, *ibid.*, pp. 241–42; Hull to Roosevelt, August 15, 1944, *ibid.*, p. 242; Halifax to Stettinius, August 25, 1944, *ibid.*, pp. 242–43; Stettinius to Hull, August 9, 1944, 845.00/8–944.

[24] *Hindustan Times*, ca. August 3, 1944, cited in a telegram from New Delhi, August 4, 1944, 845.00/8–444; *People's War*, August 13, 1944; *Bharat Jyoti*, August 13, 1944; *Bombay Sentinel*, August 15, 1944; *Bombay Chronicle*, August 14, 1944.

stir, a State Department spokesman reiterated that Phillips had resigned for family reasons.[25]

Such assurances failed to quell the controversy. The resignation had come too close to the July 25 report to be taken as coincidental. On the floor of the Senate, A. B. "Happy" Chandler of Kentucky asserted that Phillips had been declared *persona non grata*. Agreeing with Phillips that India was America's concern, Chandler demanded that Roosevelt offer a full account of conditions in India. Chandler's role resulted mostly from personal and political considerations, rather than from any convictions about India. The ambitious and publicity-conscious senator took advantage of a breach in security at the British Embassy. Perhaps emboldened by the July 25 column, some staff member interested in causing further Anglo-American differences over India provided information for Pearson and Chandler. Bajpai, who occasionally attempted to be moderately independent of the embassy and, within the limits of his office, sought to represent Indian interests to American officials, certainly was the official with the greatest incentive to reveal the information.

When Chandler's charge met with a prompt denial by Halifax, the senator was forced to reveal his possession of a message from the Government of India.[26] On September 2 Chandler released to the press the purported text of an undated cable from Sir Olaf Caroe of the Government of India's Department of External Affairs to Amery in London. It concluded:

We understand designation of Phillips is still President's Personal Representative in India. Whether or not he was connected in any way with leakage, views he had stated would make it impossible for us to do other than regard him as *persona non grata* and we could not again receive him. His views are not what we are entitled to expect from a professedly friendly envoy. Viceroy has seen this telegram.[27]

Chandler followed this with a release giving the full text of the Phillips report of May 14, 1943.

[25] Memorandum of conversation by Berle, August 28, 1944, 845.00/8–2844; telegram to London, August 18, 1944, 123 P 54; telegram from London, August 29, 1944, 740.0011 E.W./8–2944.

[26] Memorandum of conversation by Breckenridge Long, September 2, 1944, *FRUS, 1944*, 5:245–46; *New York Times*, August 29, 31, and September 1, 1944.

[27] *New York Times*, September 3, 1944.

While anxious to avoid additional antagonism, the State Department could hardly extricate the British from an embarrassment for which they were largely to blame. Assistant Secretary Breckenridge Long informed Halifax that Chandler had acknowledged to him that the senator's source of information was an employee of the British Embassy. On September 4 Caroe in New Delhi admitted that the cable cited by Chandler had been sent and that its contents had been accurately stated. That same day the European Affairs Division of the State Department offered a memorandum of a press release which would have acknowledged that neither the British nor the Government of India had informed the U.S. government that Phillips was *persona non grata*.[28] The statement, which would have aided the British position, was never released, however, presumably by order of the president, and, despite Caroe's declaration, Roosevelt conspicuously retained Phillips as his "personal representative" to India. In permitting the story to be reported without any official denial and by keeping Phillips in the position in which he had been declared *persona non grata*, Roosevelt helped to enhance the Indian image of America. For several weeks prior to the Pearson columns the State Department had received reports of increasing discontent with American inaction; this had been reflected in editorials in such prominent newspapers as *The Hindu, Star of India, Hindustan Standard, Bombay Chronicle*, and *Hindustan Times*. On August 28, when the second story appeared, a memorandum by Wallace Murray to Hull and Stettinius contended that American prestige in India had never been lower. This could be eliminated, Murray believed, only if the United States ceased to be identified with British policy. Through official silence on the Pearson-Chandler allegation and by refusing to accept Phillips' resignation as personal representative until March 14, 1945, Roosevelt did implicitly disassociate the United States from Britain.[29]

[28] Memorandum of conversation by Long, September 2, 1944, *FRUS, 1944*, 5:243–46; telegram from New Delhi, September 4, 1944, *ibid.*, p. 247; memorandum, Office of European Affairs, September 4, 1944, 740.0011 E.W./8–3144; memorandum of conversation by Hull, September 16, 1944, 845.00/9–1644.

[29] Memorandum, Office of Near Eastern and African Affairs, August 28, 1944, 845.00/8-644; *Hindu*, June 6, 1944; *Star of India*, June 4, 1944; *Hindustan Standard*, June 7, 1944; *Hindustan Times*, June 24, 1944; *Bombay Chronicle*, July 1 and August 4, 1944; *Times of India*, July 27, 1944.

What exactly had transpired in the Phillips case? Technically, the recall of Phillips had not been demanded in any official communication with the American government. The reports of the meetings of the American and British officials between August 28 and September 4 were predicated on the assumption that Pearson and Chandler's basic charge was false. Yet the Caroe message had been sent to the British Embassy, unequivocally stating that the Government of India would refuse to receive Phillips. The formality of declaring Phillips *persona non grata* thus depended on Roosevelt sending Phillips back to India. Yet Phillips' resignation was hardly coincidental and presumably was influenced by the first Pearson article. To begin with, Phillips sensed the pique of British officials, and this made it difficult for him to work effectively with them. Also, given his deep convictions about India, Phillips certainly realized that his resignation at that time would be interpreted as it was by Pearson and Chandler. Perhaps Phillips had knowledge of the Caroe message. At any rate, he knew that his resignation in these circumstances would help to keep his views prominent and might force a reconsideration of Indian policy.

Regardless of the technicalities of the incident, Indians and their American supporters accepted the Pearson-Chandler charge. According to *The New Republic* and *The Christian Century*, Phillips had been dismissed for reporting the truth about India. The nationalist journals *Voice of India, India Today*, and *Orient and the U.S.A.* devoted virtually full issues to the Phillips case. In *Voice of India* Oswald Garrison Villard endorsed Chandler's demand for an investigation, but added that Roosevelt would not act, for fear of antagonizing eastern Anglophiles and Churchill.[30]

The principal reaction to the incident came from India, however, where the Pearson-Chandler allegations received prominent attention in the press. The incident appealed to the disillusioned public for three reasons: first, it confirmed the opinion of substantial and influential American friendship; second, it fit into the pattern of thought which blamed Britain for all of India's difficulties; finally, it was

---

[30] *The New Republic,* September 9, 1944, p. 293; *The Christian Century,* September 13, 1944, p. 1044; *Orient and the U.S.A.,* September, 1944, p. 53; Oswald Garrison Villard, "The Indian Volcano Erupts Again," *Voice of India,* October, 1944, pp. 25–27.

believed that Roosevelt would now be forced into stronger assertions of Indian interests in his dealings with Churchill.

The Bombay papers *Free Press Journal* and *Bharat Jyoti*, the *Hindustan Times* of Delhi, and the Calcutta *Hindustan Standard* and *Amrita Bazar Patrika* praised Phillips' accurate reporting and his friendship to the nationalist cause. The *Bombay Sentinel, Bombay Chronicle, Hitavada,* and *Free Press Journal* foresaw Phillips and other pronationalists pressuring Roosevelt to intercede with Churchill. The incident aroused members of the Legislative Assembly to attempt to debate the questions in Phillips' letter and Caroe's cable, but the viceroy refused his sanction, which was required before issues relating to external affairs could be raised. Even in Ceylon, normally isolated from any controversy embarrassing to the British, the Phillips story was reported, with the *Ceylon Daily News* commenting that the Pearson-Chandler position was accurate. Some of the press comment was unfavorable, such as that in the semiofficial *Times of India*, which was upset with Phillips' criticisms of the civil service, and the Muslim League's *Dawn*, which recognized Phillips' lack of sympathy for the League. *People's War* warned that Phillips embodied the interest of American capitalism in exploiting the Indian market. Howard Donovan, the American consul at Bombay, whose reporting was consistently thorough and perceptive, concluded that the controversy had generally enhanced the prestige of the United States.[31]

In the end the hopes of some Indians that Roosevelt would dramatically alter U.S. policy proved illusory. Roosevelt was concerned with a multitude of problems evolving from the impending Allied

---

[31] *Ceylon Daily News*, September 2 and 22, 1944; *New York Times*, November 12, 1944; *Statesman* (New Delhi), September 7, 1944; *Blitz*, September 9, 1944; *Free Press Journal*, November 12, 1944; *Bombay Chronicle*, September 6 and November 14, 1944; *Bombay Sentinel*, September 8 and November 14, 1944; *Free Press Journal*, September 2 and 8, 1944; *Hindustan Standard*, September 5, 1944; *Hindustan Times*, September 5, 7, and 8, 1944; *Bharat Jyoti*, September 3, 1944; *Times of India*, September 5 and 11, 1944; *Dawn*, September 7 and 17, 1944; telegram from Bombay, September 11, 1944, 845.00/9-11-44.

On November 10, 1944, Pearson published the text of Phillips' plan for American, Chinese, and Russian leaders to sponsor a conference of the principal Indian groups. This report, however, attracted negligible attention in the United States and in India as well.

victory in Europe. India seemed unimportant when contrasted with the questions of the future of Eastern Europe, the establishment of the United Nations Organization, and the securing of Allied assistance against Japan. At the second Quebec Conference of September, 1944, Roosevelt and Churchill avoided India as they planned operations in Europe and Asia.

As the Phillips controversy began to recede, Indian hopes focused on the meetings between Gandhi and Jinnah. Over a period of eighteen days beginning on September 9, the two leaders discussed the various differences between the National Congress and the Muslim League. Prior to the meetings Gandhi's conciliatory spirit had led some observers, including Merrell and Donovan, to be somewhat optimistic, although they recognized the difficulties of resolving the Pakistani issue. Despite an air of friendliness, Gandhi and Jinnah could not agree on the partition question. Jinnah demanded acceptance of a sovereign, independent Pakistan, while Gandhi was willing to accept only autonomous Muslim states within a loose federal system. The talks' sole accomplishment was to enhance the status of the Muslim League to virtual equality with the National Congress.[32]

Following the unsuccessful Gandhi-Jinnah talks, Indian frustrations again became dominant. Reports that India had been ignored in the Quebec discussions led many to reiterate doubt about Roosevelt's commitment to Indian freedom. Repeatedly, editorials in the *Free Press Journal, Hindustan Times, Indian Social Reformer,* and *Hitavada* questioned whether Allied postwar planning goals included independence for India and other colonial countries. From Bombay, Donovan warned Washington of this growing suspicion of the United States. By the end of 1944 America's gain from the Phillips controversy had run its course.[33]

Although India remained in the background of American concern during the last months of the war, nationalist aspirations confronted

[32] Telegram from New Delhi, July 29, 1944, 845.00/7–2944; telegram from Bombay August 16, 1944, 845.00/8–1644; telegram from New Delhi, October 5, 1944, 845.00/10–544.

[33] *Free Press Journal,* September 20 and 22, 1944; *Hitavada,* September 20, 1944; *Indian Social Reformer,* September 23, 1944; *Hindu,* September 13, 1944; letter from Bombay, September 25, 1944, 845.9111/9–2544.

the United States in two causes: the movement to gain a quota and naturalization privileges for India, and the attempt of Mrs. Vijayalak-shmi Pandit to represent her nation at the San Francisco Conference. It was recognized that official encouragement of the second effort would be almost impossible, but Indian expectations of encouragement in the other case were considered reasonable.

In the spring of 1945 the long-delayed movement to secure a quota for India and the recognition of Indians as persons eligible for American citizenship reached its decisive moment in Congress. A few congressmen and the India Welfare League had worked for naturalization privileges for several years, but congressional and public attention had been gained only after the repeal of the Chinese Exclusion legislation in 1943. Because Congress had made that gesture in deference to Chinese nationalism, it was argued that it should do at least as much for India. For many years the Indian National Congress had protested the discriminatory treatment of overseas Indians. The United States had the opportunity to eliminate an affront to India by making a modest alteration in its immigration policy. Accordingly, when Mrs. Luce and Emanuel Celler introduced House bills granting an annual quota of one hundred and naturalization privileges, they drew wide support. The measure was backed by the India League, the National Committee for India's Freedom, the *New York Times, Los Angeles Times, Baltimore Sun,* and other newspapers. Resolutions adopted by the Council of State in Delhi, the Indian Chamber of Commerce, and four hundred Americans residing in India (mostly Protestant missionaries) reflected Indian sentiment. The Luce and Celler bills languished in committee, however, in large part because of the failure of the White House to press for approval.

Yet, when the bills were reintroduced in the first session of the Seventy-ninth Congress, the Roosevelt administration backed them. In a message to the House and Senate Immigration committees, Acting Secretary Joseph Grew contended that the measure would eliminate unnecessary antagonism in future relations with an independent India. Additional backing was given by Americans long interested in the nationalist movement, as well as by the Federal Council of the Churches of Christ, the Foreign Missions Conference (representing one hundred foreign mission boards and agencies), the Congress of Indusdustrial Organizations, and other labor groups. The only important open opposition came from the American Federation of Labor. Despite this widespread support, however, the Indian quota and naturalization bill was tabled in the House Immigration Committee on March 20, 1945. A last-minute coalition of southern Democrats and midwestern Republicans opposed to any change in the immigration policy of 1924 succeeded in killing the bill. Celler urged Roosevelt to exert his influence to gain reconsideration by the House committee, but in the remaining three weeks of his life Roosevelt took no action on Celler's suggestion.

For failing to approve this modest gesture the United States suffered a greater erosion of its prestige in India. The *Free Press Journal* interpreted the congressional action as a confirmation of its apprehension of American attachment to the imperial order. *Voice of India*, the journal of the National Committee for India's Freedom, underscored the extent and ramifications of the disillusionment: "In India, where lengthy cables of individual opinions and the statements of the Office of War Information itself had led to great expectations, there is now not only the natural disappointment over the failure of the bills, but a feeling of disillusionment over the attitude of America toward India in general and even greater distrust of any security conference —so far as the problems of Asia are concerned."[34]

The mission of Mrs. Pandit to the San Francisco Conference originated in a seemingly innocuous visit to see her daughters, who were studying at Wellesley College, and to attend a conference of the Institute of Pacific Relations. As the sister of Nehru and a leader in the National Congress for two decades, she was the only important nationalist figure permitted to visit the United States during the war. Along with thousands of others, she and her husband, Ranjit S. Pandit, had been arrested in August, 1942. The British had released them because of their poor health, but Ranjit Pandit had died in January, 1944, shortly after being freed. Before departing from India, Mrs. Pandit visited with Gandhi, who suggested that she might present the Congress' position at the United Nations Conference. In a subsequent conversation with Donovan at Bombay, neither Mrs. Pandit nor B.

[34] *Voice of India*, May, 1945, p. 144.

Shiva Rao, who also planned to attend the Institute of Pacific Relations sessions, revealed any plans to visit San Francisco.

Upon her arrival in New York on December 8, 1944, Mrs. Pandit quickly took advantage of the opportunity to speak on behalf of the National Congress. At a press conference on December 10 she told reporters that only a national government could gain Indian support for the anticipated long struggle against Japan. Then, after her address to the Institute of Pacific Relations conference at Hot Springs, Virginia, received much favorable publicity, Mrs. Pandit accepted an offer by a lecture bureau to arrange a tour. From mid-January until the end of March she spoke extensively, her two most frequent and well-received lectures being "Why India Wants Freedom" and "What Kind of Postwar World?" In conjunction with Indian independence day she spoke before an India League rally in New York and addressed a national radio audience. Her charm, keen mind, first-hand experience, and sincerity made Mrs. Pandit the most effective voice of the nationalist cause heard in America during the war.

Although Mrs. Pandit was not a guest of state, the visit of such a prominent figure placed the American government in an awkward position; ignoring her would be taken as an affront to India. Moreover, Mrs. Pandit's comment that she regretted the lack of American sympathy for the nationalist movement forced an official response. On January 29 Under Secretary of State Joseph Grew issued a statement that the United States remained interested and willing to help in reaching a settlement. In addition, Mrs. Pandit was entertained at a White House luncheon given by Eleanor Roosevelt. On February 12 Phillips, who was still the president's personal representative to India, gave a reception in her honor in Boston.[35]

When the Government of India announced its delegation to the San Francisco Conference, nationalists protested; they submitted that Mrs. Pandit represented true Indian interests. The official delegates— Sir Ramaswami Mudaliar, Sir Firoz Khan Noon, both members of the viceroy's executive council, and V. T. Krishnamachari, former prime

[35] *Asia and the Americas*, July, 1945, p. 343.
January 27 and 30, 1945; *Voice of India*, March, 1945, pp. 103–4; *India Today*, January, 1945, p. 4, and February, 1945, p. 3.

minister in the princely state of Baroda—were castigated by the India League of America, the National Committee for India's Freedom, in *Asia and the Americas, Amerasia,* and by I. F. Stone in *The Nation* as stooges of the imperial regime. In the Indian Council of State a resolution demanding the inclusion of popular representatives was defeated by the nominated members, who outvoted the popularly elected members. An insight into the Indian attitude toward the delegation was provided by K. P. S. Menon, who accompanied the three men to San Francisco as an adviser but whose nationalist sympathies led him to confer with Mrs. Pandit. In his autobiography Menon later characterized Noon as a product of Muslim communal politics and Mudaliar as a man who owed his position to an anti-Congress mentality. Both the India League and the National Committee for India's Freedom delegated Mrs. Pandit as the Indian representative.[36]

Arriving in San Francisco as the conference opened on April 25, Mrs. Pandit sought to discredit the official delegation. J. J. Singh, Anup Singh, Syud Hossain, and other Indians were also on hand to help publicize her efforts. In press conferences, speeches, and petitions Mrs. Pandit presented her case effectively, attracting considerable public attention—much more than did Mudaliar, Noon, and Krishnamachari. She was invited to address the California legislature, which proved another successful effort. Because California was the home of most of the small Indian community in the United States, Mrs. Pandit also spoke before several gatherings of her countrymen.

Although she attracted much favorable publicity to the nationalist cause, Mrs. Pandit's attempt to bring the question of India before the San Francisco Conference was utterly futile. Neither the United States nor any other member was inclined to challenge the credentials of the Indian delegation. Moreover, the United States, Britain, and the Soviet Union had agreed earlier that questions concerning freedom in the colonial areas were beyond the jurisdiction of the conference. Besides extensive deliberations on the the trusteeship system, the only consideration given to the question of non-self-governing areas resulted

36 K. P. S. Menon, *Many Worlds: An Autobiography* (New York: Oxford University Press, 1965), p. 211; *Amerasia,* May 4, 1945, pp. 141–43; *Asia and the Americas,* July, 1945, p. 343; *The Nation,* April 28, 1945, pp. 478–79; *Voice of India,* May, 1945, p. 135; *New York Times,* March 22, 1945.

in the adoption of the U.N. Charter's vague Article 73, which obligated members controlling non-self-governing regions to prepare their subject peoples for self-government, depending upon circumstances and varying stages of advancement.[37] When Stettinius, who had succeeded Hull as secretary of state, expressed American approval of this equivocal commitment to self-government rather than independence, Mrs. Pandit asserted:

What is the criterion of this preparedness and who is to determine it? The imperialistic powers . . . have used the eternal alibi of the indefinite unpreparedness of their subject peoples. Great Britain . . . has created conditions in India which provide a convenient and plausible plea to go on denying the right of the Indian people to their freedom. Under British rule they will never be able to achieve that hypothetical preparedness. . . . Mr. Stettinius and other statesmen of the United Nations who are sincerely anxious to achieve a free and peaceful world would do well to address themselves realistically to the core of this matter.[38]

In the eyes of Indian nationalists the San Francisco Conference confirmed suspicions that the victorious Allies were continuing the imperialism and major-power domination which the Atlantic Charter had seemingly promised to end. The *Hindustan Times* editorialized: "San Francisco is a fiasco. It will not lay the foundation of peace and security. The world is rapidly reverting to zones of influence out of which all wars have resulted."[39]

The conference resulted in further erosion of the American image in India, but the Soviet Union, through a modest gesture, made a significant gain. At a press conference V. M. Molotov asserted that India's delegation did not represent the Indian people and that hopefully the voice of independent India would soon be heard. This Russian interest in India had developed slowly during the last stages of the war. As long as it was engaged in a battle for survival against Germany, the Soviet Union could afford no concern with Asia. In

[37] Memorandum by Leo Pasvolsky (Special Assistant Secretary of State), January 13, 1945, *Foreign Relations of the United States, 1945*, vol. 1, *General: The United Nations* (1967), pp. 18–20; memorandum of conversation by Pasvolsky with Soviet Ambassador (Gromyko), January 13, 1945, *ibid.*, p. 14.

[38] *Asia and the Americas*, July, 1945, p. 343.

[39] *Hindustan Times*, cited in *The Christian Century*, September 12, 1945, p. 1034.

September, 1944, however, the American Embassy in Moscow had reported a sudden interest in the Soviet press in Indian developments. On the eve of the San Francisco Conference, an article in *War and the Working Class* had strongly condemned British imperial policies in India. Molotov's gesture thus signaled the beginning of Russian efforts to support nationalist aspirations in Asia.[40]

On the eve of the United Nations Conference and the Allied victory in Europe, Roosevelt had died in Warm Springs, Georgia. His passing was mourned among Indians, who, like peoples throughout the world, admired the president who had represented the aspirations of the common man everywhere. Gandhi's message of condolence to Eleanor Roosevelt, however, revealed the Indians' sense of bitterness and foreboding of the postwar world. He wrote: "My humble condolence and congratulations. Latter because your illustrious husband died in harness after war had reached a point where allied victory had become certain. He was spared humiliating spectacle of being party to peace which threatens to be prelude to war bloodier still if possible."[41] Relaying the cable to the United States, Bombay consul Donovan, long sympathetic to the nationalist cause, was appalled by Gandhi's lack of tact.[42]

Even in his last months of declining health and preoccupation with problems in Europe, Roosevelt's sympathies remained with the aspirations of the Asians. He knew that the nationalist question affected America's interests. In a conversation on March 15 with a State Department official, Roosevelt's words foreshadowed impending developments. As reported by the official:

The president said he was concerned about the brown people in the East. He said that there are over 1,100,000,000 brown people. In many Eastern countries, they are ruled by a handful of whites and they resent it. Our goal must be to help them achieve independence—1,100,000,000 potential enemies are dangerous. He then added, Churchill doesn't understand this.[43]

[40] Telegram from Moscow, September 19, 1944, 845.01/9–1944; telegram from Moscow, April 18, 1945, 845.00/4–1845.

[41] Telegram from Bombay, enclosing Gandhi–Eleanor Roosevelt message, April 16, 1945, PSF: India, Roosevelt Papers.

[42] *Ibid.*

[43] Memorandum of conversation by Charles Taussig (Adviser on Caribbean Affairs), March 15, 1945, *FRUS, 1945,* 1:121–24.

As was characteristic of his diplomacy, Roosevelt had sought to secure objectives in India without paying the necessary price. His dispatch of two presidential missions had encouraged hopes of intervention, but ultimately had led only to disappointment and the cynicism expressed in Gandhi's message. In his last two years, aside from his conspicuous silence after the Pearson exposé of Phillips' reports and his statement clarifying the objectives of the American army in India, Roosevelt had failed to demonstrate a direct and personal interest in India. Understandably, the American standing in India declined and, in the immediate postwar period, reached its nadir.

VII

The End of the *Raj*, 1945–1947

BEGINNING IN JUNE, 1945, when Lord Wavell summoned Indian leaders to a meeting at Simla, Great Britain moved, hesitantly at first, but with rapidity by early 1947, to liquidate its Indian empire. This modification in British policy changed the American interest in India. Rather than attempt to force Britain's hand, the United States now sought to channel British policy by encouraging, at times, an acceleration of plans for withdrawal and endeavoring, on occasion, to influence the resolution of the Pakistani issue. No longer was it necessary for liberals or for the India League of America to push for American intervention. To the American public, the Indian question remained as it had during the late stages of the war, remote and not very pressing. The onset of the cold war understandably focused American attention on Europe. Also, Indian politics, which always had been complicated, became more incomprehensible to Americans as the Pakistani question produced widening division among the Indians and much communal rioting, strife, and bloodshed.

Several forces drew the American government, however, toward a substantial interest in the Indian situation. First, the development of a substantial anti-American sentiment in India, the result of the popular identification of the United States with European imperialism in Asia, made it imperative that the British *raj* be ended. If the British withdrew, presumably India's preoccupation with Western domination and motives would end and would enable the United States to improve its standing. Second, the Indian political unrest of 1945–46 aroused fears of increased communist influence. A peaceful transfer to a viable government (or governments) would serve to lessen communist agitation. Third, the Soviet Union improved its standing among Asian peoples, including the Indians, owing to its seeming unequivocal support of nationalism. Fourth, as the United States became more interested in the Middle East, it was recognized that the Pakistani issue could have international ramifications, and this led to some concern that any Indian settlement unfavorable to the Muslim League could harm the British and American images among the peoples of the Middle East. The United States thus closely observed Britain's actions, endorsing and in other ways supporting those which promised an early and orderly withdrawal.

In addition to these political considerations, at least some American officials and businessmen were drawn toward India by the lure of the Indian market. During the war years a few officials in the State Department and some articles in journals had speculated on the prospects for American trade and investment in India. In July, 1945, the Commerce Department's *Foreign Commerce Weekly* devoted an entire issue to the Indian market. Pointing out that during the war years exports to India had grown from 1 per cent to 5 per cent of America's total foreign sales and that the American share of India's total imports had expanded from 6 per cent to 17 per cent, the *Foreign Commerce Weekly* concluded that the Indian market should be cultivated, and would likely become more prominent as India became more industrialized. In the State Department, Assistant Secretary for Economic Affairs Will Clayton championed efforts to enhance the American position, which, it was realized, would be facilitated by ending the system of imperial preferences.[1]

[1] *Foreign Commerce Weekly*, July 21, 1945; memorandum by William D. Pawley, "Effect of the Sterling Bloc on Anglo-American-Indian Relations," Box O.F. 48-H, India, 1944, Roosevelt Papers, Franklin D. Roosevelt Library, Hyde Park, N.Y.; "India: New Economic Frontier?" *Amerasia*, September 8, 1944, pp. 243–53; "Indian Open Door?" *Business Week*, March 21, 1942, pp. 40–42. Clayton Lane, who served as director of war economic operations at the American mission in Delhi from 1941 to 1945, was skeptical of the development of the Indian market, predicting that independent India would restrict exports (*New York Times*, March 15, 1945).

Under Harry S. Truman the American approach to India became more systematic and less personal. Preferring to concentrate on the problems of Europe and East Asia, Truman generally deferred to his subordinates on South Asia. Truman never conveyed the sort of personal interest in India that his predecessor had managed to embody; even if he had been inclined to, the new president's personality did not easily lend itself to popular identification with idealistic causes.

During his first weeks in the White House, Truman supported two important initiatives regarding India. In response to strong criticism from India and nationalists groups in America when Congress tabled the Indian immigration and naturalization bill, the Truman administration resurrected, endorsed, and lobbied for the measure. To counter the criticism of opponents that Britain's attitude toward the bill was unknown, the State Department in early May asked Lord Halifax if the British objected; the ambassador stated that in fact his government would welcome the legislation as a gesture of friendship justified by India's contribution to the war effort. Truman then informed Samuel Dickstein, chairman of the House Immigration Committee, of White House support for the bills granting a quota and naturalization privileges. Truman, at Congressman Emanuel Celler's urging, met with Robert Ramspeck of Georgia, who had led the opposition earlier, and managed to gain Ramspeck's acquiescence.

After Celler introduced his bill again on June 20, William Phillips, in hearings of the House Immigration Committee, effectively presented the administration's case that discrimination harmed the United States among Asian peoples. With the opposition mostly neutralized, the bill sailed through the House by a three-to-one margin.

In the Senate, however, Richard B. Russell of Georgia, chairman of the Immigration Committee, delayed the measure in committee. Again Truman presented the administration's position, but failed to allay the senator's apprehension of any change in immigration policy. At length, under pressure from the White House as well as from Immigration Committee members, Russell permitted the bill to be reported. Finally, in early 1946, it passed the Senate without any opposition. The act granting Indians a quota of one hundred and naturalization privileges was signed by Truman on July 2, 1946. Its passage resulted from the pressures exerted by Indian nationalist groups in America and their liberal supporters, as well as from the concerted effort of the Truman administration.

Besides reviving and championing the immigration-naturalization bill, Truman, during the first weeks of his administration, also endorsed the suggestion put forth by Phillips to exert some pressure on the British government. Frustrated by his inability to induce a change in Roosevelt's policy, Phillips urged, shortly after Truman became president, that conditions in Europe made the time opportune for Stettinius to express to Foreign Minister Eden America's interest in a solution to the Indian problem. With the viceroy then in London for consultations, Phillips believed that such an overture might encourage a change in British policy. On April 28 Stettinius, with Truman's approval, raised the matter with Eden, who responded that he appreciated the American position. U.S. concern was again registered on May 17 in a conversation between Under Secretary Joseph Grew and Eden; on that occasion Eden testily replied that a settlement was unlikely as long as Gandhi lived.[2]

Yet, in London, Wavell secured a change in Britain's position. After lengthy discussions the British government announced that the viceroy had been empowered to offer proposals for the formation of an interim government. Returning to India, on June 14 Lord Wavell announced plans to reconstitute the viceroy's executive council with all Indian members, excepting the viceroy and commander in chief; assurances were added that the viceroy would exercise his powers responsibly. In an important concession to the Muslim League, Muslims and "caste Hindus" were granted parity on the executive council. Jinnah and Gandhi, together with leaders of other groups, were invited to a conference at Simla, scheduled to begin on June 25, for a full consideration of the proposals. In the meantime the members of the National Congress Working Committee were released from prison.

This change in British attitude toward the Indian problem resulted in part from American pressures, but other factors also influenced the decision. Most important, with the victory in Europe, Britain planned

[2] Memorandum by Phillips, April 19, 1945, *Foreign Relations of the United States, 1945*, vol. 6, *The British Commonwealth, the Far East* (1969), pp. 249–50; Stettinius to Grew, April 28, 1945, *ibid.*, p. 251; Grew to Winant, May 17, 1945, *ibid.*; telegram from London, May 16, 1945, 845.00/5–1645.

to give greater attention to the war in the Pacific. The defeat of Japan loomed as a costly and distant goal. Indian support in this military effort could alleviate some of the burden.

The State Department, pleased at seeing some movement toward ending the impasse, followed closely the reaction of Indian leaders to the proposal and sought close contact with the participants in the Simla Conference. In their reports, George Merrell, now the American commissioner at New Delhi, and Howard Donovan, still the consul at Bombay, expressed cautious optimism, based on the reactions of the Indian press and some of the leaders. Lampton Berry, formerly attached to the Delhi mission and now in the Division of Middle Eastern Affairs, believed that the Wavell plan had sufficient latitude to be accepted, but he did observe that trouble was likely to result from its provision of Hindu-Muslim, rather than Congress–Muslim League, parity. On June 19, while being honored at a dinner given by the viceroy, Merrell took advantage of the occasion to gain Wavell's approval for full consultation with one of the viceroy's private secretaries during the conference. After gaining that assurance, Merrell discouraged suggestions from Grew that he seek recognition of an American observer at Simla; Merrell maintained that the presence of an American official would only encourage false hopes.[3]

The Simla Conference, however, was a failure. The critical issue centered on the powers of the two principal parties to appoint members of the executive council. The Muslim League's insistence that it had the right to appoint all Muslim members was anathema to the National Congress, which was unwilling to renounce its claim as an all-inclusive party. Wavell attempted to mediate, requesting that all groups submit lists of nominees from which he would select executive council members. After failing to gain Wavell's assurance that all Muslim League nominees would be accepted (and thus precluding a Congress-Muslim representative), Jinnah refused to comply. Despite the cooperation of the other parties, Wavell permitted Jinnah's de-

[3] Memorandum by Berry, June 19, 1945, 845.00/6–1945; letter from New Delhi, June 20, 1945, 845.00/6–2045; letter from Bombay, June 16, 1945, 845.00/6–1645; telegram from Bombay, June 21, 1945, 845.00/6–2145; telegram from New Delhi, June 21, 1945, *ibid.*; telegram from New Delhi, June 23, 1945, 845.00/6–2345; telegram from New Delhi, June 19, 1945, *FRUS, 1945*, 6:252.

mands to end the conference. On July 14, after repeated efforts to win the Muslim League's cooperation, Wavell adjourned the meetings. The effect of the Simla Conference was to increase the prestige of the League; also, Jinnah had been successful in taking an uncompromising stand, which served to encourage subsequent intransigence from the League.

In New Delhi, Merrell received reports of each of the Simla sessions through his associate on the viceroy's staff. At the conclusion of the conference Grew instructed Merrell to report on whether the Wavell offer had eliminated India's distrust of the British. After soliciting information from the consuls at Bombay, Madras, and Calcutta, Merrell concluded that the suspicion of the British had been so profound that the Wavell plan had been unable to alter it significantly. Merrell added that the Simla Conference had been an important victory for the Muslim League, which won, at least implicitly, acceptance of the principle that no political settlement could be reached without its consent. This, Merrell believed, hindered the prospects for a resolution of the communal problem.[4]

In the American press, reports and editorials had generated some optimism for the Simla Conference. When it failed, *Time, Newsweek, The New Republic, The Nation,* and many newspapers concurred in blaming the Muslim League.[5]

The disappointment of Simla, however, quickly gave way to a new wave of optimism. On July 26 the British Labour party was swept to victory in the parliamentary elections. Within the next two weeks the United States dropped its atomic bombs on Hiroshima and Nagasaki, Japan surrendered, and the war suddenly ended. Indians confidently expected that steps leading to independence would be taken immedi-

[4] Telegram from New Delhi, June 26, 1945, 845.00/6-2645; telegram from New Delhi, June 29, 1945, 845.00/6-2945; telegram from New Delhi, July 4, 1945, 845.00/7-445; telegram from New Delhi, July 16, 1945, 845.00/7-1645; letter from New Delhi, July 27, 1945, 845.00/7-2745; telegram to New Delhi, July 25, 1945; 845.00/7-2545; telegram, Madras to New Delhi, August 1, 1945, 845.00/8-145; telegram from New Delhi, August 8, 1945, 845.00/8-845.

[5] *The Nation,* July 7, 1945, p. 2, July 14, 1945, p. 51, and July 28, 1945, pp. 79-81; *The New Republic,* July 15, 1945, pp. 91-92; *Newsweek,* June 25, 1945, p. 56, and July 23, 1945, p. 54; *Time,* July 9, 1945, p. 34, July 16, 1945, pp. 34, 37-40, and July 23, 1945, p. 48.

ately. Indeed, the Labour government did move quickly. On August 21, as the viceroy was summoned to London for consultations, it was announced that elections to the central and provincial legislatures would be conducted during the cool season. A few weeks later Prime Minister Clement Attlee promised that, after the elections, provincial autonomy would be restored and a constitution-making body established. The United States assumed a wait-and-see attitude toward this development. After Attlee's announcement a State Department spokesman, while endorsing the gesture, observed that "the real test will come in the months ahead when actual negotiations begin after the election."[6]

During the interlude between the British promises and the December elections, long-lingering Indian resentment of the United States came increasingly to the surface, causing much concern among American officials. Leaders of the National Congress had been distressed by America's inaction in the face of Britain's hard-line policy of 1942. As the Congress leaders were released in 1945, other developments added to the anti-American sentiment. The San Francisco Conference confirmed suspicions of American support of imperialism. Much of the nationalist press condemned the dropping of the atomic bombs. *Dawn*, for instance, compared the American action to the inhumanity of Hitler. Finally, by the fall of 1945, it was obvious that the United States was acquiescing in the efforts of the British, French, and Dutch to recover the parts of their empires which had been conquered by Japan. As nationalist elements in Indonesia and Indochina challenged the returning European powers, American prestige in South and Southeast Asia declined sharply. Although less frequently expressed, fears of American economic penetration and military expansion into Asia further stirred the anti-American mood.[7]

Nehru, destined to be the architect of India's foreign policy, defined explicitly India's disappointment with the United States. At a press conference on October 28 he talked at length of the earlier expectations of American championship of freedom and the ensuing disillu-

[6] *New York Times*, September 20, 1945.

[7] *Hindustan Times*, April 12, 1945; editorials on the atomic bomb from *Bombay Chronicle, Hindustan Times,* and *Dawn,* reprinted in *Voice of India*, October, 1945, p. 191.

sionment. After calling attention to the Soviet Union's support of the freedom of dependent peoples at San Francisco, he concluded:

At the present moment we are right in the midst of the aftermath of war and inevitably all the assurances given and the promises made during the war demand fulfillment. Yet we see the attempt to crush with armed forces the freedom movement in Indonesia and Indo-China and in this British forces are taking an active part. . . . The American government has declared that lend-lease goods used against the Indonesians should have their labels torn off. That is poor consolation for the Indonesians. They will be shot down by guns whether the guns bear this label or that. In India, the U.S.A. has kept itself clear from all entanglements. We cannot blame it for this attitude especially in wartime, but there has been something much more than this during the past few years—a passive and sometimes even an active support of British policy and British propaganda. We realise fully that India's freedom will be won by India's strength and we cannot rely on any foreign power. Nevertheless it is obvious that India's reactions to other powers will be governed by their policy to India. . . . So far as one can see American policy in regard to India has been strongly subservient to British policy. That British policy, whatever the profession is behind it, continues to be one of authoritarian rule in India, without the least trace of democratic functioning.[8]

The identification of the United States with imperialism was manifest in the frustration-inspired aggression of Calcutta mobs in late November. Calcutta University students led demonstrations protesting the British decision to bring to trial the officers of Subhas Chandra Bose's Indian National Army. The peaceful protest quickly gave way to several days of rioting in which American, as well as British, soldiers and installations were attacked. An American ambulance driver was killed when his vehicle was isolated by mobs and set on fire. More than thirty American soldiers were injured, while an American army hospital was besieged for more than twenty-four hours. Mobs burned and destroyed nine army vehicles and damaged another fifty vehicles before order was finally restored.[9]

[8] Jawaharlal Nehru, *Important Speeches of Jawaharlal Nehru: Being a Collection of Most Significant Speeches Delivered by Jawaharlal Nehru from 1922 to 1945*, ed. Jagat S. Bright (Lahore: Indian Printing Works, 1945), pp. 375–76.

[9] *Amrita Bazar Patrika* (Calcutta), November 29, 1945; *Statesman* (Calcutta), November 27, 1945; telegram from Calcutta, November 23, 1945, 845.00/11–2345; telegram from New Delhi, November 24, 1945, 845.00/11–2445; *New York Times*, November 23–25, 1945.

While at least part of the Calcutta violence could be attributed to the proximity of Americans to the British, a motion passed by the National Congress Working Committee the following month was directed at the United States. In a resolution which strongly condemned French, British, and Dutch actions in Indochina and Indonesia, the Congress also castigated the United States for encouraging the European imperial powers by its passive and indifferent attitude. American responsibility for developments in Southeast Asia also drew strong criticism from the Indian press, including the *Hindustan Standard, Statesman, Times of India,* and *Dawn.*

Reports from the Bombay and Madras consuls drew the State Department's attention to this anti-American trend. Donovan observed that American assurances of sympathy for freedom, such as Truman had offered in a Navy Day address, simply were no longer believed, while the Soviet Union's prestige was steadily increasing. John F. Cady, a leading Southeast Asian specialist serving at this time in the Division of Southeast Asian Affairs, warned the division's head about the serious extent of the resentment of the United States.[10]

In this atmosphere, the United States stood to gain from a quick settlement, for that would extricate it from an embarrassing and detrimental position. Although it did not alter its deference to the European powers in South and Southeast Asia, the U.S. government did exert economic and political pressure on the British.

In responding to a request from London for a loan to assist in postwar reconstruction, the United States insisted on certain conditions that weakened Britain's hold on India. By the terms of the financial agreement signed by the American and British governments in December, 1945, the United States granted a $3.75 billion credit and eliminated virtually all of Britain's lend-lease debt. In return, Britain agreed to end by mid-1947 the "dollar pool" (during the war the British dominions had pooled their dollar credits in London) and eventually to end the system of imperial preferences. India had built up a great surplus of dollar credits, but under the "pool" had been obligated to gain London's permission before using its credits to purchase Ameri-

[10] All-India Congress Committee, *Congress Bulletin,* January 24, 1946; telegram from Bombay, December 8, 1945, 711.45/12–845; letter from Madras, November 14, 1945, 845.00/11–1445; memorandum by Cady, November 19, 1945, 851G.00/11–1945.

can goods. The agreement thus gave the United States new opportunities in the Indian market and at the same time lessened London's economic dominance over India.

In January, 1946, through their embassy in Washington and the Government of India in Delhi, the British requested American approval of elevating the Indian and United States diplomatic missions in the two capitals to the ministerial level. While carefully disavowing any personal interest in becoming minister, Merrell suggested to Washington that the proposal would be welcomed by the nationalists and might make the Government of India more independent of the British. James Byrnes, who had become secretary of state the previous July, and Under Secretary Dean Acheson, however, overruled Merrell, on the grounds that approval of the request might be considered tantamount to approval of the political situation; they believed action should be delayed until the Indian government became more representative.[11]

Meanwhile, the elections announced by the British in August were conducted, and the results revealed a trend toward communal polarization. In late December the elections to the central Legislative Assembly provided increased prestige for the Muslim League. The League campaigned on the necessity for Pakistan, while the Congress attempted to reassure the Muslim community by promising a large degree of provincial autonomy with only a minimum of federal jurisdiction on essential items. Gaining 87 per cent of the vote in Muslim constituencies, the League won all thirty Muslim seats. In the non-Muslim constituencies the Congress pulled 91 per cent, winning fifty-seven seats. Both parties claimed victory, but the Congress, despite its over-all strong showing, lost much of its claim that it represented all Indian communities.

In the provincial elections conducted the following month the League again did well in the Muslim areas, gaining 427 of the total of 507 Muslim seats and forming provincial ministries in Sind and Bengal. Among the predominantly Muslim areas the League lost in the North-West Frontier Province, where the Congress worked effectively

[11] Telegram to New Delhi, January 7, 1945, *Foreign Relations of the United States, 1946*, vol. 5, *The British Commonwealth: Western and Central Europe* (1969), p. 77; telegram from New Delhi, January 9, 1946, *ibid.*, pp. 77–78; telegram to New Delhi, January 14, 1946, *ibid.*, p. 78.

with local Muslims to take a majority of the seats. In the Punjab the League won more seats than any party, but lacked a majority and refused to cooperate with the Congress and minority parties; a coalition of the Congress and minority parties formed the government in that province.

After the elections Prime Minister Attlee announced that a cabinet delegation would be dispatched to confer with Indian leaders on the establishment of a constituent assembly. The members of the cabinet mission were Lord Pethwick-Lawrence, secretary of state for India; Sir Stafford Cripps, president of the Board of Trade; and A. V. Alexander, first lord of the Admiralty. The British government assured the United States that these steps would lead to a settlement. On February 21, two days after Attlee's announcement, Sir Paul Patrick, under secretary of the India Office, discussed with Winant the anticipated difficulty of resolving the Pakistani issue in the forthcoming negotiations, but added that the Labour government remained determined to fulfill its pledges to India. A week later another British official suggested to a member of the American Embassy staff that Jinnah would be willing to accept a compromise on the Pakistani demand.[12]

During the period between the elections and the arrival of the cabinet mission on March 24, the State Department became concerned again about anti-American sentiment. In an interview upon her return to India in early February, Mrs. Pandit charged that the American and British governments had conspired to conceal critical facts about India from the American public. *New York Times* correspondent George E. Jones reported that Mrs. Pandit's criticisms strongly appealed to nationalists disappointed with the United States for its failure to support independence. In this atmosphere emotional talk again gave way to hostile actions. From February 12 to February 15 American army personnel in Calcutta were caught in the midst of violent protests against the conviction of an Indian National Army officer; 37 Americans were among the 400 injured during the rioting. On the other side of the subcontinent a Bombay mob, waving the flag of the Indian National Congress, tore the flag from the U.S. Informa-

[12] Telegram from London, February 21, 1946, *ibid.*, pp. 79–80; telegram from London, February 28, 1946, *ibid.*, pp. 83–84.

tion Service building and burned it in the streets. A spokesman for the demonstrators told newsmen that, while the agitation was directed against the British, Americans also should quit India.

In analyzing these incidents American officials were encouraged by the British to place the responsibility on the Indian Communist party. On February 28 in Delhi, British officials informed Merrell that evidence had been found in secret Government of India files which indicated that communist agitators had been instrumental in the recent Bombay and Calcutta riots. On the same day in London, Patrick reiterated this observation to American Embassy officials, adding, however, that Indian Communist party operations were largely independent of Moscow. The Soviet Union, however, continued its appeal to Indian nationalists. In a message to Washington on March 1 Merrell called attention to the fact that Hindustani anti-imperialist radio broadcasts were being beamed to India from Moscow. According to Merrell, the Soviet Union sought to cause disruption without itself becoming involved in Indian politics. Unwilling to rely on British assertions of communist agitation, Washington cabled its diplomatic representatives to report extensively on the communist influence. Merrell and Donovan found that in Delhi and Bombay the communists had taken advantage of volatile situations, but had not initiated the protests. Karachi consul Clarence E. Macy and Roy Bower, his counterpart at Madras, concluded that in those cities the communists had organized and planned demonstrations and violent actions. This information was relayed to the director of the Office of Near Eastern and African Affairs.[13] The specter of communist influence, seemingly certain to increase as long as the British held onto power, added another compelling reason for the United States to encourage a quick and orderly withdrawal.

In an important subsequent report on the same topic, however, Merrell warned Washington that it was inaccurate to blame anti-Americanism on communist agitators. The fault, Merrell held, rested

[13] Telegram from New Delhi, February 28, 1946, *ibid.*, pp. 80–82; telegram from London, February 28, 1946, *ibid.*, pp. 82–83; telegram from New Delhi, March 1, 1946, *ibid.*, pp. 84–85; memorandum by Berry to Director, Office of Near Eastern and African Affairs, April 4, 1946, *ibid.*, pp. 85–86; *New York Times*, February 6, 12, 15, and 19, 1946.

squarely with the United States for overselling itself to Indian nationalists during the war, and for then permitting its objectives to become identified with those of the European powers. Correctly or not, the United States was seen as embracing British objectives in the Middle East as well as British, French, and Dutch imperial drives in South and Southeast Asia.[14]

The experience of the noted American historian Merle Curti, who toured India in 1946 as a visiting professor at several universities, substantiated Merrell's analysis. Upon his return to America, Curti wrote:

But I was asked on innumerable occasions why the American government had, in view of America's own revolutionary revolt against England, done so little to help the Indians in their struggle for freedom. The report of the Phillips mission during the War was indeed known and appreciated, but the preponderance of opinion was definitely critical.[15]

The cabinet mission offered renewed hopes for a settlement, which would be as welcome in Washington as in Delhi or London. During its first month in India the mission discussed the political situation with leaders of all the political parties. These sessions gave rise to much speculation in the press, including a report on April 12 in the British-owned *Statesman* that the United States favored submitting the Pakistani issue to international arbitration. Merrell discussed the possibility of U.S. intervention and its possible support of arbitration with Asaf Ali, a close associate of Nehru and a prominent Muslim member of the National Congress; Liaqat Ali Khan, Jinnah's chief lieutenant; and Major Woodrow Wyatt, private secretary of the cabinet mission. Not surprisingly, Merrell found no support for American intervention. Yet, in his report to Washington on April 15, he added another consideration to the formulation of a U.S. position: the ramifications on American interests in the Middle East should the United States be associated with a settlement that proved unfavorable to the Muslims.[16]

Americans were only dimly aware of these political developments and communal divisions. In a sample of public opinion conducted in

[14] Telegram from New Delhi, June 10, 1946, *FRUS, 1946,* 5:88–92.
[15] Merle Curti, "My Discovery of India," *The American Scholar,* Autumn, 1947, p. 423.
[16] Telegram from New Delhi, April 15, 1946, *FRUS, 1946,* 5:86–87.

the spring of 1946, 48 per cent of the public reported that it was following discussions between the British and Indian parties. When those following developments were asked what Britain should do about India, two-thirds responded that India should be given its independence. While independence and a variety of intermediary solutions were suggested, significantly none of the alternatives considered the Pakistani issue. The ignorance of the public regarding communal politics was underscored in another poll, conducted a few months earlier, in some fifty Iowa communities. In that sample 82 per cent could not name an Indian leader other than Gandhi, 70 per cent had never heard of Jinnah, and, of the 30 per cent who had heard of Jinnah, two-thirds could not name the group or party he headed. When asked if they had heard of Pakistan, 85 per cent replied negatively. Of the 15 per cent to whom Pakistan sounded familiar, nine out of ten could not identify it. The press was partly responsible for this lack of knowledge. The sparse reports on India after the war generally paid little attention to the enhanced stature of the Muslim League. In April, 1946, *Time* did a cover story on Jinnah in which he was presented as an aloof, arrogant, wealthy troublemaker. In the *New York Times*, several editorials on India in early 1946 strongly supported British objectives, but gave minimal consideration to the difficulties caused by the increase in communal tensions.[17]

The United States endorsed the cabinet mission plan, which seemed to promise a reasonable compromise. Presented to the presidents of the League and the Congress on April 27, the plan called for a government of three tiers: (1) a union government, which would be responsible for foreign affairs, defense, and communications; (2) two groupings of India's provinces—one of the predominantly Hindu provinces and the other of the predominantly Muslim provinces—which could deal with all subjects that the provinces in each group desired to handle in common; (3) provincial governments, which would be responsible for all other matters and have all residual sovereign rights. The League and the Congress were asked to send representatives to a

[17] Statistics prepared by Mildred Strunk for *Public Opinion, 1935–46*, ed. Hadley Cantril (Princeton: Princeton University Press, 1951), p. 328; S. Chandrasekhar, "What Does Iowa Know of India and China?" *Asia and the Americas*, June, 1945, pp. 298–300; *Time*, April 22, 1946, pp. 28–31; *New York Times*, February 23, 25, and June 16, 1946.

conference at Simla, where the formulation could be fully discussed. Meeting at Simla from May 5 to May 12, the Congress and the League did not agree, and the efforts of the cabinet mission to adjudicate their differences failed. At the heart of the division remained the divergent views on a unified versus a divided India. Congress leaders pressed for a strong central government, while minimizing the provincial groupings, but the League sought a weak central government and assurances of compulsory provincial groupings.

Charged by London with responsibility for reaching a settlement, the cabinet mission redoubled its efforts. On May 16 it announced plans for a long-range settlement which reiterated the formulation of April 27 but included some modifications intended to reassure both the League and Congress. In addition, it called for the immediate establishment of an interim government in which all cabinet positions would be held by Indians. On May 17 acting Secretary of State Acheson praised the cabinet mission announcement as a constructive and statesmanlike step.[18]

Except for Acheson's statement, the United States left the negotiations and resolution of the cabinet mission plan to the British and Indian parties. By June 25 the League and the Congress had accepted the May 16 long-range plan, but the agreement was subject to their interpretations of the clauses pertaining to the grouping scheme. The League's approval was based on the assumption that the revised plan guaranteed compulsory provincial groups, which was tantamount to the acknowledgment of Pakistan. Yet other provisions stipulated a voluntary basis for the groupings; these were parts on which the Congress Working Committee predicated its acceptance. In reality the two parties were still far apart, but the cabinet mission interpreted their "acceptances" as the completion of its task. On June 29 the mission left India.

A few days later, on July 4, the United States granted independence to the Philippines. The American government anticipated that this action would offset doubts about its dedication to self-determination. Suspicion of U.S. motives had become so profound, however, that in India, and elsewhere, nationalists expressed skepticism rather than

[18] *New York Times*, May, 18, 1946.

praise for the U.S. policy. Nehru, who had been elected president of the National Congress in May, sent a message of congratulations to the Philippine Republic, stating:

We hope that this really signifies independence for this word has become rather hackneyed and outworn and has been made to mean many things. Some countries that are called independent are far from free and are under the economic or military domination of some great power. Some so-called independent countries carry on with what might be termed "puppet regimes" and are in a way client countries of some great power. We hope that is not so with the Philippines.[19]

A few weeks later *New York Times* correspondent George E. Jones reported that educated Indians remained convinced that the United States was supporting imperial policies in the Middle East and Southeast Asia, and that they were highly critical of the continued economic dependence of the Philippines on the United States.[20]

Meanwhile, the cabinet mission's failure became an inescapable reality. The All-India Congress Committee met in Bombay on July 6 to consider the Working Committee's position on the proposal. As expected, the Committee's conditional approval of the plan was overwhelmingly endorsed. In his concluding statement to the representatives Nehru vigorously asserted that the mission plan would inevitably lead to greater powers for the central government. Moreover, the Congress-dominated provinces (North-West Frontier Province and Assam) within the "Muslim group" would certainly opt out of the group as soon as possible. (According to the May 16 formula, provinces could opt out of their group after provincial elections were conducted under new provincial constitutions.)

Nehru's speech expressed the sentiments and expectations of the Congress, but it effectively ended any prospects for a settlement under the cabinet mission plan. Moreover, it enabled Jinnah to seize the initiative and press the Pakistani demand. The former result likely was inevitable; the plan would have invited an endless struggle for power among the central government, the groups, and the provinces.

[19] All-India Congress Committee, *Congress Bulletin*, August 3, 1946.
[20] *New York Times*, August 9, 1946.

Jinnah, however, now could point to the Nehru speech as evidence of the Congress' determination to dominate India. On July 27 the League's acceptance of the plan was withdrawn, and Jinnah announced that August 16 would be designated "Direct Action Day" to achieve Pakistan.

Direct Action Day brought Muslim League–sponsored meetings to nearly all the major towns of India. The League's leaders and press encouraged communal bitterness and defiance of authority, while the League ministries in Bengal and Sind declared August 16 a holiday. In Calcutta, League spokesmen incited attacks on the Hindu community which led to four days of chaos, destruction, and death. Approximately 5,000 persons were killed, another 15,000 were injured, and more than 100,000 were left homeless. Direct Action Day widened the breach, perhaps irreparably, between the Hindu and Muslim communities.

The League's campaign of violence also produced a measure of cooperation between the British and the National Congress. The Congress worked with Lord Wavell in the formation of the All-Indian Executive Council as an interim government, while the League refused to participate. Still, the British and the Congress attempted to bring the League into the government. When the new council took office on September 2 with Nehru as *de facto* prime minister, five vacancies remained for the League to fill with its appointees. In a broadcast on September 7 Nehru appealed to the League to join the government.

The United States also strongly supported this effort to salvage a united India. When the council was announced, Acheson issued a statement praising the British and the Congress for their statesmanship. Terming the League's non-participation "regrettable," the acting secretary of state expressed the hope that it would soon cooperate.

As the All-Indian Executive Council assumed office, the United States reversed its earlier position on the elevation of the American and Indian diplomatic missions. In a memorandum to Truman, Acheson suggested that, considering the representative character of the new government, an exchange of ambassadors would be appropriate. While not mentioned by Acheson, this diplomatic support also could conceivably serve to help strengthen the interim government in its effort to include all Indian parties. With White House approval the

State Department on September 9 informed Bajpai in Washington and Patrick in London that it would welcome the appropriate request from the Government of India. After some negotiations on the details it was announced on October 23 in London, Washington, and New Delhi that the American and Indian missions would be elevated to embassies. Merrell became chargé d'affaires, pending the appointment of the the first U.S. ambassador.[21]

In the following weeks, however, relations between the League and the Congress deteriorated, leading the United States to take a more direct role in Indian developments. On October 15 the League joined the interim government, only to press more stridently for recognition of Pakistan. When Wavell attempted to placate the League, Nehru threatened to resign and charged that the British were allied with the League against the Congress. In this atmosphere of mutual distrust the fragile coalition became unworkable. With the convening of the Constituent Assembly scheduled for December 9, Attlee summoned representatives of the League and the Congress to London for a brief conference.

On November 30, two days before the talks began in London, Acheson sent identical messages to Merrell and Waldemar J. Gallman, the chargé in London, outlining the position of the State Department. Acheson added a new reason for America's interest in reaching a quick settlement—namely, the apprehension that further delays in India could have world-wide repercussions; they could have, the acting secretary averred, an effect on China. Presumably the State Department officials believed that hesitancy toward independence in India would delay the resolution of other colonial questions in Asia and would increase the appeal and strength of communism. To break the Indian deadlock the United States shifted its position and became more sympathetic to the Muslim League. Suggesting that Gallman establish contact with the Indian leaders, Acheson stated that the Congress should accept the British and Muslim League interpretation pertaining to compulsory provincial groupings as the only means of securing

[21] *Department of State Bulletin,* September 8, 1946, p. 463, November 3, 1946, p. 827, and November 24, 1946, p. 971; memorandum, Acheson to Truman, August 30, 1946, *FRUS, 1946,* 5:92–93; telegram from London, September 9, 1946, *ibid.,* pp. 93–94; telegram to New Delhi, October 16, 1946, *ibid.,* pp. 95–96.

the League's participation in the Constituent Assembly. If the groupings meant the end of the Congress governments in Assam and the
North-West Frontier Province, that result, Acheson suggested, would
be of little importance.

On December 2 Gallman replied that the United States would be
wise to avoid any action which might be construed as interference or
taking sides. Instead, he urged that the State Department issue a statement affirming its interest in the talks. The chargé did inform the
India Office of the position taken by Washington in Acheson's message. At a press conference on December 3 Acheson affirmed the American government's hope that the League and the Congress would
cooperate, under the general formula of the cabinet mission plan, to
achieve a settlement granting all elements of the population their
sovereign political and economic rights.[22]

This change in the American government's attitude apparently resulted from the conviction that the League's demonstrated following
in India warranted giving it the assurances Jinnah was demanding. To
officials in Washington, Direct Action Day had revealed the extent to
which the League could stir the Muslim masses. Jinnah's repeated
threats that the only alternative to Pakistan was civil war registered
in America as well as in India and Britain. Also, the Muslim League
had finally managed to gain some attention in America. In November,
Jinnah dispatched Hassan Ispahanai and Begum Shah Nawaz to New
York as unofficial delegates to the United Nations. In speeches before
various groups and at rallies organized by the India Welfare League,
the Muslim League's representatives did advance the Pakistani demand.[23]

The trend in American thinking paralleled that of the Attlee government. After four days of fruitless discussions, the London meetings
ended on December 6 when the British issued a statement which
further enhanced the League's standing. After reaffirming that provinces would be compelled to meet in groups (but could still opt out
after the first elections under the new group constitutions), the declara-

[22] Telegram to London, November 30, 1946, *ibid.*, pp. 97–98; telegram from London, December 2, 1946, *ibid.*, pp. 98–99; telegram to London, December 3, 1946,
ibid., pp. 99–100; *Department of State Bulletin*, December 15, 1946, p. 1113.

[23] *New York Times*, November 16, 24, and 26, 1946.

tion also reversed Attlee's assurance of the previous March that the minority could not impose a veto on the majority. If a constitution was drafted by a constituent assembly which did not include any substantial minority, the British government now asserted that it would not force that constitution on an unwilling minority. The effect, of course, was to encourage the League's non-participation in the Constituent Assembly convening on December 9.

The Attlee government's statement supporting the League would likely have been made regardless of Washington's position. It followed the traditional pattern of standing with the Muslim minority against the Congress. The League's appeal and strength also encouraged concessions. In addition, knowledge that the nation on which Britain depended for financial assistance also supported the League's demands certainly facilitated the position taken in the December 6 declaration.

By the end of the London talks, British policy seemed to embrace Pakistan as the only solution to the Indian deadlock. At the time, however, Pakistan could still mean Muslim provincial groupings within a comparatively weak central government or complete independence for the Muslim areas. Perhaps Britain had already decided on partition, for subsequent statements from London gave that alternative greater impetus.

The United States, however, was not yet prepared to accept partition. The State Department sought to help alleviate the disagreements between the League and the Congress over the cabinet mission plan. On December 7 the State Department cabled Merrell to establish contact with Nehru immediately upon his return from London and to inform him of the position expressed by Acheson in his November 30 message. In a brief meeting with Nehru on December 10 Merrell presented the view that the Congress should accept compulsory grouping. The circumstances did not permit a discussion, but Nehru invited Merrell to join him for dinner on December 13. In the interim Merrell met with Jinnah, who expressed appreciation for America's interest but refrained from discussing how the League's differences with the Congress could be settled.

Convinced that inducing the Congress to moderate its stand remained the prime hope, the State Department cabled extensive instructions to Merrell for his December 13 meeting with Nehru. To remove any suspicions that the United States was acting at the behest of the British, Merrell was to make it clear that the U.S. overture was its own. While the United States recognized the serious limitations of the cabinet mission plan, particularly in the powers it delegated to the central government, Merrell was to tell Nehru that America's own federal experience had revealed that the central government of neces-ity gradually acquires more authority. This American gesture occurred at an inopportune moment, for Nehru's recent experiences had con-vinced him that, as long as the British remained, attempting to work with the League was almost futile. Nehru had recognized that the central government would likely gain authority, but when he had sug-gested that development in July, the League had responded with Direct Action Day. Moreover, the parallels between the American federal system and that anticipated under the cabinet mission plan were at best tenuous; the United States had no counterpart to the Muslim minority and had never attempted to function under anything resembling the three-tier arrangement. Accordingly, the Nehru-Merrell meeting proved disappointing. In a lengthy and dispassionate dis-course Nehru expressed exasperation with Jinnah, who, he said, had never adequately defined the meaning of Pakistan. Nehru also charged that the British, by calling the London conference at the moment when it seemed that the League might participate in the Constituent As-sembly, had effectively sabotaged any possible cooperation.

From Merrell's report the State Department realized, much more fully than it had earlier, the frustration and despair of the Congress. It then decided to seek compromise from the other side. On December 19 Merrell was instructed to inform Jinnah or Liaqat Ali Khan that the reservations of the Congress could be eliminated only if the League issued a statement affirming its willingness to work within the federal union embodied in the cabinet mission plan. At the same time, Merrell was to reassure the League of America's interest in making certain of adequate safeguards for the "legitimate" economic and political rights of the Muslim community. A week later Thomas Weil of the embassy staff presented these views to Liaqat Ali Khan, who, for nearly two hours, held forth against the Congress, charging that it intended to establish a Hindu *raj*. At another meeting between the two men on December 29 Weil requested that the American position be conveyed to Jinnah. Again, the response was wholly negative, for Liaqat Ali Khan held that Jinnah would not be receptive to the idea.

The reports of the sessions with Liaqat Ali Khan and those of the discussions with Nehru convinced officials in Washington of the irreconcilability of the National Congress and the Muslim League. As Weil concluded in his last message, the crisis called for statesmanship from Jinnah, but profound bitterness and distrust made statesmanship too much to expect.[24]

By the end of 1946 a note of despair also prevailed in the limited press reports on India. The Muslim League had generally been criticized for its policies since Direct Action Day, although *Newsweek*, more than other journals, apportioned responsibility equally between the Hindu and Muslim communities for the riots and killings. After the London talks *Time*, *Newsweek*, and *The Nation* speculated on the likelihood of civil war.[25]

In 1947, however, events moved quickly and the British *raj* finally ended. The process began on February 20 and 21—turning points in the histories of Britain, India, and the United States. On those days the Attlee government began the liquidation of the British Empire, which resulted in new responsibilities for India and the United States. On February 20 Attlee announced that the British government planned to take the necessary steps to effect a transfer of power in India no later than June, 1948. To implement the transition Lord Louis Mountbatten would replace Wavell as viceroy. The next day the British ambassador Lord Inverchapel met with Secretary of State George C. Marshall and discussed in detail Britain's plans and the

[24] Telegram to New Delhi, December 7, 1946, *FRUS, 1946*, 5:100–101; telegram from New Delhi, December 11, 1946, *ibid.*, pp. 101–3; telegram to New Delhi, December 11, 1946, *ibid.*, pp. 103–4; telegram from London, December 12, 1946, *ibid.*, p. 104; telegram from New Delhi, December 14, 1946, *ibid.*, p. 105; telegram to New Delhi, December 19, 1946, *ibid.*, p. 106; telegram from New Delhi, December 27, 1946, *ibid.*, pp. 106–9; telegram from New Delhi, December 29, 1946, *ibid.*, pp. 109–12.

[25] *Newsweek*, August 26, 1946, p. 38, September 2, 1946, p. 28, and December 16, 1946, pp. 50–51; *The New Republic*, August 26, 1946, p. 214; *Time*, August 26, 1946, p. 32, October 28, 1946, p. 40, and December 16, 1946, p. 32; *The Nation*, December 21, 1946, pp. 717–18, and December 28, 1946, pp. 757–58.

situation in India. The same afternoon the first secretary of the British Embassy delivered two notes to the State Department, informing the United States of the British government's intention to end its traditional policy of supporting Greece and Turkey. The British withdrawal led to President Truman's decision to assist Greece and Turkey and to launch the far-reaching policy of containment.

As the United States assumed responsibilities and commitments in Europe, it renewed its efforts to make certain that the political transition in India was carried out peacefully. Instability in India could invite more communist activity there and could easily affect other areas, particularly the Middle East. On February 25 Marshall publicly praised the British promise and urged the Indian parties to accept the challenge and resolve their differences. When Asaf Ali, India's first ambassador, presented his credentials to Truman on February 28, the President took the occasion to reiterate Marshall's sentiments and to pledge American assistance in India's economic development. The statements of both Marshall and Truman avoided any position on the Pakistan issue. Apparently after the futile effort at inducing a reconciliation the previous December, the State Department had decided to let the Indian parties and the British work out that problem.[26]

Indeed, the Indians were quickly moving toward agreement. By the time Mountbatten arrived on March 22, more and more Indians had come to accept partition as the only alternative to civil war. As Mountbatten soon deduced, the Congress was more inclined to compromise than was the Muslim League. The Congress leadership, notably Nehru and Patel, now were willing to concede, at least privately, that Pakistan had to be accepted. A variety of forces were working on the Congress: the spread of communal warfare to the Punjab, the exhaustion of trying to work on compromise schemes with the Muslim League, and the pressures from Congress leaders in Muslim majority provinces to accept Pakistan but to seek communal division of their provinces.

In discussions with Nehru, Patel, Jinnah, Gandhi, and Liaqat Ali Khan the new viceroy managed to gain agreement on partition. On June 2 Mountbatten presented the partition plan to the Indian pub-

[26] *New York Times*, February 21 and March 1 and 9, 1947; *Department of State Bulletin*, March 9, 1947, p. 50.

179

lic. It offered a measure of self-determination for the minorities in the Muslim majority provinces destined to become part of Pakistan. In Bengal and the Punjab the legislative assemblies were to divide into two groups, one representing the Muslim majority areas and the other the non-Muslim majority areas; if either group voted to partition the province, both groups had to accept the decision. In practice this assured the division of the two strife-ridden provinces. Within two weeks of Mountbatten's announcement the Muslim League and the National Congress gave their formal assent.

This resolution of the Indian dilemma was greeted with relief among American officials and in the press. In a statement on June 10 the State Department praised the agreement and pledged American friendship with all Indian groups. En route to India as the first United States ambassador, Henry F. Grady was interviewed in Singapore and affirmed that the partition plan had full American support. Upon arriving in Bombay on June 25, Grady spoke of American sympathy and understanding of the problems facing India as it prepared to implement the partition decision. In a press conference a few days later at New Delhi, the American ambassador reaffirmed Truman's offer to assist India in its economic development. In American newspapers and journals the acceptance of Pakistan was regarded as the only possible solution. *Chicago Daily News* correspondent Phillips Talbot (reporting from New Delhi) and editorials in the *New York Times* and *The Nation*, however, called attention to the serious economic, political, and administrative problems caused by partition.[27]

With the commitment to partition secured, Mountbatten moved quickly to work out the troublesome details: the allocation of resources, the establishment of the boundaries, the status of the princely states, and the division of the vast administrative bureaucracy. The date of the transfer of power was advanced to August 15. The British, who had been reluctant for so long to give up India, now were perhaps too hasty in transferring power, for the ten weeks between the June 3 announcement and the date of independence were insufficient to pro-

[27] *Department of State Bulletin*, June 22, 1947, p. 1249; *New York Times*, June 10, 11, 25, and July 8, 1947; *Time*, June 16, 1947, pp. 39–40; *Newsweek*, June 16, 1947, p. 38; *The Nation*, June 14, 1947, p. 702; Phillips Talbot, "Report from New Delhi," *The New Republic*, June 6, 1947, p. 7.

vide for an orderly withdrawal. Behind Mountbatten's actions were understandable motives, most important of which was his determination to carry out his plan before either the Muslim League or the Congress had second thoughts.

The long-awaited day of independence was celebrated with unrestrained enthusiasm throughout India. For the National Congress and its followers the occasion marked the fulfillment of years of a determined effort to end British rule without resorting to violence. Partition, which the Congress had opposed until a few weeks earlier, detracted only slightly from the spirit of the moment. In his address to the Constituent Assembly on the night of August 14, Nehru spoke for his countrymen:

Long years ago we made a tryst with destiny, and now the time comes when we shall redeem our pledge, not wholly or in full measure, but very substantially. At the stroke of the midnight hour, when the world sleeps, India will awake to life and freedom. A moment comes, which comes but rarely in history, when we step out from the old to the new, when an age ends, and when the soul of a nation, long suppressed, finds utterance. It is fitting that at this solemn moment we take the pledge of dedication to the service of India and her people and to the still larger cause of humanity.[28]

India's independence, which many American officials, political leaders, and journalists had believed and had argued ought to be a paramount American objective, had finally been achieved. In the final acts of the Indian drive for independence, the United States, in contrast with its earlier deep involvement and interest, remained more in the background. Americans, of course, welcomed the event, and newspapers everywhere gave it front-page coverage. President Truman sent congratulations to the two new dominions and their peoples. In a message to the American public on August 15, 1947, which also happened to be the second anniversary of V-J Day, Mountbatten related Britain's withdrawal to the Allied pledge in the Atlantic Charter.[29]

[28] V. P. Menon, *The Transfer of Power in India* (Princeton: Princeton University Press, 1957), p. 413.

[29] *Department of State Bulletin*, August 24, 1947, p. 396; *New York Times*, August 14–16, 1947.

Mountbatten's remarks were ironic, considering Churchill's wartime stand, but the British could now claim fulfillment of the Atlantic Charter. As Mountbatten stated:

Two years ago today I had just returned from the Potsdam Conference and was in the Prime Minister's room in 10, Downing Street, when the news of the Japanese surrender came through. Here, as I speak to you tonight from Delhi, we are celebrating an event no less momentous for the future of the world—India's Independence Day. In the Atlantic Charter, we—the British and Americans—dedicated ourselves to champion the self-determination of peoples and the independence of nations. Bitter experience has taught us that it is often easier to win a war than to achieve a war aim; so let us remember August 15th—V.J. Day—not only as the celebration of a victory, but also the fulfillment of a pledge.[30]

The leaders of India and Pakistan soon learned that blaming imperial masters or one another for their troubles was easier than governing themselves. The aftermath of partition brought communal warfare of horrendous proportions. The migration of some twelve million persons from one section of the Punjab to the area of their co-religionists led to atrocities throughout the divided province and the western United Provinces. Riots, lootings, and murders came to Delhi less than a week after independence. Before the end of the year, when a measure of stability was finally achieved, half a million persons had been killed. Simultaneously, the struggle to control Kashmir brought Indian and Pakistani soldiers into conflict. The glowing promises uttered in Karachi and Delhi on August 15 to work together closely had given way to a state of undeclared war, which the two nations have yet to end.

[30] Menon, *Transfer of Power*, p. 415.

VIII

America and Indian Nationalism
in Retrospect

FROM THE TIME OF PEARL HARBOR until the French withdrawal from
Indochina in 1954, the United States continually faced the challenge
of responding to Asian nationalist movements directed against its
European allies. In its first test the United States substantially failed.
Because of its equivocation the nation appeared uncertain of its own
espoused ideals, and, indeed, seemed to be a partner in imperialism.

This conclusion is based on the assumption, which seems as clear
now as it did to many observers in and out of the government during
and after World War II, that the interests of the United States necessitated supporting the irresistible force of nationalism. This conclusion does *not* rest on the romantic assumption, frequently expressed
by nationalist leaders and some of their more fervent spokesmen in
America, that independence provides an end to the problems of a
people. The experience of the "emerging nations" attests the profound
difficulties of building politically and economically viable nations. Yet,
because nationalist movements everywhere in Asia gathered momen-
tum during World War II and the European nations were no longer
capable of holding their colonies, the interests of the United States
dictated moving with the times by encouraging an end to the European empires.

As the first people to revolt against a modern empire, the United
States stood in a unique position. The American Revolution had

183

indeed been heard round the world; and the words of the Declaration of Independence had inspired generations of colonial peoples. Moreover, America's avowed idealistic aims in World War II, expressed in the Atlantic Charter, encouraged nationalist leaders to look to the United States for inspiration, guidance, and support. In the case of India, ideals and self-interest coincided, but the United States failed to respond effectively and thus produced disenchantment and a lessening of American prestige.

The critical American test in India occurred during the war years. By the summer of 1945 India's independence had become a certainty, and the Truman administration, to its credit, encouraged the Attlee government in its determination to withdraw quickly. Yet, during the war, when the United States had been in a position to influence Indian developments, Roosevelt declined opportunities and suggestions to advance an unequivocal policy and to pressure the Churchill government. During the Cripps mission, Roosevelt waited until Churchill had already decided to recall Cripps before attempting to salvage a settlement. That gesture, to be certain, took some courage, but it came so late that Churchill could easily brush it aside. Prior to the crisis of August, 1942, George Merrell and other American officials in India warned repeatedly that only Roosevelt's intervention could avert widespread unrest and suppression. Chiang Kai-shek, who had just visited India, implored Roosevelt to use his prestige and leverage to insist upon a mediated settlement. Beyond informing Churchill of Chiang's plea, Roosevelt took no action.

The subsequent British imprisonment of National Congress leaders was one of the dark pages of the Allied history of World War II. In waging a war against fascist tyranny a principal Allied government suppressed, with the acquiescence of the only nation in a position to prevent it, a political movement whose dedication to the Allied cause was unquestioned and whose only crime was its refusal to accept prolonged foreign rule.

In 1943 William Phillips attempted to bring about a change in American policy, seeking Roosevelt's intercession to prevent Gandhi's possible death, urging Roosevelt's mediation and guarantee of a political settlement, and, after failing in those endeavors, attempting to get at least endorsement of his effort to visit Gandhi and Nehru. Phillips, however, gained no support from Washington.

It would have been difficult to force a modification in Churchill's policy. The prime minister's warning that intervention risked an open rupture between the two allies, as well as the military situation of 1942–43, led Roosevelt to retreat from the Indian question. Yet most American diplomats in India, several officials in the State Department, and many journalists recognized the importance of the Indian question and believed it should be given priority over Anglo-American harmony. Given Britain's dependence on the United States, it is likely that America's insistence that power be transferred to India's leaders would have produced only a temporary rift between the allies. Phillips, Merrell, Louis Johnson, Howard Donovan, and, at times, Adolph Berle and Sumner Welles, all argued that intervention was worth the risk.

Short of such intervention, the United States could have affirmed its support of the aspirations of the Indian people. Even that gesture would have caused consternation in London, but it would have clarified the American position. Roosevelt, however, avoided any such affirmations. Instead, America's dedication to self-determination became conditional, beginning with Cordell Hull's statement of July 23, 1942, and concluding with the United Nations Charter.

By acquiescing in British imperial policy, the United States influenced developments in India and elsewhere in Asia. The suppression of the National Congress facilitated the rise of the Muslim League. As it became stronger, the prospects for partition also increased, and by 1947 became a reality. Moreover, if the British had granted the Indian demands in 1942 and if the U.S. position had been evident, the other imperial powers would have been forced to act more realistically in dealing with their own colonies. In other words, the futile postwar efforts to regain predominance in South and Southeast Asia would have been discouraged.

This is not to suggest that Indian leaders were free from responsibility for the impasse of the war years. Both the Muslim League and the National Congress claimed greater popular backing than was justified. The League did not represent all Muslims, and the National Congress' pretension to speak for all Indians ignored the growing strength of its rival group. Within the National Congress the divergence between the idealistic and somewhat provincial Gandhi and the pragmatic and internationally oriented Nehru over participation in the war weakened the Congress in its dealings with the British and in presenting its case to the world. Nehru's final deference to Gandhi in the summer of 1942 led to the fateful "Quit India" movement, which seemed extreme to Americans and paved the way for British suppression.

The events of 1947, however, illustrated that the Indians were correct on a fundamental point of difference with the British. Churchill and Amery repeatedly maintained that the Indians had to resolve their differences before any definite transfer of power could be planned. The Congress argued that, once the British left or set a time-table for withdrawal, the Indian parties could reach an understanding. When the British announced such a date in 1947, the National Congress and the Muslim League quickly resolved their differences. If such a stand had been taken by the British five years earlier, the two groups would have been forced to face realistically the issues that divided them. Because the Cripps offer left ultimate power in the hands of the British, the Indian groups were encouraged to assert extreme positions. The results of meaningful negotiations among the Indian parties in 1942 probably would have been different from what they were in 1947, for Jinnah, Nehru, Azad, and Gandhi, shrewd as they all were, would have been compelled to act responsibly.

After independence was finally attained the Indians' disenchantment with the United States passed. In retrospect, appreciation for the moral encouragement rendered by many Americans and for the known support of Johnson and Phillips came to outweigh the disappointment over Washington's equivocation between 1942 and 1945. When Nehru visited the United States in 1949 he spoke warmly of the support given by private Americans to India's struggle and of the interest shown by President Roosevelt.[1]

Unfortunately, America's deference to Britain on the Indian question proved to be but the first instance of its insensitivity to the aspirations of the emerging peoples. During the postwar years the United States faced the dilemma of responding to the attempts of its European allies to regain their empires, and again failed to take a position

[1] Dorothy Norman, ed., *Nehru: The First Sixty Years, Presenting in His Own Words the Development of the Political Thought of Jawaharlal Nehru and the Background against Which It Evolved* . . . , 2 vols. (New York: John Day Co., 1965), 2:500–501.

based on its prime interests in Asia. In terms of prestige and influence the United States was the major loser, for, while the European nations acted as the nationalist leaders had anticipated, it was the United States which seemed to act inconsistently with its own ideals. Disillusionment with the United States became as common in Indochina and Indonesia as it had been in India. After independence came to the rest of Asia, the United States continued to have difficulty understanding the aspirations of those emerging nations. Its political, economic, and military policies frequently revealed a prevalent insensitivity to the determination of the newly independent nations to resist alignment in the cold war and any semblance of Western domination.

By its actions in South and Southeast Asia during World War II and the early cold war, the United States indicated that European interests warranted priority over those in Asia. The determination to hold onto its European allies largely accounted for the nation's inconsistent and ineffectual response to nationalism, beginning with India. Recent frustrations, however, have underscored the fact that U.S. objectives in Asia need to be calculated on a clear understanding of the political, ideological, and economic forces in the countries and regions of that vast continent.

Bibliography

This Bibliography is Divided into two parts: (1) a summary of the documents; (2) a discussion of secondary sources. The numerous references in the footnotes to articles in newspapers and journals and to books pertaining to India published during the 1940–47 period are not repeated.

PRIMARY SOURCES

The Department of State decimal files are, of course, the major source. The Roosevelt Papers at the Franklin D. Roosevelt Library, Hyde Park, N.Y., add important details. The Papers of William Phillips at the Houghton Library of Harvard University are available, but add little information. The Papers of Louis Johnson are at the Alderman Library of the University of Virginia, but will not be available until 1977.

The Historical Office of the Department of State publishes selected documents in the *Foreign Relations of the United States* series. Volumes in that series which pertain to this topic and their years of publication by the Government Printing Office are as follows: *FRUS, 1941*, vol. 1, *General: The Soviet Union* (1958); *FRUS, 1941*, vol. 3, *The British Commonwealth, the Near East and Africa* (1959); *FRUS, 1942*, vol. 1, *General: The British Commonwealth, the Far East* (1960); *FRUS, 1942: China* (1956); *FRUS, 1943*, vol. 4, *The Near East and Africa* (1964); *FRUS: The Conferences at Cairo and Teheran, 1943* (1961); *FRUS, 1944*, vol. 5, *The Near East, South Asia and Africa, the Far East* (1965); *FRUS, 1945*, vol. 1, *General: The United Nations* (1967); *FRUS, 1945*, vol. 6, *The British Commonwealth, the Far East* (1969); *FRUS, 1946*, vol. 5, *The British Commonwealth: Western and Central Europe* (1969).

Although the British documents and Churchill Papers are not available to the public, the British government has begun publication of a projected multivolume series: *Constitutional Relations between Britain and India: The Transfer of Power, 1942–47*. The first volume, *The Cripps Mission, January–April, 1942* (London: Her Majesty's Stationery Office, 1970), adds much important information.

SECONDARY WORKS

It is hoped that this section will serve three purposes: (1) to summarize the principal scholarly works dealing with Indo-American relations; (2) to acknowledge the secondary sources utilized in writing this study; (3) to suggest a few important similarities and differences in interpretation on some of the questions considered in this volume. For convenience the discussion is divided by chapters, although that has necessitated some arbitrary decisions as to where certain studies should be cited and has resulted in the repetition of several major sources.

Chapter I

There is no general history of Indo-American relations from the early contacts to recent developments. W. Norman Brown's *The United States and India and Pakistan*, 2nd ed. rev. (Cambridge, Mass.: Harvard University Press, 1963), was intended primarily to introduce Americans to India, and it admirably accomplishes its goal. Phillips Talbot and S. L. Poplai, *India and America: A Study of Their Relations* (New York: Harper & Bros., 1958), focuses on political and economic relations during the first decade after independence. Norman D. Palmer, "Ups and Downs in Indo-American Relations," *Annals of the American Academy of Political and Social Science*, July, 1954, pp. 113–30, is a brief survey of early postindependence problems. Norman D. Palmer, *South Asia and United States Policy* (Boston: Houghton Mifflin, 1966), provides an excellent statement of India's contemporary importance to the United States. Lawrence Rosinger, *India and the United States: Political and Economic Relations* (New York: Macmillan, 1950), emphasizes the 1947–50 period. L. Natarajan, *American Shadow over India* (Bombay: People's Publishing House, 1952), a Marxist interpretation, charges American economic exploitation of India.

A number of dissertations, books, and articles trace Indo-American relations to World War II. The American view of India is carefully presented in Harold R. Isaacs, *Scratches on Our Minds: American Images of China and India* (New York: John Day Co., 1958). Some specialized studies provide

190

details on American attitudes: Dorothy B. Jones, *The Portrayal of China and India on the American Screen, 1896–1955: The Evolution of Chinese and Indian Themes, Locales, and Characters as Portrayed on the American Screen* (Cambridge, Mass.: M.I.T. Center for International Studies, 1955); Shyama Deodhar, "The Treatment of India in American Social Studies Textbooks" (Ph.D. diss., University of Michigan, 1954); Bernard S. Stern, "American Views of India and Indians, 1857–1900" (Ph.D. diss., University of Pennsylvania, 1956); Richard Howard Schramm, "The Image of India in Selected American Literary Periodicals: 1870–1900" (Ph.D. diss., Duke University, 1964).

Earl Robert Schmidt, "American Relations with South Asia, 1900–1940" (Ph.D. diss., University of Pennsylvania, 1955), covers economic, political, and cultural developments, but is marred by imprecision and factual errors. Commercial relations are surveyed by Holden Furber, "Beginnings of American Trade with India, 1784–1812," *New England Quarterly*, June, 1938, pp. 235–65, and Dwijendra Tripathi, "The United States and India: Economic Links, 1860–1900" (Ph.D. diss., University of Wisconsin, 1963). On diplomatic contacts, the Historical Office of the Department of State has issued "Official United States Representation in India, 1776–1963" (mimeographed).

The role of missionaries has not been fully explored. Sushil Madhava Pathak, *American Missionaries and Hinduism: A Study of Their Contacts from 1813 to 1910* (New Delhi: Munshiram Manoharlal, 1967), provides a thorough survey of early Protestant work. Muhammad Mohar Ali, *The Bengali Reaction to Christian Missionary Activities, 1833–1857* (Chittagong: Mehrub Publications, 1965), deals with the efforts of British-based missionaries and contributes to an understanding of acculturation as a function of missions. Gary R. Hess, *Sam Higginbottom of Allahabad: Pioneer of Point Four to India* (Charlottesville: The University Press of Virginia, 1967), studies the influence of the foremost agricultural missionary in India. A survey of the agricultural phase is Gary R. Hess, "American Agricultural Missionaries and Efforts at Economic Improvement in India," *Agricultural History*, January, 1968, pp. 23–33. C. Chacko Thomas, "The Work and Thought of Eli Stanley Jones, with Special Reference to India" (Ph.D. diss., State University of Iowa, 1955), is a competent biography of an important missionary figure.

The experience of the Indian community in America and its political activity during the early twentieth century have been rather thoroughly examined. Gary R. Hess, "The 'Hindu' in America: Immigration and Naturalization Policies and India, 1917–1946," *Pacific Historical Review*, February, 1969, pp. 59–79, traces the restrictive measures and the struggle for an immigration quota and citizenship privileges. Stephen N. Hay, "Rabindranath Tagore in America," *American Quarterly*, Fall, 1962, pp. 439–63, is an excellent survey of Tagore's influence. Sujit Mukherjee, *Passage to America: The Reception of Rabindranath Tagore in the United States, 1912–1941* (Calcutta: Bookland Private, 1964), details the diverse American reactions to Tagore. On the moderate nationalist movement in America during World War I, Naaen Gul Rathore has written a first-rate study: "Indian Nationalist Agitation in the United States: A Study of Lala Lajpat Rai and the India Home Rule League of America, 1914–1920" (Ph.D. diss., Columbia University, 1965). The evolution and activities of the "Hindu conspirators" are traced in three articles: Giles T. Brown, "The Hindu Conspiracy, 1914–1917," *Pacific Historical Review*, August, 1948, pp. 299–310; Mark Naidis, "Propaganda of the Gadar Party," *ibid.*, August, 1951, pp. 251–60; and Kalyan Kumar Banerjee, "East Indian Immigration into America: Beginnings of Indian Revolutionary Activity," *Modern Review* (Calcutta), November, 1964, pp. 355–61. Haridas T. Muzumdar, one of the founders of the India League of America, has written *America's Contribution to India's Freedom* (Allahabad: Central Book Depot, 1962), a useful compilation of nationalist activities.

A few works detail the American response to Indian nationalism during the pre–World War II period. Harnam Singh, *Indian National Movement and American Opinion* (New Delhi: Central Electric Press, 1962), is a thorough survey of the comment in periodicals. Walter C. Mackett, "Some Aspects of the Development of American Opinion on India, 1918–1947" (Ph.D. diss., University of Southern California, 1957), summarizes the reaction of major journals and several, mainly West Coast, newspapers. Diwakar Prasad Singh, "American Official Attitudes towards the Indian Nationalist Movement, 1905–1929" (Ph.D. diss., University of Hawaii, 1964), surveys the responses of American officials in India to political developments there.

The other side of the picture—the development of Indian nationalist attitudes toward the United States—is included in Bimla Prasad, *The Origins of Indian Foreign Policy: The Indian National Congress and World Affairs, 1885–1947* (Calcutta: Bookland, 1960).

Roosevelt's attitudes toward imperialism are well summarized in Foster Rhea Dulles and Gerald Ridinger, "The Anti-Colonial Policies of Franklin D. Roosevelt," *Political Science Quarterly*, March, 1955, pp. 1–18. Lowell Thomas Young, "Franklin D. Roosevelt and Imperialism" (Ph.D. diss., University of Virginia, 1970), is a more comprehensive treatment. Morton Frisch, "Roosevelt on Peace and Freedom," *Journal of Politics*, August, 1967, pp. 585–96, stresses the continuity between Roosevelt's interest in India and his efforts, late in the war, to limit Russia's influence in Eastern Europe. Cordell Hull's position is presented in his *Memoirs of Cordell Hull*, 2 vols. (New

York: Macmillan, 1948); Donald F. Drummond, "Cordell Hull," in *An Uncertain Tradition: American Secretaries of State in the Twentieth Century*, ed. Norman A. Graebner (New York: McGraw-Hill, 1961), pp. 184–209; and Julius W. Pratt, *Cordell Hull*, vol. 13 of *The American Secretaries of State and Their Diplomacy*, ed. Robert H. Ferrell and Samuel Flagg Bemis (New York: Cooper Square Publishers, 1964).

The work of Lord Halifax as Ambassador is traced in Earl of Birkenhead, *Halifax: The Life of Lord Halifax* (London: Hamish Hamilton, 1965), and Lord Halifax, *Fullness of Days* (New York: Dodd, Mead & Co., 1957). A unique diplomatic relationship between the Government of India and the United States began in 1941. That and subsequent changes are summarized in Raymond L. Thurston, "U.S. Relations with the Government of India: A Reference Article," *Middle East Journal*, July, 1947, pp. 292–306; and Lawrence Rosinger and H. M. Trivedi, "Indian-American Relations," *Far Eastern Survey*, January 25, 1950, pp. 9–12.

The Atlantic Conference and the drafting of the Atlantic Charter have been definitively studied by Theodore A. Wilson, *The First Summit: Roosevelt and Churchill at Placentia Bay, 1941* (Boston: Houghton Mifflin, 1969).

Chapter II

On political developments in India, two works are indispensable: V. P. Menon, *The Transfer of Power in India* (Princeton: Princeton University Press, 1957), a thorough and factual history; and Michael Brecher, *Nehru: A Political Biography* (London: Oxford University Press, 1959), a superb biography and history of the Nehru era. K. P. Bhagat, *A Decade of Indo-British Relations, 1937–1947* (Bombay: Popular Book Depot, 1959), also is authoritative. On Gandhi, Louis Fischer, *The Life of Mahatma Gandhi* (New York: Harper & Bros., 1950), remains the best biography, at least in terms of understanding Gandhi's actions during the war years. B. R. Nanda, *Mahatma Gandhi: A Biography* (Boston: Beacon Hill Press, 1958), and Rajendra Prasad, *At the Feet of Mahatma Gandhi* (New York: Philosophical Library, 1955), add some insights. The multivolume biography by [Nair] Pyarelal has not yet examined Gandhi's career in the early part of the period studied here, but volumes covering the last four years of his life have been published: *Mahatma Gandhi: The Last Phase*, 2 vols. (Ahmedabad: Navajivan Publishing House, 1956–58). Robert Payne, *The Life and Death of Mahatma Gandhi* (New York: E. P. Dutton, 1969), adds little on Gandhi's political activity during this period. D. G. Tendulkar, *Mahatma: Life of Mohandas Karamchand Gandhi*, 8 vols. (Bombay: Jhaveri & Tendulkar, 1951–54), is helpful. Other important biographies include: Hector Bolitho, *Jinnah, Creator of*

193

Bibliography

Pakistan (London: John Murray, 1954); Frank Moraes, *Jawaharlal Nehru: A Biography* (New York: Macmillan, 1956); Narhari D. Parikh, *Sardar Vallabhbhai Patel*, 2 vols. (Ahmedabad: Navajivan Publishing House, 1956). Maulana Abul Kalan Azad, *India Wins Freedom: An Autobiographical Narrative* (Bombay: Orient Longmans, 1959), is a candid and revealing memoir.

Churchill's position on India is well presented in his *The Second World War*, vol. 3: *The Grand Alliance* and vol. 4: *The Hinge of Fate* (Boston: Houghton Mifflin, 1950). The British concern over American interest is also reflected in Sir Llewellyn Woodward, *British Foreign Policy in the Second World War* (London: Her Majesty's Stationery Office, 1962); Lord Ismay, *The Memoirs of General Lord Ismay* (New York: Viking Press, 1960); Arthur Bryant, *The Turn of the Tide: A History of the War Years Based on the Diaries of Field-Marshal Lord Alanbrooke, Chief of the Imperial General Staff* (Garden City, N.Y.: Doubleday & Co., 1957); Earl of Avon, *The Memoirs of Anthony Eden, Earl of Avon: The Reckoning* (Boston: Houghton Mifflin, 1965).

On the Cripps Mission the distinguished constitutional historian Reginald Coupland provides a brief narrative from the British viewpoint in *The Cripps Mission* (New York: Oxford University Press, 1942). Eric Estorik, *Stafford Cripps: Master Statesman* (New York: John Day Co., 1949), is also helpful.

America's interest in India and the resultant problems in Anglo-American relations are placed in proper perspective in two accounts of World War II: James MacGregor Burns, *Roosevelt: The Soldier of Freedom* (New York: Harcourt, Brace, Jovanovich, 1970), a masterful biography; and Gaddis Smith, *American Diplomacy during the Second World War* (New York: John Wiley & Sons, 1965), an excellent synthesis of wartime problems. Other general histories of the war ignore or minimize the Indian question. One exception, William L. Neumann's provocative *After Victory: Churchill, Roosevelt, Stalin, and the Making of the Peace* (New York: Harper & Row, 1967), touches briefly but cogently on the colonial issue. Burns, Smith, and Neumann all call attention to the lack of a systematic decision-making process in Roosevelt's conduct of foreign policy and the frequent divergence between the White House and State Department; this is further underscored in Robert E. Sherwood, *Roosevelt and Hopkins: An Intimate History*, rev. ed. (New York: Grosset & Dunlap, 1950); Julius Pratt, "The Ordeal of Cordell Hull," *Review of Politics*, January, 1966, pp. 76–98; and in Hull's *Memoirs*.

American policy in India after Pearl Harbor has been summarized in several studies. A. Guy Hope, *America and Swaraj: The U.S. Role in Indian Independence* (Washington, D.C.: Public Affairs Press, 1968), covers principally the 1941–47 period, but is uncritically and wholly favorable to American actions. In a series of articles, M. S. Venkataramani and B. K. Shrivastava have evaluated various phases of U.S. policy, basing their work extensively on published State Department documents. Their first article deals with the material covered in this chapter: "The U.S. and the Cripps Mission," *India Quarterly,* July, 1963, pp. 214–25. Despite its title, Somendu K. Banerjee's "American Interest in Indian Independence, 1930–43," *ibid.,* October-December, 1968, pp. 311–32, focuses on 1942–43, but it fails to make use of published documents and is of little value. The development of Indo-American relations during and after the war has been the subject of several dissertations. Mohammad Abdul Khair, "United States Foreign Policy in the Indo-Pakistan Subcontinent, 1940–1955" (Ph.D. diss., University of California at Berkeley, 1963), and Shiwaram Krishnarao Kshirsagar, "The Development of Relations between India and the United States, 1941–1952" (Ph.D. diss., American University, 1957), provide fair summaries, but are outdated, at least in their coverage of the 1941–46 period. The dissertation of Mrs. Frances Harper Mullins, "American Diplomacy and Indian Independence, 1941–45" (Fletcher School of Diplomacy, Tufts University, anticipated date of completion, June, 1971), makes extensive use of archival materials and examines in detail economic and political relations and the decision-making process of the Roosevelt administration.

The role of the United States in the Cripps mission has triggered some controversy among scholars. Some Indians have judged American pressure on the British as the most important, if not the sole, reason for dispatching the mission. This interpretation leads easily to the conclusion that the mission was a gesture for the benefit of the American audience. See Bimla Prasad, *The Origins of Indian Foreign Policy: The Indian National Congress and World Affairs, 1885–1947* (Calcutta: Bookland, 1960), pp. 158–63; Shiwaram Krishnarao Kshirsagar, "The Development of Relations between India and the United States, 1941–1952" (Ph.D. diss., American University, 1957), pp. 94–96; and Narhari D. Parikh, *Sardar Vallabhbhai Patel,* 2 vols. (Ahmedabad: Navajivan Publishing House, 1956), 2:457. Other writers have seen U.S. influence as one of three principal considerations, the others being the tide of the war in Asia and pressures from within Britain. See M. S. Venkataramani and B. K. Shrivastava, "The United States and the Cripps Mission," *India Quarterly,* July, 1963, pp. 226–27; Michael Brecher, *Nehru: A Political Biography* (New York: Oxford University Press, 1959), pp. 276–77; and V. P. Menon, *The Transfer of Power in India* (Princeton: Princeton University Press, 1957), pp. 115–18.

The opinion that Hopkins, through his conversation with Churchill, was responsible for the failure of Johnson as a mediator and hence of Cripps as well, is expressed by M. S. Venkataramani and B. K. Shrivastava, "The United States and the Cripps Mission," *India Quarterly*, July, 1963, pp. 248–50. The opinion that the British and the National Congress were in such fundamental disagreement that a settlement was almost impossible is offered in the following: Michael Brecher, *Nehru: A Political Biography* (New York: Oxford University Press, 1959), pp. 279–80; Reginald Coupland, *The Cripps Mission* (New York: Oxford University Press, 1942), pp. 78–80; V. P. Menon, *The Transfer of Power in India* (Princeton: Princeton University Press, 1957), pp. 130–33; Eric Estorik, *Stafford Cripps: Master Statesman* (New York: John Day Co., 1949), pp. 281–85; Rajendra Prasad, *At the Feet of Mahatma Gandhi* (New York: Philosophical Library, 1955), pp. 301–2; and Rajendra Prasad, *Autobiography* (Bombay: Asia Publishing House, 1957), pp. 523–27.

Chapter III

For tracing political developments I have again relied most heavily on V. P. Menon, *The Transfer of Power in India* (Princeton: Princeton University Press, 1957), and Michael Brecher, *Nehru: A Political Biography* (New York: Oxford University Press, 1959). Louis Fischer, *The Life of Mahatma Gandhi* (New York: Harper & Bros., 1950), and Maulana Abul Kalan Azad, *India Wins Freedom: An Autobiographical Narrative* (Bombay: Orient Longmans, 1959), also were useful. Amba Prasad, *The Indian Revolt of 1942* (Delhi: S. Chand & Co., 1958), summarizes the August disturbances.

American policy is considered in two articles by M. S. Venkataramani and B. K. Shrivastava: "America and the Indian Political Crisis, July–August, 1942," *International Studies* (Bombay), July, 1964, pp. 1–48; and "The United States and the 'Quit India' Demand," *India Quarterly*, April, 1964, pp. 101–39. In the first article Venkataramani and Shrivastava are very critical of Roosevelt's August 1 letter to Gandhi. They are also concerned with the delay in dispatching the letter and question why, if it was written on August 1, it was not dispatched until August 5 and had not reached Gandhi by August 9. Since Roosevelt knew of the British plan to arrest the Congress leaders, Venkataramani and Shrivastava suggest that the delay may have been intentional. I examined the documents in the State Department and the Roosevelt Papers, but could find no indication of an intentional delay. Roosevelt apparently reconsidered his India policy for several days after drafting the message to Gandhi. On August 4 Welles informed a White House staff member that the Indian matter had been before the president for several days but that no decision had been reached (M. J. McDermott to Early, August 4, 1942, Box O.F. 48-H, India, 1942, Roosevelt Papers, Franklin D. Roosevelt Library, Hyde, Park, N.Y.). Perhaps the letter to Gandhi was delayed to allow the president this period of contemplation.

Chapter IV

Owing to the political stalemate that existed by 1943, the mission of William Phillips has received little attention. James MacGregor Burns, *Roosevelt: The Soldier of Freedom* (New York: Harcourt, Brace, Jovanovich, 1970), pp. 379–81, discusses it and is critical of Roosevelt's failure by 1943 to recognize fully the growing strength of nationalism in India and elsewhere in Asia. A. Guy Hope, *America and Swaraj: The U.S. Role in Indian Independence* (Washington, D.C.: Public Affairs Press, 1968), pp. 75–84, briefly treats the mission, but minimizes Phillips' frustrations in attempting to force a change in American policy. William Phillips' memoir, *Ventures in Diplomacy* (Boston: Beacon Press, 1952), includes a substantial chapter on his experience in India. While it includes important details and the earliest full account of his messages to Roosevelt, the memoir regrettably fails to offer any detached reflections on the mission. Mohammad Abdul Khair, "William Phillips' Mission to India 1942–43," *Journal of the Asiatic Society of Pakistan*, December, 1964, is a brief survey based on Phillips' memoir and a few other sources.

Chapter V

The propaganda activities of the British and the nationalists have not received systematic consideration. Much of the writing that has been done on the subject has come from nationalists critical of the British and of the Indian "stooges" who endorsed British policy in America. N. G. Jog, *Judge or Judas?* (Bombay Thacker & Co., 1945), is a scathing denunciation of British propagandists. Chaman Lal, *British Propaganda in America* (Allahabad: Kitab Mahal, 1945), is another, if more measured, indictment. K. P. S. Menon, *Many Worlds: An Autobiography* (London: Oxford University Press, 1965), includes noteworthy observations on Bajpai and other Indian supporters of the British.

Robert Shaplen, "One Man Lobby," *The New Yorker*, March 24, 1951, pp. 35–36, 38, 40–55, is a first-rate account of the activities of the enterprising J. J. Singh. Haridas T. Muzumdar, *America's Contribution to India's Freedom* (Allahabad: Central Book Depot, 1962), is useful for its recounting of nationalist activities in America.

Bibliography

Chapter VI

On the official American reaction to the Indian famine the judgment of scholars has been harsh. M. S. Venkataramani, "The Roosevelt Administration and the Great Indian Famine," *International Studies,* January, 1963, pp. 241–64, a thorough study, is highly critical of Roosevelt and the British. James MacGregor Burns, *Roosevelt: The Soldier of Freedom* (New York: Harcourt, Brace, Jovanovich, 1970), p. 381, describes Roosevelt's policy of deference to the British as reaching, in this instance, "tragic lengths."

In tracing military developments that affected India the studies by Charles F. Romanus and Riley Sunderland are basic: *United States Army in World War II: China-Burma-India Theater,* vol. 1, *Stilwell's Mission to China,* vol. 2, *Stilwell's Command Problems,* and vol. 3, *Time Runs out in CBI* (Washington, D.C.: Office of the Chief of Military History, Department of the Army, 1953–56). On the reaction of the GIs to India and the response of Indians to the Americans, the following provide much information: Ulysses Lee, *United States Army in World War II, Special Studies: The Employment of Negro Troops* (Washington, D.C.: Office of the Chief of Military History, Department of the Army, 1966); Albert Mayer, "Americans in India," *Survey Graphic,* March, 1947, pp. 202–6; Merle Curti, "My Discovery of India," *The American Scholar,* Autumn, 1947, pp. 419–23.

The immigration-naturalization struggle is detailed in Gary R. Hess, "The 'Hindu' in America: Immigration and Naturalization Policies and India, 1917–1946," *Pacific Historical Review,* February, 1969, pp. 71–77.

The controversial mission of Mrs. Pandit is considered rather fully in the three biographies of her career: Robert Hardy Andrews, *A Lamp for India: The Story of Madame Pandit* (Englewood Cliffs, N.J.: Prentice-Hall, 1967); Vera Brittain, *Envoy Extraordinary: A Study of Vijaya Laksmi Pandit and Her Contribution to Modern India* (London: George Allen & Unwin, 1965); Anne Guthrie, *Madame Ambassador: The Life of Vijaya Laksmi Pandit* (New York: Harcourt, Brace & World, 1962).

Chapter VII

For the basic narrative of Indian developments, V. P. Menon, *The Transfer of Power in India* (Princeton: Princeton University Press, 1957), and Michael Brecher, *Nehru: A Political Biography* (New York: Oxford Univercity Press, 1959), were again heavily relied upon. The following also proved helpful: Michael Edwardes, *The Last Years of British India* (London: Cassell & Co., 1963); Leonard Mosley, *The Last Days of the British Raj* (London: Weidenfeld & Nicholson, 1961); Alan Campbell-Johnson, *Mission with Mountbatten* (London: Robert Hale, 1951); Penderel Moon, *Divide and Quit* (Berkeley and Los Angeles: University of California Press, 1962); Francis Williams, *Twilight of Empire: Memoirs of Prime Minister Clement Attlee* (New York: A. S. Barnes & Co., 1962).

The development of the Pakistani movement is placed in perspective in two studies: Khalid B. Sayeed, *Pakistan: The Formative Phase, 1857–1948*, 2nd ed. (New York: Oxford University Press, 1968), a balanced and detached account which, among several important observations, suggests that Jinnah was not as averse to the cabinet mission plan as has been commonly believed; Chaudhri Muhammad Ali, *The Emergence of Pakistan* (New York: Columbia University Press, 1967), the work of a former prime minister of Pakistan, presents the arguments of the Pakistani adherent.

America's economic interest in India and the 1945 loan to Britain is discussed, in the chapter on Will Clayton, in Lloyd C. Gardner, *Architects of Illusion: Men and Ideas in American Foreign Policy, 1941–1949* (Chicago: Quadrangle Books, 1970).

The completion of the drive for an immigration quota and naturalization privileges is detailed in Gary R. Hess, "The 'Hindu' in America: Immigration and Naturalization Policies and India, 1917–1946," *Pacific Historical Review*, February, 1969, pp. 71–77.

The position that American prestige had sharply declined by 1945 contrasts with the interpretation of several authors. W. Norman Brown, *The United States and India and Pakistan*, 2nd ed. rev. (Cambridge, Mass.: Harvard University Press, 1963), pp. 367–68, Norman D. Palmer, *South Asia and United States Policy* (Boston: Houghton Mifflin, 1966), p. 13, and Phillips Talbot and S. L. Poplai, *India and America: A Study of Their Relations* (New York: Harper & Bros., 1958), pp. 1–2, maintain that the United States was popular because of its efforts to induce a settlement during the war. It seems, rather, that criticism of the United States and anti-Americanism prevailed until after independence, when American prestige increased, as is mentioned in Chapter VIII of the present volume. The view that, in terms of its standing with the Indian people, America suffered during 1945–47 for its wartime policies is shared by Raymond L. Thurston, "U.S. Relations with the Government of India: A Reference Article," *Middle East Journal*, July, 1947, p. 297, and Lawrence Rosinger, *India and the United States: Political and Economic Relations* (New York: Macmillan, 1950), pp. 21–22. Thurston was vice consul at Bombay from 1941 to 1945.

199

Bibliography

Chapter VIII

Roosevelt's general anticolonial policies during World War II have drawn varied comments in the principal studies of his diplomacy. James MacGregor Burns, *Roosevelt: The Soldier of Freedom* (New York: Harcourt, Brace, Jovanovich, 1970), pp. 593 and 609, observes Roosevelt's failure to coordinate ends with means and his mistaken assumption that colonial questions could always be postponed. William L. Neumann, *After Victory: Churchill, Roosevelt, Stalin, and the Making of the Peace* (New York: Harper & Row, 1967), pp. 102–3 and 187, criticizes Roosevelt for his willingness to dispose of colonial and other political questions without full consideration of the details, and his failure to comprehend Britain's weakened position. Gaddis Smith, *American Diplomacy during the Second World War* (New York: John Wiley & Sons, 1965), pp. 83 ff., notes Roosevelt's indirection and constant shifting on colonial issues.

America's responses to other specific colonial problems in Southeast Asia have also been studied: in J. A. L. Sullivan, "The United States, the East Indies and World War II: America's Efforts to Modify the Colonial Status Quo" (Ph.D. diss., University of Massachusetts, 1969); Edward R. Drachman, *United States Policy toward Vietnam, 1940–1945* (Rutherford, N.J.: Farleigh Dickinson Press, 1970); and in my forthcoming "Franklin Roosevelt and Indochina," *Journal of American History*. On Southeast Asia generally, Edwin O. Reischauer, *Beyond Vietnam: The United States and Asia* (New York: Random House, Vintage, 1967), comments that American indifference to the growing strength of nationalism encouraged the French and Dutch in their efforts to regain their empires.

A full account of the disillusionment among South and Southeast Asian peoples with the United States after World War II is provided in Harold R. Isaacs, *No Peace for Asia* (New York: Macmillan, 1947).

The ideological bond between the United States and nationalist movements in the last two centuries has been explored by Richard B. Morris, *The Emerging Nations and the American Revolution* (New York: Harper & Row, 1970). Morris concludes that the United States must recapture its dedication to anticolonialism. Similar thoughts are expressed in Arnold Toynbee, *America and the World Revolution* (New York: Oxford University Press, 1962). R. R. Palmer, "The Revolution," in *The Comparative Approach to American History*, ed. C. Vann Woodward (New York: Basic Books, 1968), pp. 47–61, notes the intellectual impact of the American Revolution, but also stresses the differences between the American experience and the anticolonial movements of Africa and Asia.

Addendum

Two recent publications need to be cited. Relative to the material discussed in Chapter I, Goberdhan Bhagat's *Americans in India: Commercial and Consular Relations, 1784–1860* (New York: New York University Press, 1971), provides a comprehensive treatment of early Indo-American relations. On the role of the United States in Indian independence, R. C. Jauhri has written *American Diplomacy and Independence for India* (Bombay: Vora & Co., 1970), a thorough account, based on published sources, of the 1941–47 period. Jauhri reaches conclusions similar to those expressed in this volume; he finds American policy during World War II "a tragedy of high intentions self-defeated" (p. 129).

Index

THE JOHNS HOPKINS PRESS

Composed in Baskerville text and display
by Monotype Composition Company

Printed on 60-lb. Sebago MF, Regular
by Universal Lithographers, Inc.

Bound in Joanna Kennett, #39450
by L. H. Jenkins, Inc.

E
183.8 Hess, Gary R
I4   America encounters India, 1941–1947 ₍by₎ Gary R. Hess.
H58   Baltimore, Johns Hopkins Press ₍c1971₎

           xi, 211 p.   24 cm. $9.50

           Bibliography : p. 189–201.

251093

           1. U. S.—Foreign relations—India. 2. India—Foreign relations—
       U. S.   I. Title.

           E183.8.I 4H4   327.73′054   72–163196
           ISBN 0–8018–1258–3   MARC

           Library of Congress   72 ₍4₎